Rural Data, People, and Policy

RURAL STUDIES SERIES
of the
Rural Sociological Society

Rural Studies Series

Rural Data, People, and Policy: Information Systems for the 21st Century, edited by James A. Christenson, Richard C. Maurer, and Nancy L. Strang

Economic Adaptation: Alternatives for Nonmetropolitan Areas, edited by David L. Barkley

Persistent Poverty in Rural America, Rural Sociological Society Task Force on Persistent Rural Poverty

The Future of Rural America: Anticipating Policies for Constructive Change, edited by Kenneth E. Pigg

Rural Policies for the 1990s, edited by Cornelia B. Flora and James A. Christenson

Research, Realpolitik, and Development in Korea: The State and the Green Revolution, Larry L. Burmeister

Whose Trees? Proprietary Dimensions of Forestry, edited by Louise Fortmann and John W. Bruce

Rural Data, People, and Policy

Information Systems for the 21st Century

EDITED BY

James A. Christenson,
Richard C. Maurer,
and Nancy L. Strang

Routledge
Taylor & Francis Group
LONDON AND NEW YORK

First published 1994 by Westview Press

Published 2019 by Routledge
52 Vanderbilt Avenue, New York, NY 10017
2 Park Square, Milton Park, Abingdon, Oxon OX14 4RN

Routledge is an imprint of the Taylor & Francis Group, an informa business

Library of Congress Cataloging-in-Publication Data
Rural data, people, and policy : information systems for the 21st
Century / edited by James A. Christenson, Richard C. Maurer, and
Nancy L. Strang.
p. cm. — (Rural studies series of the Rural Sociological
Society)
Includes bibliographical references and index.
ISBN 0-8133-8797-3
1. Rural population—United States—Statistical services.
2. United States—Rural conditions—Statistics. 3. Rural
development—United States. I. Christenson, James A., 1944- .
II. Maurer, Richard C. III. Strang, Nancy L. IV. Series.
HB2385.R87 1994
304.6'0973'091734—dc20 93-41559
CIP

ISBN 13: 978-0-367-28626-2 (hbk)

ISBN 13: 978-0-367-30172-9 (pbk)

To three scholars who have made
significant contributions to the
development of rural information systems:
Jim Bonnen, Tom Ford, and Jim Hildreth.
We salute you!

Contents

Foreword

Despite the myriad of data-collection and archiving activities sponsored by federal, state, and local agencies and universities, our capacity to understand the problems and needs of rural Americans is seriously wanting. The federal government, long involved in collecting and publishing data on Americans, has never provided an adequate mechanism for social scientists to accurately measure and interpret the status and well-being of rural communities and their citizens. Current and proposed reductions in resources dedicated to the collection of national statistics are further eroding information on rural areas and people in this country. The end result is that policy initiatives, designed to address the current and emerging needs of rural residents, too often remain ineffective because they rely on data that mask the diversity and complexity of rural America.

Recognition of these problems prompted James A. Christenson, Richard C. Maurer, and Nancy L. Strang to focus their attention on the information needs of rural America as we approach the twenty-first century. By painting a critical view of the current state of rural data systems in this country, this volume in the Rural Sociological Society's Rural Studies Series places an important wake-up call to all social scientists engaged in rural research and to all who use it. Given the limited resources with which most social scientists must work, it is not surprising that research agendas often are organized around existing information sources. Unfortunately, the manipulation and interpretation of secondary data sets often become ends in themselves, both limiting researchers' vision and scope, and perpetuating confidence in the adequacy of existing data systems.

While alerting researchers and practitioners to the problems of existing data systems is useful in its own right, the added utility of this volume rests with its articulation of key strategies that can further advance the application of rural data systems and serve to clarify the unique policy needs of people and places in rural America. Tapping the expertise of leading scholars in the social sciences arena, the editors have assembled a collection of contributions that will be valued by both practitioners and scholars. These contributions incorporate cutting-edge methodologies and information technologies that can further our efforts to collect, analyze, and disseminate practical, scientifically sound data in a timely fashion.

Among the important messages that Christenson, Maurer, and Strang leave with us is that overcoming the problems they identify will require us to operate far differently than we have in the past. No longer can federal and state agency officials, along with faculty in mission-oriented land-grant institutions in this country, afford to carry out their data collection efforts in isolation from one another. Rather, these key players must work in concert to create information systems that can better guide policy activities at all levels of government. The capacity of these individuals to engage the confidence of taxpayers and policymakers in their work will depend on their commitment to make this collaborative effort a reality.

Lionel J. Beaulieu
Forrest A. Deseran
Board of Editors
Rural Studies Series

Acknowledgments

This book is dedicated to three scholars—Jim Bonnen, Tom Ford, and Jim Hildreth—who have made significant contributions to the development of rural information systems. These eminent individuals have challenged old ways of looking at or gathering information. They have struggled to build bridges between the university and the government. They have stimulated the gathering of new types of data on new subjects to better represent the changing conditions of the American hinterland. They have looked at old problems in new ways. They have served as mentors for several generations of students and colleagues. They have made the social sciences and people involved in the social sciences better because of their integrity, their insistence on quality, and their devotion to improving the documentation of the social, economic, and cultural conditions of rural America. We salute them!

Dr. James T. Bonnen, professor of agricultural economics at Michigan State University, has contributed greatly to the development of rural data systems. His research, publication, and teaching of public policy have made major impacts on his students and on the academic world. However, he is especially noted for his distinguished career in restructuring the agricultural data system. In addition to his position as senior staff economist on the President's Council of Economic Advisers, he has held positions with the National Academy of Sciences and the President's Office with the specific purpose of making federal statistics more usable for public policy. Jim has received many awards throughout his career, but he is especially recognized here for his dedication to using statistics for the betterment of people in the United States.

Dr. Thomas R. Ford has served over 40 years as a demographer with a particular concern for rural areas. He was one of the first to conduct a comprehensive survey of people living in Appalachia, which served as a cornerstone for legislation related to rural conditions and services. Over 30 years of his career were carried out at the University of Kentucky, where he held various positions, including professor in and chair of the Department of Sociology and director of the Center for Developmental

Change. He has also served as president of the Rural Sociological Society and the Population Association of America. Tom's work epitomizes the importance that data can have for rural people and provides a model for the use of data as discussed in this book.

Dr. R. James Hildreth is best known for his 30 years of leadership with the Farm Foundation. In this role, he prodded the social sciences to be relevant, responsive, and realistic to the evolving needs of rural America. Jim worked hard to bring the concerns of the private sector to bear on the research and extension issues in the university sector. Through his role as president of the American Agricultural Economics Association, his many books and articles, and his frequent attendance at every meeting ever held, Jim has made a difference. He truly stimulated scholarship and thoughtful investigation that has tremendously impacted the lives of rural people.

Finally, we would like to thank Dr. Richard Stuby of the Cooperative State Research Service of the U.S. Department of Agriculture, who played a major role in stimulating ideas for the development of this book. He also provided support under a CSRS cooperative agreement (89-COOP-2-4273) for the Rural Data Needs conference in Lexington, Kentucky, which laid the foundation for this book.

James A. Christenson
Richard C. Maurer
Nancy L. Strang

PART ONE

The Politics of Data

Because data drive policies, lack of information often results in nonresponsive or biased public policies. The first three chapters suggest that the methods we are using to gather and interpret data are insensitive to the diversity and needs of Americans living in our hinterlands. Data are political, perishable, and permanent. We suggest how federal and state agencies and public universities can work together to create a more appropriate information system for developing a policy agenda sensitive to rural needs and circumstances.

Rural policy often has been a matter of personal antidotes, political expediency, and institutional neglect. Without a rural information system to capture and highlight rural situations, antidotes and expediency will perpetuate past neglect.

Data drive policy, but people interpret what data are gathered, how they are processed, and whether they should be distributed. Information systems require data and interpretation. The philosophical discussion about and the theoretical needs for rural information systems provide the basis for the first three chapters of this book.

1

Rural Data Needs: The Comparative Advantage of University Research

James A. Christenson and Edwin H. Carpenter

This book is concerned with rural people and communities and how we gather and interpret information about them. Current methods of gathering and interpreting data are not sensitive to the diversity and needs of people living in America's hinterland. National data-gathering efforts have inherent biases that are rooted in the methods of data collection and analysis and the approaches to interpretation. As a result, the twentieth century has been marked by the failure of policies and programs directed at rural people and places.

Rural poverty is a good example of a national data system misrepresenting issues in rural areas. From census data we find that the average American household in poverty is headed by a single nonworking parent. However, data from rural America indicate that a household in poverty is made up of an intact family with both parents working (see Chapter 5). Data drive policy. Lack of data and the failure to develop an integrated information system based on available data can misdirect policy and undermine program intent. In the case of rural poverty, the gap in our knowledge about the characteristics of the rural poor and how they differ from the urban poor lead to public assistance programs that fail to address the needs of the rural working poor.

This book examines how the many players (federal and state agencies and public universities, especially land-grant universities) involved in data collection and the development of information systems can work together to create a more appropriate information base for developing a policy agenda for rural people and places sensitive to their particular needs and circumstances.

This book is guided by three themes. The first theme is *complementarity*. How can research and related activities in public universities complement, extend, and reinforce national data and information systems? Further, how can they reorganize, refocus, and restructure data and information as they pertain to rural people and places?

The second theme is *cooperation*. How can academicians involved in research and related activities be encouraged to collaborate in interdisciplinary, interuniversity, and interagency endeavors to provide data and information required to inform rural policy. This book attempts to answer the following questions: What is the role of public universities in providing data and information on rural needs? What kind of rural data will be needed in the years ahead? What do the national data sets reveal about rural America and what can't they reveal? In what areas do public universities need to provide information to complement, extend, and reinforce national research efforts? In what ways can the new microcomputer-based tools be used to collect data, turn data into information, store and update the information, make retrieval of the information as easy as asking a question, and display the information spatially using geographical information systems (GIS)?

The third theme of this book is *responsiveness*. American society is becoming more urbanized and less responsive to the needs of "uncounted" Americans. Rural Americans do not show up in most counts. Part of the problem is that information from national data systems is adequate for urban policy but of limited value for informing rural policy. For a particular rural place or area, data from national data sets are either too sparse to draw reliable conclusions or unavailable, except as part of a larger picture, to assure the anonymity of individuals from low-density population areas. This latter situation, known as "aggregation," is required by law to protect the privacy of individuals in the data set. The result of these inadequate data is a pronounced lack of responsiveness to the needs of rural Americans. If data are not available, then it is virtually impossible for anyone to make a persuasive case that informs policy. Increased responsiveness, then, is highly dependent on data and information systems that can represent rural people, places, or areas. Such data can be provided by using increasingly automated primary-data collection and analysis technologies, which are fast and easy to use (see Chapters 9–11).

This book does not seek to criticize ongoing national data and information systems. Such systems have a role in charting and monitoring the state of the nation, which is predominantly urban. However, these national information systems, most of which emanate from the Bureau of the Census, are limited by the conceptual basis of their counting procedures—a conceptual basis that was conceived in the 1930s for different people, places, and times. And they are mandated by a mission to provide information systems that monitor and project certain conditions for all of American society, rural and urban.

The federal agencies, with guidance from the Office of Management and Budget and other groups, appear to be performing roles within the constraints of their funding bases and missions. This is not to say, however, that all is well at the federal and state levels. Much of the information processed is not relevant to the evolving problems of today. And, federal agencies have been less than eager to create cooperative endeavors with state and university researchers in monitoring or studying unique conditions or changing situations.

What Kind of Rural Data Do We Have?

The data that serve as the basis for most decisions by federal and state governments are found in our national longitudinal data sets. These are the best, and virtually the only, information systems available. These systems include the National Longitudinal Surveys, Panel Study of Income Dynamics, Survey of Income and Program Participation, Census of Population, and many others (Chapter 4). However, these systems are limited in their applicability to rural areas and in their ability to provide geographical specificity. Likewise, while national longitudinal studies are able to provide valued information over time, they are not responsive to changing times. The lack of responsiveness stems from the fact that the studies are historically mandated counts of people that have not been altered to meet the evolution of the problems and concerns that afflict rural people and places.

State government data are unsystematic. A few states, such as Wisconsin and Pennsylvania, have developed excellent information systems and some cities, like Phoenix and Cincinnati, have made major strides in information systems, especially GIS, but most states and cities do not have a system at all. In most states and cities, little liaison exists between universities and state agencies in developing information systems. In fact, most states and cities focus on gathering data for cities and are much less concerned with rural implications.

Public university data systems are an embarrassment. In colleges of agriculture and other mission-oriented sectors of the university, a lot of data are gathered. Some data are routinely transmitted to state and federal agencies, but this is clearly the exception rather than the rule. Academic research is, for the most part, individualistic and opportunistic. Data gathering is labor intensive and expensive. Most university professors do not want to spend the time nor do they have the financial resources to generate data. Instead, they use existing data or simulate model data, which tend to be disciplinary bound. We may be moving beyond this narrow base because the national funding agencies and foundations are encouraging interdisciplinary research and interdisciplinary programs. But only in time will we know how strong their commitment is to interdisciplinary efforts. Besides the five Rural Development Centers and a few regional research projects, little interstate or interuniversity research is performed. In short, we have the existing national longitudinal information systems, and we have a smorgasbord of state and university efforts. Specifically, there is no university-based rural information system that informs either the federal or state governments.

Problems with Existing Rural Data

Longitudinal data are desperately needed to monitor and interpret rapidly changing conditions in rural areas. Rural areas are heterogeneous, belying the aggregate comparison so often applied. Rural problems are complex, both spatially and contextually. We need to know more about the variety of activities (human, social, economic, and environmental) occurring in rural places. And, we know that rural places are very different from urban places. Contextually, rural areas offer a unique laboratory to assess what is going on, what is working, and what is not working in different parts of the country. These kinds of contextual studies are not possible in ongoing longitudinal national data efforts. In addition, many of the concepts central to ongoing national systems are questionable to the extent of the phenomena under study. We only have to ask what is a farm, a standard metropolitan area, a household, or poverty to launch a lively discussion.

Second, we lack primary data. Most university research efforts are shotgun projects with considerable variability in the quality of data, in the procedures utilized, and in the compatibility with any other ongoing efforts. The last three chapters discuss methodological, conceptual, and statistical standards to address such problems.

Third, we lack qualitative insight. At times, we become so accustomed to counting and using the computer that we forget the situation in rural society is changing. Our perception of rurality may be colored more by myths and assumptions than by what is really going on. We need to listen to people. We need to critically assess our assumptions and values in light of the words and actions of real people when interpreting data and formulating our agenda (see Chapter 8).

Finally, we lack panel data on individuals in a rural context (see Chapter 6). The Survey of Income and Program Participation (SIPP) and other information systems do have individual-level data, but without controls on rurality. We have similar problems in many ongoing data systems because of sample size, geographical specificity, or conceptual design.

Problems in Obtaining New Data

Costs, standards, technology, political constraints, and lack of appreciation inhibit efforts to generate rural data systems. At the national level, costs are clearly a major deterrent to broadening existing information systems to include rural information needs. Likewise, at the state level, it is difficult to generate new funds for information systems that are sensitive to rural areas if such systems are not already in place. Since most states have little existing data on rural areas, new information systems are often pipe dreams. Once an information system is in place, the likelihood that it will be maintained over a long period is very low. Information systems are often among the first programs to get the budget axe when economic times are difficult.

For many in the university research community, standards and coordination seem to be an irrelevant concept. People receive so many surveys from so many different sources, sometimes from different disciplines within the same university, that they cannot reasonably respond to all of them. There have been more than a dozen farm polls conducted simultaneously in the United Sates, each using a completely original set of questions and response categories. Mail surveys of the public vary greatly in their response rates, from as low as 35 percent to as high as 75 percent. Lack of coordination is clearly evident in university studies. We need university-wide or interuniversity standards on sampling, survey response elicitation techniques, questionnaire design, measurement scales, and background information questions. But, more important, we need standards that address comparability and compatibility among research projects and programs, without which we cannot build cumulative information systems (see Chapter 10). For example, questions on household income or the amount of education completed should have comparable response categories across surveys.

Technology provides increasingly better ways to gather information effectively. The social science research process can be likened to the physical science research process of years ago. For example, a few decades ago gas chromatography was accomplished by a laboratory full of technicians and equipment—very similar to the social science research process of today. However, the physical sciences now have a black box, known as the "gas chromatograph," that takes the place of the lab full of technicians and equipment. Simply stated, to determine the chemical make-up of a substance, one merely has to insert a sample in the gas chromatograph and wait for the result. The social science research process eventually may be automated in a similar way.

Today, many steps in the social science research process can be computerized (like computer-assisted interviewing) and linked so that it takes only a few minutes from the time of the last interview to when the findings are presented. However, knowledge of new procedures to gather and process information is lacking across social science disciplines. We tend to conduct research the way we were taught in graduate school. The lack of common methodological and statistical standards in gathering and analyzing rural data continues to plague academic research. Transferring social science technology to those who could make the most use of it is slow. The third section of this book addresses these issues.

Little support exists for building information systems. We seem to be driven by the need for data rather than the need for information. *Data* are raw information that need a conceptual basis before they can be treated as information (see Chapter 2). There appear to be few systematic efforts within disciplines, across disciplines, or between levels of government and universities. Each researcher wants to do his or her own thing, precluding the possibility of building data into an ongoing information system. Insensitivity to this issue frustrates efforts to build a rural information system; however, the situation may be changing.

One of the impediments to forming and maintaining information systems has been the cost of the hardware, software, and personnel to make such a system work. Inexpensive microcomputers, easy-to-use software (such as search and retrieval systems), and inexpensive massive storage capability in the form of read/write optical disks, compact disks with read-only memories (CD-ROMs), and gigabyte hard drives provide new opportunities for the development of information systems, including those that will inform rural policy. The most difficult part is providing the information that will go into the system, updating the system, and providing easy access to the contents of the system. For example, Internet, which links university computers around the world, is a possible starting point for providing access to an information system that resides on a microcomputer at a university site.

This new technology opens the way to systematically analyze and evaluate text-based information that relates to policy in rural America. Such a capability opens the systematic inquiry and tracking of government documents, legal opinions, research reports, and any other text items that have been prepared over the years. If these new information-archiving procedures are activated to analyze historical and contemporary textual information relative to rural policy, then we can forge ahead with new insights from a historically grounded context.

How to Improve the Rural Information System

First, to improve the rural information system, we must make existing national information systems more accessible, more flexible, and more sensitive to the heterogeneity of rural areas. Clearly, concepts such as "rural" and "farm" need both conceptual and methodological clarification. Disaggregation of information systems for geographical specificity is crucial.

Second, primary information is needed to expand and build national information systems so they can be responsive to rural needs. Likewise, new data generated in state studies should be designed to complement ongoing national information systems. In addition, we need qualitative information to assess the accuracy of ongoing systems to the changing conditions. Further, we need to continually test old concepts with new data.

Third, rural data systems need to be established in each state. Each agriculture college or other mission-oriented center or institute should have a unit to coordinate all data into an information system, one that informs and is informed by ongoing national information systems.

Fourth, standards for the design and collection of data should be strongly encouraged by federal agencies and agriculture colleges alike. Extension surveys should conform to the same standards as those of the Bureau of the Census, although we would hope they would not be as elaborate or as confusing. Ignorance is no excuse for professors or others to gather information of dubious quality and relevance.

The Comparative Advantage of University Research

We have spoken at length of the need for rural information systems. Where do universities fit into this scheme? Universities are the institutions entrusted with the mission to stimulate unique research. National research efforts are mandated to maintain an ongoing information system to monitor the condition of the nation. Universities are mandated to generate new knowledge and apply this knowledge to local, state, and national problems. Most professors are not very concerned with the applied mission of universities, but most centers of learning—whether public or private, large or small—have an applied utilitarian mission statement in their charter. This mandate needs to be revisited.

University research is responsive to rapid change. Most universities tend to be conceptually dynamic and substantively innovative. Most primary data-gathering efforts, outside of private research projects, are likely to be found in universities. Most of the attempts to test and modify concepts and issues involved in an ongoing national information system are found at universities. And, most policy-relevant test cases are evaluated by university researchers.

Universities often have the funds and the mandate to conduct research and, thus, the potential to play a complementary role in the development of national information systems. With leadership, incentives, and guidance, universities could facilitate cooperation among disciplines, across states, and with federal agencies. Utilizing new data designs and technology, universities could make research more cost efficient and provide high-quality data while, at the same time, encouraging faculty to develop and undertake unique and innovative studies.

We are not encouraging universities to control the creative elements involved in generating knowledge. Rather, we are suggesting that universities begin to emphasize the applied mission by encouraging their faculty to assume a greater role in this responsibility. Further, we are advocating that researchers take advantage of existing technologies that facilitate primary data collection and analysis and then apply the time and resources saved to creative research endeavors that contribute in some way to ongoing rural information systems. Universities need to encourage a climate that stimulates researchers to contribute appropriate data to information systems.

To summarize, data must be transformed into information before they can be useful. In the academic community, there does not seem to be much effort to stimulate the various disciplines to generate a rural information system. Clearly, public university people who write books and articles become experts in an area, and many testify before Congress on various programs. But there is no concerted effort to standardize the kinds of data that are gathered, nor is there a concerted effort to monitor or control what happens to data after they are collected. That is, there is no committee within colleges or universities that monitors what goes out of the academic institutions to prevent many different questionnaires from being sent to one individual at the same time and to ensure that high standards are maintained.

The federal system has not been very receptive to working with universities in making their information systems relevant to rural America. There are clearly some liaison problems. We need administrators who will facilitate ongoing efforts to develop information systems relevant to the needs of rural America.

Finally, we need to be more sensitive to the values underlying our choices of data gathered, data processed, and data used in information systems. What data are not gathered is as important an issue as what data are gathered. Oftentimes studies are not conducted because people do not want to know the answers. Typically, these are political situations where someone fears the findings will run counter to desired (valued) political decisions of local, state, or federal policy. At other times, segments of the general public do not want data for fear the findings may not conform to their desired myths or beliefs (e.g., religious organizations that oppose the National Science Foundation study on human sexuality). We need to be more active in framing our data so that they can serve as information for public policy recommendations at the national and state levels. It's a little embarrassing when popular entertainers testifying before Congress have more influence on public policy than does the university community. What does this say about the influence of good research and insightful thinking on public policy decisions? What does it say about the attempts of public universities and, in particular, land-grant institutions to fulfill their charter and mission of serving the taxpayer?

Looking Ahead

In attempting to improve the situation, we hope that this book will provide some ideas to stimulate coordination and collaboration of efforts. We also need coordination and collaboration within colleges and across disciplines to obtain a greater return for the tax dollar as well as the grant dollar. Most of us in the land-grant system who have worked with federal and state money know the problems related to declining research dollars. Working across disciplines has two goals: to get a better return for the dollar and to bring in more intellectual expertise to address complex issues.

Public research should be policy relevant, should be responsive, and should be rewarded. These are the sentiments we need to generate both among our disciplines and among our administrators. The system, as it is set up now, neither rewards scholars for attempting to make their research relevant to societal needs nor to ongoing national efforts. In fact, researchers are often penalized for gathering primary data, for writing popular articles, and for looking beyond the discipline.

To put some concrete ideas and structural changes as underpinning to these statements, we are proposing three "immodest" proposals. Concern for complementarity, cooperation, and responsiveness is great, but unless money and sanctions begin to move us toward the vision outlined in this book, nothing will come of it. Thus, the following proposals provide carrots, hammers, and operational procedures for implementing such sentiments.

Proposal 1. One cent of each dollar allotted for research by the federal government would be earmarked to archive and to make federally funded research available to the public.

Two components—money and information systems—make up this proposal. Money drives the research enterprise. If data and information systems are to be made publicly available, a funding mechanism must be built into the system to expedite the process. Second, all publicly funded research must be placed in an archive and made available in a user-friendly format within two years of the termination of the grant or contract. Local or university libraries might be a good repository for such information. CD-ROM could provide a readily available format for dissemination.

Many positive benefits, and only a few negative consequences, can be derived from such a proposal. First, adoption of this proposal would strengthen the importance and legitimacy of major research institutions. Making publicly funded data accessible through information systems can demonstrate that public dollars benefit the public as well as researchers. Adoption of the proposal would increase public trust. This might overcome some of the fraud (i.e., the tampering of research results) as has been recently reported in *Science* magazine and in the popular press. Second, providing an archive system would allow scientists to assemble and organize large information systems to address critical issues. Research would cease to be an elitist enterprise, making data available to a much broader range of scientists. Third, the availability of a broad range of data would allow cross-sectional analysis to facilitate historical research.

One negative consequence of this proposal is that the availability of such archiving systems will likely generate more public debate on the use and meaning of data, particularly in the social science arena where explained variance is not high and where public debate over interpretation may initially generate public skepticism and mistrust. Another negative consequence is that those who spend a considerable amount of time gathering data may not get the credit they have been accustomed to receiving. We believe new ways of evaluating and rewarding researchers' efforts should be developed. In the end, the positive elements will outweigh the negative consequences.

Proposal 2. University libraries should receive the one cent per dollar check-off allocation from research grants and contracts to systematize research findings. This money would help establish an entity independent of research projects and programs to set standards for archiving, accessibility, and responsiveness. Libraries would be conceived as telematic centers for an information age. Certain libraries would focus on particular issues and topics to facilitate organizational substance in information systems.

Proposal 3. Land-grant universities would be mandated to provide information systems sensitive to the particular needs of the state and relevant to rural issues and people in that state. USDA-funded research programs could make a major contribution in this area, both with the institutionalized annual formula funding and with the scientific legitimacy traditionally brought to rural studies. Land-grant universities already have a delivery system in place and are mandated to serve the people of their state. States vary considerably in topography, people, and issues. Implementation of this proposal would facilitate the development of information systems which would help overcome problems of aggregation, diversity, and uniqueness inherent in rural areas and in rural people. This proposal could provide the funding and organizational basis for a rural information system.

Conclusion

We believe it is essential to have rural data information systems that will be responsible to rural Americans' needs. We see these proposals as additive and complementary. They are proposals for public access and research legitimacy and not for research reallocation. Public universities must take an active role in supporting the development of rural information systems that complement, extend, inform, and enhance ongoing state and national information systems. Each level of government and each university has an important and unique role to play. We need liaisons between these groups. We need cooperation, complementarity, and responsiveness. We need to work together. We need mechanisms, reward structures, incentives, and leadership to implement such ideas. We hope the discussions and insights generated in this book will lead to a better understanding of the roles, the responsibilities, and the actions that might be taken to facilitate implementing such proposals and generating information systems, in general, and rural information systems, in particular, to meet the rural data needs of the twenty-first century.

2

The Politics of Information

Jerry R. Skees and Louis E. Swanson

The pop futurist Alvin Toffler (1990) has once again gained recognition, this time for being among the first to state that the capacity to process and interpret information has become a major source of economic and political power in advanced industrial societies. Rapid technological advances in computers and telecommunications technology have made once unmanageable amounts of data and information accessible and manipulatable. Moreover, the disciplines of economics and sociology have developed more complex conceptual frameworks for understanding social and economic phenomena. Such conceptual frameworks have legitimized demands for more precise socioeconomic data. However, the disciplinary and technical capacity to provide informed analysis of our society has been retarded by the continuing problems of providing accurate measures of these phenomena.

Information is a source of power in several respects. In market transactions, new information can give a margin of advantage to those who have the economic power to act—which tends to reproduce existing patterns of political and economic power. Given the massive amounts of seemingly meaningless information, people who can access and process appropriate data have a comparative advantage at providing timely information on markets and public policy debates. Consequently, in this age of information overload and information anxiety, the value of the right type of information in the right circumstance has greatly increased.

In public policy debates, information becomes a type of propaganda tool. Marshaling information to achieve political agendas takes many forms, ranging from anecdotal information, which is often conveniently used to validate society's beliefs and biases, to complex econometric models, which are designed to predict the consequences of government regulations and market interventions. Moreover, information can be perceived either with suspicion or accepted as social fact without criticism.

Because developing and interpreting information is a social process, values mediate the usefulness and character of any given piece of information. As such, information has value in all political processes. That information is not value-free is not a disturbing conclusion. Rather, imbedded in the recognition of the role of values in assessing the politics of information is the search for whose interpretation will have the greatest legitimacy. Consequently, it is in society's interest for some institutions to provide a broader set of values than those with the greatest currency in the policy arena. It is quite logical that policy actors who currently have the greatest legitimacy often peddle information that is formed to protect and foster their interests.

Although an underlying theme of this book is that those in the land-grant universities have a responsibility to champion causes for those with less or no currency in the policy arena, there is a certain irony in that theme. Researchers within the land-grant universities also respond to incentives that are conditioned by the political arena. The research agenda is shaped by the availability of funding. Funding availability has always been influenced by those with the greatest political currency. Sometimes such incentives have been purposely negative in their intent and effect. Walter Golschmidt's Bureau of Agricultural Economics 1944 study of Arvin and Dinuba in California, which documented the negative social consequences of industrial farming, was quarantined by the secretary of agriculture. This information was not released until it was read into a congressional committee's record. Similarly, the demise of the Bureau of Agricultural Economics is often traced to a community study in Congressman Jamie Whitten's Mississippi district that documented the social pathologies of racial segregation—hardly a surprising conclusion for the early 1950s. The fate of these studies sent a clear message to social scientists, especially sociologists and anthropologists: do not tread among politically explosive issues.

This dilemma presents certain constraints that must by identified. No one should expect land-grant researchers to respond without funding. It is not enough to simply say that land-grant social scientists have some kind of vague moral responsibility to assess the plight of society's disenfranchised groups. These social scientists are unlikely to conduct controversial research without sufficient funding and without evidence that they will not be severely penalized in their promotion and merit reviews. Therefore, the data needs for rural social issues are made complex by the interaction between the reward structures of disciplines and universities, on the one hand, and the dearth of useful measures of social phenomena, on the other. In combination, these factors conspire to limit effective social science and policy research on rural social problems.

To understand the importance of university activities in rural data, it is useful to develop a framework that incorporates the philosophical dimensions of data and information as well as the politics of information and information systems. Good information can lead to improved public policy; however, any improvements in information are constrained by the political and economic environments in which they are developed. The political economy is conditioned by the cultural and social segments in society that dominate the underlying ideology. In turn, the prevailing ideology influences the development of information. In short, the types of data and information systems that society designs are subjective.

To challenge conventional wisdom, we believe society needs a balance of ideas, including opportunities for those with different perspectives, to influence our data and information systems. A major thesis of this chapter is that such tensions in the information development process can lead to improved information and improved public decisions. Further, we argue that universities, and land-grant universities in particular, can foster pluralism by using these tensions to contribute to new and improved information systems. Academicians must take a more aggressive role in informing decision makers about the data and information that are needed to address rural problems. Thus, this chapter attempts to provide some insights into the role of politics in the information development process.

Philosophy of Science and Data and Information Systems: What Is Valid Knowledge?

First, it is important to distinguish between information and data. Data, as raw numbers, are information only when given meaning as measures or indicators of socioeconomic forces and characteristics. The interpretation of data, a hermeneutic process, gives meaning to the numbers. Interpretation is a social and often a political process. The collection of data by government agencies is usually preceded by a political screening process. While most experts readily agree on the measures of some characteristics (e.g., population size, age, and gender), measures of poverty, unemployment, income, wealth, land ownership, and so on undergo considerable political scrutiny before agreement is reached.

Bonnen (1975:758) observes that "an information system includes not only the production of data but also analysis and interpretation of these data in some purposeful policy decision or problem solution context. The demand for data is generated by the need to make decisions on problems, but decisionmakers rarely use raw data." This is why an information system is important. For data to be useful, they must be transformed into information that is relevant to a particular problem.

Bonnen's contributions to information systems have been significant. One of the most important challenges he presents is that the discipline helps identify concepts that can be measured. In this model, social scientists continually reevaluate concepts and measures to improve information systems. The flow of the model is presented in Figure 2–1. In essence, the model rests with the ability of social scientists to operationalize concepts in some measurable way. In short, contributions of social scientists should be focused on bridging the gap between theory and empirical verification. Research clearly plays a major role in this process because information is developed for policy decisions.

Bonnen helps us consider the epistemological underpinnings of concepts we try to measure but omits the role of politics from this framework. The political dimension of rural data is added to the framework in Figure 2–2. That is, some of the forces that influence the decision-making process in a federal information system are introduced. Although the dynamics of the schematic are incomplete, a number of linkages are developed. First, the political economy forces, which influence the choice and design of the data that are collected, are explicitly recognized. Further, development of the potential role of these forces is developed below. Finally, social scientists recognize that the system is incomplete and there are people who are left out. In Figure 2–3, our perceptions of the role of bureaucrats in the information system are developed. The actors that influence the behavior of the bureaucrat are depicted on the right and the factors that motivate the bureaucrat are presented on the left.

Introducing Politics in Information System Models

Bonnen (1975) uses the outdated concept of the family farm as one example of conceptual obsolescence in our agricultural database. The Census of Agriculture still considers any unit with $1,000 of gross farm sales or more a farm. The Census of Agriculture's change of the definition of a farm in 1974 serves as a reminder of the political aspects of this

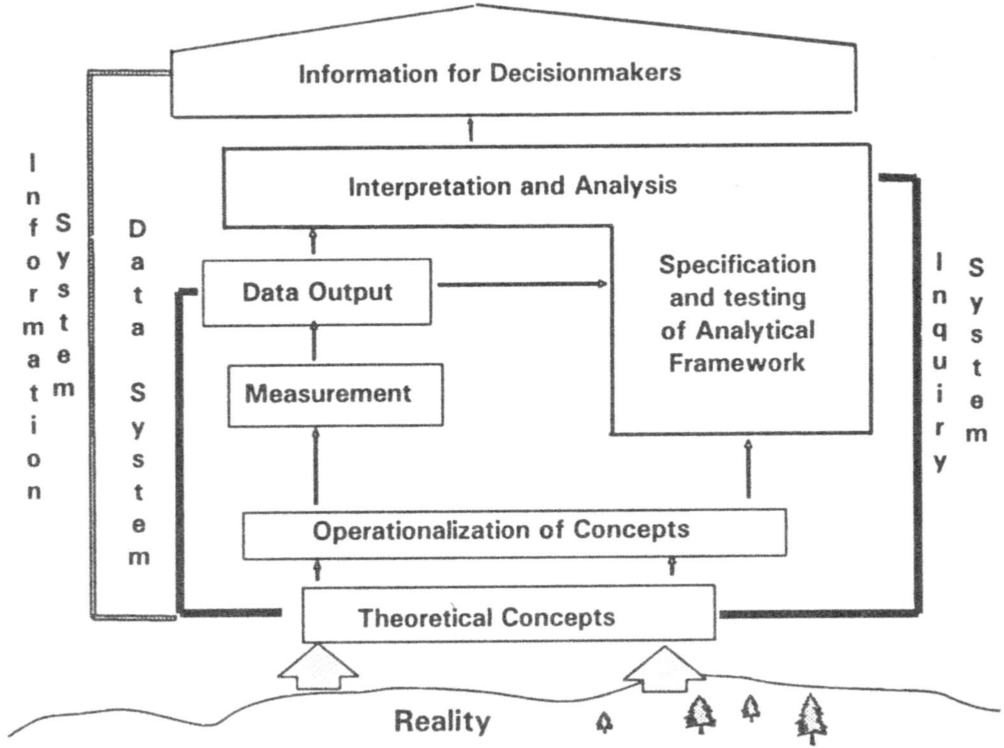

Figure 2–1. An illustration of Bonnen's information system. (Adapted from Bonnen, 1975.)

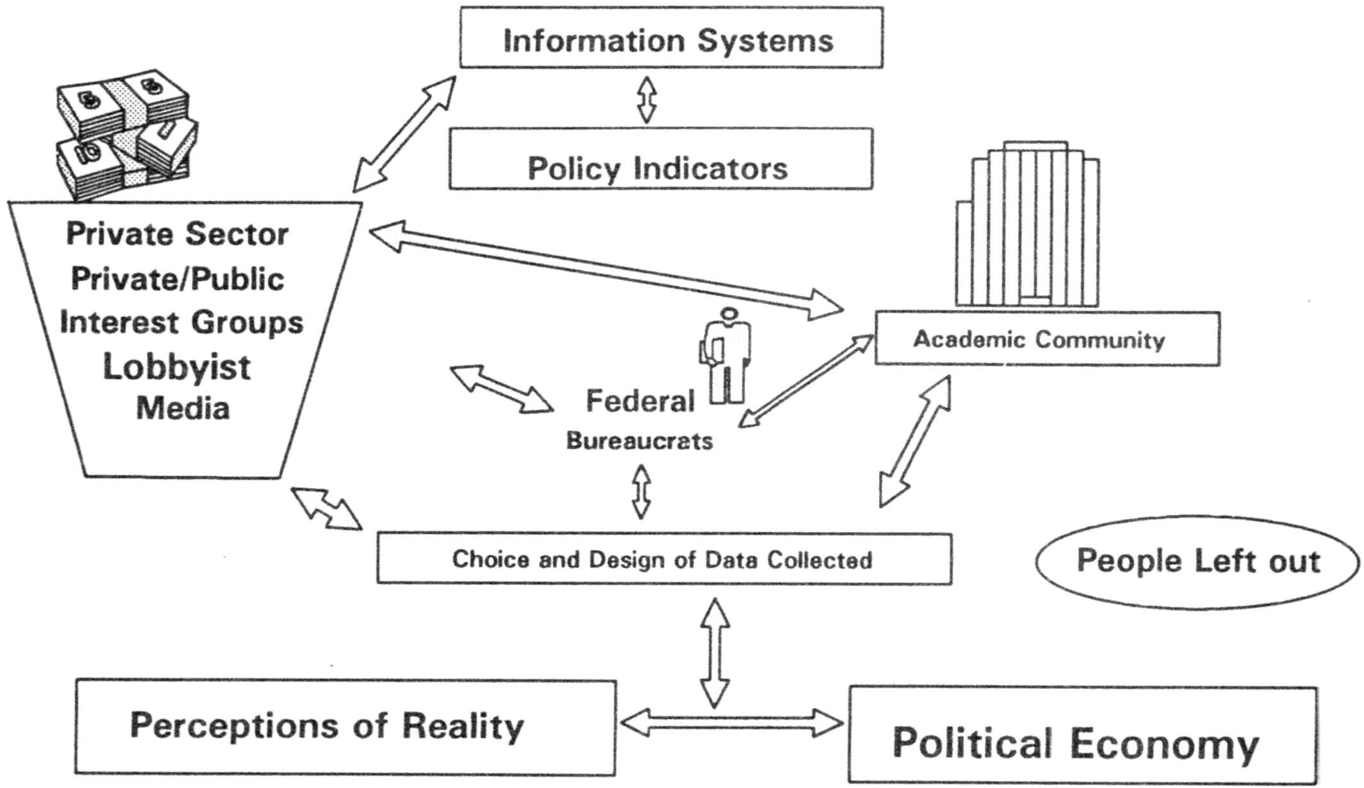

Figure 2–2. An illustration of public policy and rural data choices.

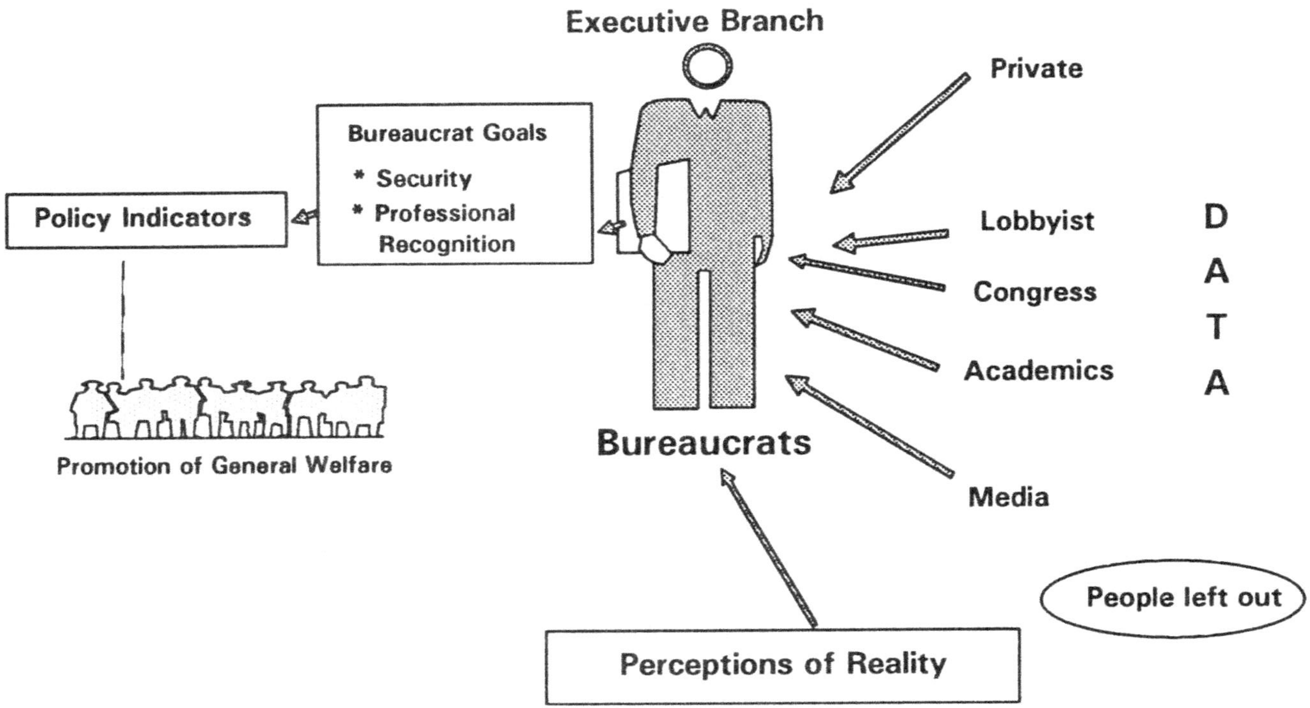

Figure 2-3. An illustration of information, bureaucrats, and policy choices.

concept. At that time, the sales criterion was increased from $250 of gross farm sales to $1,000. This relatively modest change in the definition of a farm was not implemented without tremendous political resistance. Many of the federal benefits to states had been tied to the number of farms. It was in the best interest of many to retain the old definition of a farm, despite its conceptual obsolescence.

Most scholars would agree that the census definition of a farm continues to be outdated. Those involved in agricultural structure research have adjusted to these conceptual problems by reporting classes of farms and focusing on the contribution of various classes to show that many of the smallest units that are considered farms make very little contribution to agriculture. Still, in a political world where numbers matter, it is much more palatable to speak of 2.1 million farm families than the 300,000 commercial operations that produce nearly 80 percent of our food. Similar conceptual problems are pervasive in a political economy that is responsible for developing and modifying federal information systems.

Another example of a major policy indicator with conceptual problems is the official U.S. unemployment rate. Ideally, this measure should provide policymakers with information about the number of people who are out of work. However, given the way this figure is calculated, it underestimates the actual number of unemployed people. That is, a major condition for achieving unemployment status is for individuals to verify their job-seeking efforts for four weeks prior to applying for unemployment benefits. Thus, those who live in areas with few opportunities (i.e., primarily rural areas) become discouraged more quickly and curtail their job searches early, thereby never showing up in the official unemployment counts. Most would agree that such people who would like to be employed should be counted in the unemployment statistics. Of particular interest to rural research scientists is that this measure provides a systematic bias, causing unemployment statistics in rural areas to be more under-represented than those in urban areas (see Chapter 5). Preissing, Skees, and Smith (1990) demonstrate the potential magnitude of this bias for metropolitan versus nonmetropolitan counties using Kentucky data.

Given the pervasive nature of conceptual problems in major policy indicators, it is important to investigate some of the political reasons for these problems. Some common models of political behavior can be used to explain this problem and to highlight the potential role of universities in this system. At least three commonly accepted models of politics (interest group theory, incrementalism, and elite theory) can help us understand federal information systems.

Interest Group Theory and Information Systems

Interest group theory involves the interplay of conflicting interest groups in the political process. The potential power of interest groups in developing federal information systems can be understood best by looking at the demand for data.

The demand for data in a democratic enterprise economy is driven by its value. Private firms collect data because they anticipate an economic return. However, constraints such as scale economies make collection of certain types of data by private firms uneconomical. Or, more simply, the value of the data cannot offset the economic costs incurred by individual firms collecting and processing the data. Since data that are processed into information can reduce uncertainty and improve decisions, society has an interest in subsidizing data to be shared with private sector firms. In other words, the public cost of collecting and maintaining such data and information systems can be offset by the public gain that results from better private sector decisions and, thus, more efficient allocation of society's resources. This type of data and information system, referred to as *public/private data*, is maintained by the public but has direct economic value to the private sector.

The other type of data and information system is almost exclusively public in nature and is referred to as *public data*. This information has little or no direct value for private sector firms. Rather, the value of this information is to improve public decisions (whether they are made by the local, state, or federal government). For public/private sector-oriented information, it is generally easy to identify private sector interest that can use the information directly. For example, price and production information is easily used to reduce uncertainty in markets. In general, private sector interests provide a clientele for this type of data and information because they can more easily reap economic value from it. The United States has a long history of supporting high-quality price and output data for a variety of industries and agricultural commodities. However, even these data have been shown to be lacking; that is, the value of improved estimates far exceeds the costs of generating those estimates.

Because the private sector generally does not use public data, it is more difficult to obtain support for collecting these type of data. Since the private sector user is missing, there are no natural clientele groups who will support such information systems. Socioeconomic indicators are a major example. Generally, private sector interest groups will not use this type of information directly, although they may find such information useful in planning or they may have access to federal money that is tied to the measure. The major distinction is that they typically cannot use these data or information for the most visible economic benefits. Yet the public sector can realize benefits from such information, even though these benefits are usually difficult to measure. Thus, we need to examine the political economy of public sector-oriented information to understand the value of such information systems in a democratic enterprise economy.

In a democratic enterprise economy, information and access to information help make policy. Without the appropriate public support for information systems, special interest groups will have greater access to decision makers and, thus, greater influence. Thomas Jefferson, who long ago emphasized the importance of an educated populace in a democracy, recognized these principles.

In *The Economic Foundations of Political Power*, Randall Bartlett (1973) develops a useful framework for understanding why interest groups have power. In short, special interest groups can expect a greater return from providing "subsidized information" to the policy process than can diffuse citizens groups. By providing subsidized information, special interest groups can have greater influence. In economic jargon, the marginal return from investing in developing and presenting information to decision makers exceeds the marginal costs.

Policymakers commonly make major policy decisions based on inadequate or even wrong information. Much of what happens in the public-policy-making process, as well as in the public-opinion-making process, is conditioned by anecdotal information. Events surrounding the U.S. welfare programs during the 1980s are a good example. At that time, Congress heard a lot of anecdotal stories and testimony about abuses within the welfare system. Although good analysis and factual information were lacking, the pervasiveness of the alleged abuses in the welfare system led Congress to enact reform legislation.

Making national policy based merely on testimony about cases of abuse is questionable without balanced information about what proportion of the welfare recipients abuse the system. The socioeconomic information systems should be adequate to help researchers determine other dimensions of this problem, such as welfare recipients' ability to use welfare payments as a vehicle to become productive members of society. Without such information, public policy actions will generally be misinformed and misdirected.

Given the existing information overload and the limitations of decision makers at processing information, it is only natural that they seek already processed information or naive criteria with which to make decisions. This tendency increases the influence of special interest groups in the policy process because policymakers rely heavily on interest groups to supply and synthesize information as well as to act as barometers.

This begs the question as to the role of public institutions, such as the land-grant universities, as information brokers. Should public institutions address information needs of people who have neither the economic nor technical capacity to process and understand information? Does the public have a right to demand that public institutions research disenfranchised special interests? In short, our society has roughly equated economic power with the power to generate and control the dissemination of information. Those who can pay for the collection and analysis of information have clear advantages both in markets and in articulating public policy debates. In market economies, people without economic resources cannot influence demand and those without economic power have little influence on the social processes of creating and articulating information.

Incrementalism and Information Systems

The economist Charles Lindblom first advanced the idea that decisions made in the political arena are not made with a continual reassessment of the system. Rather, public policy is made from an existing set of past government actions leading only to incremental modifications. This understanding of the policy process also helps us understand changes that may be possible in our public information systems. It is unlikely that we could expect major changes in the existing information systems. Further, the issue of maintaining a consistent series of data through time is also an important constraint to major changes. An exception to the incremental change model has evolved in recent years. The federal budget process has introduced a force that can result in fairly significant departures for national policy. Tight budget conditions have forced many programs out of existence. Further, much of the information-gathering budget has been subject to significant budget cuts. In short, the budget process can result in significant policy changes to the detriment of federal information systems needed by researchers and policymakers to understand rural issues.

Elite Theory and Information Systems

The premise of elite theory is quite simple: only a few members of society have the economic or political power, or both, to influence policy decisions. To understand this theory with regard to public information systems, it is important to identify the actors (see Figure 2-3). The primary message here is that the actors are the elite. It is important for academicians to know that they are included in this group. This knowledge carries both opportunities and responsibilities. In one sense, it means that we should be more politically active in our attempts to inform decision makers about the types of data we need to deal with rural problems. The extent that academicians are willing or able to take leaves of absence that immerse them in the process will, in large part, determine their ability to both understand and influence federal information systems.

The Role of Public Universities

In an environment where special interest groups have a political advantage in supplying information and where decision makers are inclined to seek out such information for expediency, the case for public investment in information systems is strong. This book introduces some of the many issues about such investments. On the national level, it has been argued that clientele support for public-oriented information systems will be weak at best. This, in part, explains the current state of such information systems. An underlying theme of this book is that state universities can make contributions to public-oriented information systems in a variety of ways.

However, determining who in the state universities makes the decisions concerning the types of information made available should involve democratic and pluralist processes. The threat may come from special interest groups who have the capital resources to bend capital-short public institutions to do their bidding. University administrators and faculty may want to set up advisory panels that represent the dispossessed and politically weak members of society as well as those who sit on boards of trustees. At the outset of this chapter we argued that information is by its very nature political. The type of information we do not collect can blind us to possible policy options.

For public universities to be responsive to all aspects of rural social and economic problems, existing incentives for promotion and funding must be reformed. Without such incentives, it is unreasonable to expect such research to be forthcoming. As noted earlier, improving data and analysis of rural social problems involves reform not only of the institutions that conduct rural social science research but of the collection system of rural socioeconomic data. Both of these dimensions need to be addressed simultaneously.

The absence of strong clientele support for public information systems enhances the opportunities for universities to contribute to public debate and decision-making. For example, work is needed that challenges national decision makers and reduces the cynical use of "designer" information. More effort is needed to demonstrate the public value of improved public sector-oriented information systems. Academicians must take on a more aggressive role in informing decision makers about the data and information that are needed to address rural problems. Finally, academicians must be more sensitive to the data needs of those unable to generate their own information.

References

Bartlett, Randall. 1973. *Economic Foundations of Political Power*. London: Collier Macmillan.

Bonnen, James. 1975. Improving information on agriculture and rural life. *American Journal of Agricultural Economics* 57(5):753–763.

Golschmidt, Walter. 1978. *As You Sow: Three Studies in the Social Consequences of Agribusiness*. Montclair, N.J.: Alanheld, Osmun, and Co.

Lindblom, Charles. 1968. *The Policy Making Process*. Englewood Cliffs, N.J.: Prentice-Hall.

Preissing, John F., Jerry R. Skees, and Eldon Smith. 1990. Problems with unemployment statistics for rural areas. *The Kentucky Journal of Economics and Business* 10:55–63.

Toffler, Alvin. 1990. *Powershift: Knowledge, Wealth, and Violence at the Edge of the 21st Century*. New York: Bantam Books.

3

Rural Data Needs in Rapidly Changing Times

James T. Bonnen

Statistics are perishable. If not continually renewed and improved, they inevitably deteriorate. Why? Economic and social statistics track the structures and behavior of society over time. Because society's economic and social structures and behaviors change with time, statistical measurement is an effort to capture a moving target. The faster the target moves, the more rapidly the statistical descriptor deteriorates, losing both accuracy and relevance. All attempts to describe phenomena statistically must periodically be evaluated and adapted in concepts, in real world proxies selected to represent those concepts, and in the techniques of measurement, if the statistics produced are to remain accurate representations of that changing real world. However, for at least two decades or longer, we have allowed our national statistical capacity to deteriorate. At the same time, the rate of change in our society and economy has never been greater. As a consequence, the quality of much of our national database has declined (Bonnen, 1984; Wallman, 19881).

Between 1980 and 1988, the real resources budgeted for national statistics declined by 15 to 20 percent. Personnel numbers dropped by 9 percent. Over the same period, the real resources expended on agricultural statistics declined by about 20 percent, if the budgets of the National Agricultural Statistics Service (NASS) are any indicator (Bonnen, 1988; Wallman, 1989). NASS personnel were reduced 17 percent. Statistical agencies were forced to drop individual series and to reduce sample sizes and the detail in many national data sets, thereby eliminating much small-area data (Wallman, 1988). In addition to dollar budgets and personnel ceilings, irrationally administered paperwork budgets have further constrained and injured statistical quality and capacity. During the Reagan administration, the Office of Management and Budget (OMB) mounted an assault on federal statistics. We will live with the consequences for a long time, even though the Bush administration had returned most of the lost resources to the statistical system by 1992.

Agricultural statistics have lost important ground in the last fifteen years. Statistics for quite a few crops considered minor at the national level, but that are significant at state levels, were dropped. The frequency of some collections has been reduced, and the size of samples, and therefore the accuracy of some agricultural collections, has been reduced.

Our agricultural statistics are still undoubtedly the best in the world. We have made some progress in specific areas but we have lost ground in others. The agricultural database has long had a number of chronic weaknesses. Data on labor inputs and conditions of employment almost do not exist. This problem was partially exposed by the new Immigration Control Act, which requires estimates of labor needs in agriculture that cannot even be guessed at intelligently without new collections. In fact, the whole area of data on human capital in agriculture and rural society is weak. Another weakness is the lack of distributions for many financial aggregates, although as the NASS-Economic Research Service (ERS) Farm Costs and Returns Survey increases its sample size, some real improvement is possible. The moment an equity question arises, agricultural data are frequently inadequate. Politically strong economic interests in agriculture have not wanted equity questions explored.

National Academy of Sciences Panel Recommendations

Data on rural society have so many weaknesses that they cannot be listed here. Instead, this chapter will begin by discussing some of the recommendations from a 1979–1980 National Academy of Sciences (NAS) panel attempt to assess the statistical database for rural development policy. That panel report, *Rural America in Passage: Statistics for Policy*, starts with several useful observations.

The first idea is that the term "rural" is what philosophers call an ill-defined concept—that is, it is a term arising out of common experience that is broadly understood but not capable of a single, precise definition. The panel report pointed out that our knowledge of rural people and their environment is imperfect and incomplete, consisting mostly of annual statistics for large aggregations of areas with only occasional benchmark data for small areas in decennial census years.

The report further concluded that aggregated data are often misleading because rural areas are so heterogeneous. In fact, the panel concluded that rural America today is more heterogeneous than is urban America, although it had no objective way of measuring that conclusion. This heterogeneity compounds the basic problem inherent in rural data; that is, it inevitably involves small-area data collection. For the same level of accuracy, small-area data require larger samples and are far more expensive to collect than national aggregates. They are usually the last numbers collected and the first affected by cutbacks. With the exception of major agricultural statistics, the rural database has long been quite inadequate. And it is a poorer database today than it was in 1980 because of budget and paperwork-driven reductions in sample size and in small-area data collected for health, housing, education, employment and income statistics, and for the various censuses.

This National Academy report also argued that it makes little sense, in a society in which rural and urban areas are so interdependent, to develop any single comprehensive rural database or system separate from the data systems for the rest of the nation. Rather, we need to make the existing data system more flexible, accessible, and capable of addressing rural issues. The panel made a number of specific recommendations designed to improve the database for rural society. What follows is a discussion of some of the more important general recommendations.

All federal and state data should be recorded with a county code to permit tabulations for individual counties and groups of counties. Current reporting practices with respect to geographic coding are highly variable and often frustrate rather than facilitate aggregation and comparisons. Most microdata sets are not county-coded at all. Because no single definition of rural is feasible or desirable, data should be organized in a flexible, building block approach. The county is the most commonly used geographic unit for reporting small-area data. A federal standard requiring county coding would facilitate aggregation regardless of how rural is defined.

A standard classification of nonmetropolitan counties relating to level of urbanization (Hines, Brown, and Zimmer, 1975) should be developed to analyze and evaluate programs at each level of government. The panel also suggested that the county classification should be supplemented by a distinction between urban and rural areas within counties.

A system of standard statistical areas (an extension of the present set of metropolitan statistical areas, MSAs) to encompass the entire geographic area of the nation should be developed and implemented. The panel argued that the difficulties of defining rural should not be allowed to result in inequitable treatment for rural people. Procedures for obtaining, analyzing, and reporting data should be developed to provide data for rural people and problems that are comparable in scope and reliability to those for metropolitan areas. Designation of standard statistical areas (SSAs) encompassing the entire geographic area of the nation would provide continuous, inclusive, and systematic data based on boundaries that would be changed less frequently than the present, continually abused MSA criteria. Nonmetropolitan statistical areas (NMSAs) are determined after MSAs are determined, and statistical coverage and reliability are much poorer for NMSAs than they are for MSAs.

The panel also recommended that the federal government should take a more active role in coordinating statistical activities and in developing and promoting common definitions and other statistical standards that are appropriate for implementation at the federal, state, and local levels. As it turns out, OMB has since defaulted on its responsibility, even for the federal government, to say nothing of state and local statistics (Bonnen, 1984).

Statistical activities and standards must be managed at not only the federal but also at the state level. States are solely responsible for many statistical programs, and state officials have a major interest in many other statistical activities in which the state shares responsibility for producing data with other levels of government or for which the state is a major user of data produced by other governmental levels.

Each state should designate or develop an organization for managing the state's role in statistical coordination in establishing and implementing standards, if such an organization does not already exist. The panel also identified the following specific data needs.

The Survey of Income and Program Participation (SIPP) should be expanded to include samples of clients of rural development programs and rural clients of general programs as well as to the Current Population Survey (CPS) and the Panel Study of Income Dynamics (PSID).

The Bureau of Labor Statistics should develop an index of underemployment. The much greater incidence of underemployment in rural areas has long biased any comparisons of unemployment. Even measures of unemployment are often lacking or quite unreliable for rural areas.

A rural cost-of-living index should also be developed. The panel recommended that the Bureau of Labor Statistics provide an annual index of cost of living differentials between each of eight to ten rural areas and selected urban areas.

The academy panel made quite a few other recommendations, but those identified here define the larger deficiencies that affect the rural database. Thirteen years later, none of these recommendations have been achieved. They should be on our agenda for action today. In addition to the now thirteen-year-old National Academy of Sciences recommendations, other improvements are needed today.

Other Needed Improvements

In the general database for rural areas, there are a number of additional needs. By far the most preeminent need affects everything and has already briefly been discussed in the first three recommendations from the National Academy of Sciences panel. The database for rural decision-making will remain incoherent until two general characteristics are imposed on the various kinds of data collected nationally, from education and health to housing and agriculture. One of these is a common geographic code on practically every major national collection identifying the county from which the individual microdata set comes. Until we have the capability of sorting our data by any preferred geography, service to rural decision makers and rural units of government will be very difficult and, in general, the data will be unavailable. This, of course, is not enough. Sample sizes are far too small to provide accurate data at the county level in most collections. Samples for many collections need to be increased.

Closely related is the need for a multidimensional measure of the degree of urbanization stretching from highly rural to highly urban that will allow us to classify these diverse counties properly and to deal with the changes that occur over time. The metropolitan/nonmetropolitan or urban/rural definition, in which rural or nonmetropolitan is simply the residual left over after you define urban or metropolitan, is naive and not only useless but even dangerous. The binary concept to which the Census Bureau continues to cling, namely that all locations are either urban or rural, flies in the face of the obvious relative nature and complexity of what is being measured. The failure to update these concepts has reached outrageous proportions. Even some of the smallest countries in Europe (such as Belgium, which is smaller than most of the states in the Union) have multiple measures of the degree of urbanization. If Belgium can afford to produce such a measure, surely we can.

Finally, if the use of MSAs is continued, and politically it is difficult to imagine how they can be dropped, they need to be subsumed into a stable system of SSAs covering the entire United States. We need a standard geography that aggregates to the entire nation and which is stable, consistent, and comparable. In general, what happens now is that reliable, detailed data are collected for MSAs but not for NMSAs. In addition, the MSA boundaries are under chronic political pressures for change. The MSA standard has been politicized so frequently that it is an unstable, and thus unsuitable, base for statistical measurement and aggregation. If there were a standard set of reasonably fixed statistical areas to account for all of the United States and this were combined with a multidimensional measure of degree of urbanization, it might be possible to create a far more useful national data set. Little else matters if we cannot improve the general context within which data are collected from that part of the nation we now call nonmetropolitan. In addition, other important general database needs for rural areas include the following:

1. Better measures of major economic sector activity for nonmetropolitan counties and better measures of their influence on rural community welfare. These sectors include forestry, fisheries, recreation, mining, manufacturing, and services at a minimum.
2. Better environmental database for rural areas, including an improved ability to measure groundwater quality and quantity and to track waste disposal problems and toxic chemical movement and disposal in rural areas. Rural America has become the dump site for urban America.
3. Better measures of rural income and assets, housing quality, poverty and deprivation (which is rising), education, health and nutrition, and other dimensions of human welfare for small areas.
4. Better measures for rural access to credit and capital, to transportation by mode, to public services and community facilities, and to natural resources and energy use.
5. Household time budgets and better measures of the human resources of rural society.
6. Improved demographic data that are available more frequently than every ten years, which the census now provides. In the last five years of each decade following a census, these data are essentially useless in every environment in which rapid changes have been occurring, which is fairly frequently in the United States. A mid-decade census or preferably a large survey of population is necessary.

The agricultural database needs a number of additional improvements as well, such as the following:

1. Improved labor market data. As indicated, labor market data are almost nonexistent in any comprehensive form.
2. Improved data on services to farming, including financial services. As purchased inputs grow, many of the service inputs are now escaping our data collection.
3. Better performance indicators for the agribusiness sector. In terms of value added, the agribusiness sector is now so much larger than the farm sector that future improvements in productivity within agriculture will have to come mainly from agribusiness, the performance of which we know relatively little.
4. Additional performance indicators for the farm sector. Despite the many measures we now have, we also need size distributions of farms by input categories; size distributions of income and assets deflated over time; better measures of price and income stability; measures of productivity that internalize major well-recognized externalities; and measures of access to credit and credit market performance.
5. Improved measures of food consumption. Current disappearance measures are relatively crude. This is a difficult area of measurement.
6. Better measures of international market performance. These measures are becoming more important as our markets become more global.
7. Improved international trade and finance measures because our dependence on trade and international finance has increased dramatically in agriculture.

A Major Challenge

We face a major challenge in achieving these goals, with very real obstacles to overcome. But it is urgent that we move now to improve our databases. In fact, we have little choice but to do so. Why?

We are passing the point of no return on many options in rural development and viability. This can be seen in the extreme depopulation of the Great Plains and parts of the Far West, in the urban sprawl that is devouring the rural landscape in the Midwest and the East and in the exploitation of resources in the South and West without concern for external effects. There is, as well, a rising crisis of rural access to various transportation modes as the result of deregulation. In addition, the deregulation of banking has not been assessed adequately. It is already clear that in many states, rural savings are draining out of branch banks in the rural areas and access to credit has declined. This problem is especially obvious in the Southwestern oil states where the liquidity of many large banks has been impaired by mismanagement and defaults on oil and real estate loans.

Another reason why we must move now is that the land-grant institutions must deal soon and effectively with a number of challenges or they will lose legitimacy and face long-term decline. The first of these challenges are the agricultural externalities for which land-grant universities are, in general, held partly accountable. This is especially so with respect to the environmental movement, which is rapidly taking over the farmers' role in the stewardship of the land. In addition, natural resource use issues are becoming more and more controversial and cannot be avoided. Finally, the governors of the states are increasingly asking whether the universities are capable or willing to contribute to solutions of the states' more pressing problems. The initiative in economic development is now in the hands of the governors. If the universities do not respond to their states' needs, they will very likely lose much of their legitimacy and financial support in the state legislatures.

We must move rapidly to deal with the changing demographics of the United States and its rural sector. It is increasingly clear that we face a decline in the quality of U.S. human capital and ultimately in our productivity. This decline is perhaps a function of the rising disorder in the American family, rural and urban. It can be seen in the decay of the nuclear family. Today, fewer than half of all children live with two parents. The problems of delinquency, drugs, and teenage pregnancy are growing. Many youth lack the motivation and values that make an individual effective in society. The formation of values and the development of motivational structures that form effective, functioning human beings are primarily a product of the family and its socialization of children.

Past discussions of human capital development have tended to focus on the formal institutions of society that are primarily responsible for education and health. We have been taking for granted the contribution of the family to human capital formation, but we can do so no longer. By the year 2,000, more than one-half of all new entrants to the labor force will be minorities, primarily blacks and Hispanics, a very high percentage of whom will be low income, low skilled, poorly educated, and often in poor health (Fullerton, 1987). Clearly, these deficiencies in human capital will constrain our ability to extract greater productivity out of improvements in technology or greater investments in physical and biological capital. If you think we have a problem of inadequate productivity improvement today, just wait until these human capital problems have their full impact on the labor force.

Problems in Providing Rural Databases

Reliable rural statistics cost more per capita and per data set produced. In addition, the more heterogeneous nature of rural society requires more descriptors. Thus, in calling for better rural data, we are talking about providing more data at higher per unit costs than we do in metropolitan areas.

Another problem we face is that the demand for publicly provided rural data is weak and the interest in it diffused. There is little policy-driven demand, since we have no coherent national rural development policy worth noting. This, in turn, suggests that the political support for a rural development policy is lacking and is commonly confused with agricultural policy (Bonnen, 1992). On top of this, state and local resources for data collection are limited and statewide rural community statistical needs lack clear focus due to the great heterogeneity of rural communities.

Even if we can assert clearly that some specific types of data need to be collected, conceptual development is often lacking. Many of the data needs mentioned here require the development of new concepts such as underemployment, a standard statistical geography for the United States, or improved environmental data measures for rural areas.

Finally, the federal statistical system and its product is fragmented, lacking the institutional capacity for effective coordination and exceedingly lacking in statistical standards for rural data. Therefore, we lack the capacity to address many problems (Bonnen, 1984).

The Politics and Economics of Statistics

The economics of statistical information is very poorly understood. Nowhere has this ignorance been as complete as it has been at the highest policy levels in the federal government over the decade of the 1980s.

Statistics are to a very substantial degree public or quasi-public goods in nature. There are, indeed, many private information goods, but they involve highly specialized, often single-problem–related data and analysis. We would have no demographic measures of any consequence were it not for the U.S. Census of Population. The same is true of almost all the major public surveys and census collections. Private sector firms and industries cannot afford to collect such data for themselves or for resale to others; they would not recover their costs (Bonnen, 1986). As indicated, the demand for rural data is often diffused and weak, in part because we have no coherent rural policy.

On the other hand, where Congress establishes specific public policies, intense interests tend to form around the benefits or costs imposed by the law on groups in society. Such examples range from farm policy to the tax laws. The conventional public program areas in housing, health, education, agriculture, and social security generate very substantial demands for statistics to manage the programs. A decade or so after the original legislation, the demand for these data will often extend well beyond the minimum necessary for running the program. New institutions related to the policy area develop in both the private and the public sectors beyond the federal government and they depend on such information to function effectively. Indeed, they come to constitute major users of that data. Large-scale, multiple purpose, national databases have high benefit-cost ratios and cannot be mounted as efficiently, if at all, from the private sector.

Large private sector firms express an intense demand for statistics driven by their vested-interest or private policy concern. These firms need very specific numbers, some publicly, others privately produced. They will lobby for data they want that can only be provided by public efforts, and they will pay for the collection of those data that can be produced efficiently on a private basis. They also can take very active policy positions to prevent the analysis or collection of public data that impairs their efforts in public policy or informs their customers or competitors who would otherwise be disadvantaged. Even when such data are collected and analyzed, these firms will often attempt to limit public access (Starr and Corson, 1987).

Much of the demand for privately provided data is very narrow and specific. Such data are needed to market some specific product or to illuminate some policy issue or a specific niche in a market and none of these data are likely to be provided publicly. Thus, private firms ranging from consultants, who do analysis using existing data, to statistical consultants, who will collect data for you, exist to service the needs of the private sector and, in some cases, the public sector. These data are usually needed for a specific decision and are thus focused on one specific problem. The final point that needs to be made about the private sector is that it is very dependent, even in the production of privately provided data, on the existence of good public data provided by national censuses, surveys, and the national accounts (Bonnen, 1986).

Ideology Drives Policy

Every administration reflects some ideology, consciously or unconsciously. Any decision involves prescriptive beliefs. The Reagan administration had a clear attitude toward information. It did not want data broadly available on poverty, housing, health, education, or even agriculture. As recently as the FY 1990 budget review, NASS was told by an OMB political appointee that they had no business collecting data for use in private markets. The U.S. government has been collecting, analyzing, and disseminating agricultural market information to improve the efficiency and performance of those markets (i.e., in the public interest) for a century and a half. Have we been in error for 150 years? Are these markets so completely different today? Imagine the price instability and increased concentration that would follow the elimination of NASS programs.

The Reagan OMB statistical policy aim was to eliminate all data collected or paid for by the U.S. government except those needed for federal policy and program decisions—as OMB defined those needs. The private sector information industry would take care of all other needs—as long as you could afford the price (Starr and Corson, 1987). The presumed need for an informed electorate in a democracy counted for nothing. The administration did not want any central capacity in OMB to coordinate an informed statistical policy or to develop new statistical standards or statistical products. The only purpose of OBM's role in statistics was to privatize federal data collection and eliminate every data set it could in the name of reducing paperwork. In eight years, the administration did more damage to federal statistical quality and product availability than benign neglect did in 40 to 50 years (Wallman, 1988; Bonnen, 1984).

These OMB leaders are economic illiterates blinded by their ideology. They do not understand the economics of information. They do not recognize that public and private data are complements in productive use, and they do not realize that private sector productivity depends on public data. This stupidity did not continue in the Bush administration, which took federal statistical responsibilities seriously.

Such an ideological outlook on data collection, analysis, and dissemination, as in the Reagan administration, is destructive of the nation's productive capacity and development and must be rejected. We must combine with other professional groups and business organizations aggressively to establish a public ideology to sustain necessary national data collection. Our allies in this matter include the Council of Professional Associations on Federal Statistics (COPAFS) and the Council of Social Science Associations (COSSA), as well as various academic professional associations and private sector organizations with interests in public data. That public data collection is a national necessity has been part of the conventional wisdom of this nation from the founding of the Republic. It arose out of the values of the eighteenth-century Enlightenment and rationalism. It has been part of the very air we breath. It has been taken for granted. It is clearly a complex matter involving more than economics and politics (Kellman, 1987). We must develop such a philosophic statement and broadcast it. It needs to be embedded in law.

Ideological or social movements generally precede and drive policy innovation. The time is right for an equity-based expression of outrage over the treatment of rural people and their communities. To succeed, this effort should be combined with the values of the environmental movement already underway. By itself, it is only a cry in the wilderness. The time is ripe for this movement. The state governors are taking over the initiative in economic development and human welfare policy from a federal government in default. The National Governors Association is in search of common ground for pursuing national policy. Rural poverty and homelessness have increased dramatically. Rural poverty has been increasing faster since 1978 than has central city poverty (O'Hare, 1988). As a consequence, today there is a slightly higher incidence of poverty in nonmetropolitan or rural areas than there is in the central cities in the United States (Greenstein, 1989). The public needs to know this. Rural people have had it with their landscape being used as a dump for urban waste. Rural people and state legislators are now increasingly active in an endless number of issues. But little of this has been expressed in a coherent policy at the national level.

What Is the Role of the University?

Where problems are well defined and the moral imperatives clear, we need to encourage people to organize for action. The land-grant university has played a limited role in such matters in the past, but it can play an important role today. More central to the university's capability is the need to define clearly the plethora of rural problems, both for research purposes and for action. After the problems are defined, we need to communicate them clearly and repeatedly to the public and to the decision makers. In addition to defining the problems, the university has another role: to develop concepts and empirically test the concepts needed to define and act on rural problems. Many of the issues that have been identified lack the necessary conceptual focus. Examples include the need for an underemployment index and a measure of rural cost of living as well as a need for an improved rural environmental database.

Another natural university role in these matters is the development, through modeling and empirical analysis, of the best real world representations of the relevant concepts. Generally, analysis leads the refined design of data collection. Another potential university role involves some pioneering collaboration with federal and state statistical and action agencies in the design and development of new data systems. Federal and state agencies are underfunded and are under great pressure. Most now have reduced capacity with which to do the research needed before new data systems can be developed. Their researchers usually have more than they can do to keep up with demands for improvements in existing data systems. We can help by collaborating with them in research. Limited investments by university researchers in the design of needed new data systems could accelerate the implementation and collection of new data.

Another role, generally not thought of by academics, but where they have the capability, is in the development of standards for data collection and analysis. Researchers are often at the cutting edge in dealing with the various kinds of problems. The need for statistical standards in new data development is always one of the early problems encountered. University researchers can have a decisive role in setting these standards. Finally, universities have the potential to serve as the neutral ground and convener of conflicting public and private interests. These conflicting interests need to be brought together in order to address problems and act on them. Interests in conflict will rarely, if ever, convene on one or another's turf. But the university is usually seen as neutral ground. This has substantial power in settling conflicts and getting on with the job.

The range of these examples implies the need for something that universities often do not do very well, that is, maintaining a reasonably balanced investment in the continuum of knowledge that ranges from disciplinary through subject-matter to problem-solving research. Disciplinary research is work that improves the theories, basic measurement, databases, and the techniques of a basic discipline such as sociology, chemistry, economics, physics, or philosophy. Subject-matter research is concerned with multidisciplinary subjects that are important to some decision makers concerned with reasonably well-defined sets of problems such as rural development, agronomy, or farm management. Subject-matter research produces useful results but is still general enough that it is not directly relevant to solving specific practical problems. Problem-solving research deals with a specific problem and involves much more highly specialized and processed information. Problem-solving knowledge is highly relevant to a single problem but has little power of generalization. Subject-matter knowledge is relevant to a general set of problems and in many cases is more generalizable by virtue of being less specific. Disciplinary knowledge, on the other hand, has the greatest power of generalization but usually has the lowest relevance to any particular problem (Johnson, 1986). The continuum of knowledge is a process by which the power of basic knowledge is transformed into useful and tested information products for solving problems. The land-grant system has been committed to maintaining this entire continuum and transferring to users the knowledge necessary for solving major societal problems.

Historically, the land-grant mission focused on agriculture and rural society; however, since World War II, the university increasingly linked its reward system to disciplinary research. Most disciplinary research becomes embedded in journal articles that are transformed into usable and tested subject-matter and problem-related knowledge rather slowly by a poorly coordinated process involving many actors. As one moves from disciplinary toward problem-solving research, private sector responsibilities increase and the universities' responsibilities decline, but the university must collaborate to assure effective and rapid transfer of knowledge. In addition, as can be seen in the research and development (R&D) literature, the coordination of that collaboration produces very high returns (Evenson, Waggoner, and Ruttan, 1979). Universities are not doing well at this today, not only because many are focused almost exclusively on generating disciplinary knowledge, but others, especially some professional schools, have concentrated on the other end of the continuum on subject-matter and problem-solving knowledge, ignoring investment in disciplinary knowledge that is necessary to maintain the long-term intellectual vitality of subject-matter and problem-solving activities.

It is worth making a distinction here between data and information. Data are the direct products or outputs of measurement or counting. They may or may not have direct relevance to a specific decision. Information, on the other hand, is a decision input, which integrates data from various sources as well as integrating data with analysis in order to transform it into knowledge that is relevant to and can inform a specific decision. Thus, information has a very strong teleological content having been processed to develop its relevance for a specific decision.

Far too frequently, policymakers and sometimes analysts treat data as if they were something that you dig up, put in a sack, and deliver as is, to a user. This is nonsense. Data must be transformed into information before they have much utility. Thus, information processing systems are an absolute necessity. Raw data must be cleaned, debugged, and validated. Data must be compared to past data sets for comparability to know what they mean and to test their reliability. This process is often referred to as *data analysis*.

One of the great weaknesses, both in statistical systems and in research, is that statisticians and analysts often fail to analyze data adequately. Quantitative technicians often seem to think they know what data mean before even looking at them, simply as a result of having designed their collection (or worse, even without having collected them), which is a fundamental error. Data analysis is essential before statisticians can understand and explain what their data can be used for and what the data's limitations are. Data analysis is absolutely essential to the analyst's ability to select and use data that are appropriate to the specification of models and other analytic formats. Data can be used to test alternative analytical or model designs within an information system. Conversely, previously validated analytical models can be used to test the accuracy and appropriateness of various data designs.

Information systems do many other things. Data must be formatted, which implies a specific purpose. Alternative uses are eliminated by the decision to select a specific format. Data must be integrated with other primary and secondary data. Data must be integrated with standard decision rules, as in the national accounts and in other imputational systems such as for the disappearance data that we use for food consumption measures. Data must be analyzed, organized, and shaped for some general purpose to become subject-matter information. Data must be further analyzed, organized, and shaped into problem-solving information for a specific decision. Most private sector, information industry firms are clustered toward the user end of information systems.

There are a number of obstacles to an effective university role in improving rural data. The reward systems of many universities recognize only disciplinary research, usually in the form of peer-reviewed articles in disciplinary journals. Today, after two decades of inflation-eroded budgets, slow economic growth, and actual budget cuts, there are limited operating dollars for research. Most of the existing budgets go into personnel with little left for operational costs. There also is only a limited tradition of multidisciplinary and multiuniversity collaboration as well as collaboration with private sector firms in the history of higher education. Certainly the colleges of agriculture represent a very high percentage of what tradition does exist, but the shift toward a disciplinary focus has eroded their historic capability. Ironically, the university is now under increasing pressure to improve its ability to move knowledge into practical use. Needless to say, this presents the universities with substantial difficulties in changing their current practices.

Finally, we face a dilemma. Without clear policy goals for rural America, a coherent policy database cannot be developed. But without a good database, it is not possible to develop a clear statement of the problem to be addressed, policy prescriptions, or means of implementation. Thus, databases in policy must develop together in an iterative, interactive manner if their interdependence is not to be a major constraint (Johnston and Clark, 1982). We are unlikely to have a fully adequate rural database until we have a coherent, consistent rural policy, and vice versa. Thus we must act on several fronts at once: data development, policy creation and evaluation of alternative options, problem identification and definition, development of moral and ethical justification for policy action, and the organization of social movements for policy action, to name but a few. We must work on all of the constraints in a continuing and energetic manner. It can be done. We've done it before for other problems.

References

Bonnen, James T. 1984. Federal statistical coordination today: A disaster or a disgrace? *Milbank Memorial Fund Quarterly/Health and Society* 62(1):1–41.

______. 1986. Agriculture in the information age. Keynote address to the Agricultural Institute of Canada, Saskatoon, Canada, July 7. Michigan State University Agricultural Economics Staff Paper No. 86-78.

______. 1989. The statistical database for rural America. Pp. 25–34 (Senate print 101-50) in *Towards Rural Development Policy for the 1990s: Enhancing Income Employment Opportunities*. Washington, D.C.: U.S. Congressional Research Service and Joint Economic Committee of Congress.

______. 1992. Why is there no coherent U.S. rural policy? *Policy Studies Journal* 20(2):190–201.

Evenson, Robert E., Paul E. Waggoner, and Vernon W. Ruttan. 1979. Economic benefits from research: An example from agriculture. *Science* 205(September 14):101–107.

Fullerton, Howard N. 1987. Labor force projections: 1986 to 2000. *Monthly Labor Review*. U.S. Department of Labor, September, pp. 19–29.

Greenstein, Robert. 1989. Welfare reform in rural areas. Pp. 35–59 (Senate print 101-50) in *Towards Rural Development Policy for the 1990s: Enhancing Income Employment Opportunities*. Washington, D.C.: U.S. Congressional Research Service and Joint Economic Committee of Congress.

Hines, F. K., D. L. Brown, and J. M. Zimmer. 1975. *Social and Economic Characteristics of the Population in Metro and Nonmetro Counties, 1970*. Agricultural Economic Report No. 272. Washington, D.C.: U.S. Department of Agriculture.

Johnson, Glenn L. 1986. *Research Methodology for Economists*. New York: Macmillan.

Johnston, Bruce F., and William C. Clark. 1982. *Redesigning Rural Development: A Strategic Perspective*. Baltimore: The Johns Hopkins University Press.

Kellman, Steven. 1987. The political foundations of American statistical policy. Pp. 275–302 in *The Politics of Numbers*. New York: Russell Sage Foundation.

National Research Council (NRC). 1981. *Rural America in Passage: Statistics for Policy*. Edited by D. M. Gilford, G. L. Nelson, and L. Ingram. Panel on Statistics for Rural Development Policy, Committee on National Statistics, National Research Council. Washington, D.C.: National Academy Press.

O'Hare, William P. 1988. *The Rise of Poverty in Rural America*. Population Trends and Public Policy Paper No. 15. Washington, D.C.: Population Reference Bureau.

Starr, Paul, and Ross Corson. 1987. Who will have the numbers? The rise of the statistical services industry and the politics of public data. Pp. 415–447 in *The Politics of Numbers*. New York: Russell Sage Foundation.

Wallman, Katherine K. 1988. *Losing Count: The Federal Statistical System*. Population Trends and Public Policy Paper No. 16. Washington, D.C.: Population Reference Bureau.

______. 1989. Federal statistics in the FY 1990 budget. *AAAS Report XIV: Research and Development, FY 1990*. Washington, D.C.: American Association for the Advancement of Science.

PART TWO

Data for Rural Information Systems

The following five chapters explore both the kinds of rural data that are gathered and the kinds of data that are not gathered, as well as the policy implications of such decisions. We clearly do not have sufficient data in quantity, breadth, or continuity to formulate policy issues for rural people. The authors point out the need to modify existing longitudinal files, to use synthetic estimates to augment existing data, to have greater access to existing rural data in large data sets, to make greater use of panel studies, and to refine sampling frames and qualitative data to supplement longitudinal quantitative indicators. As Bonnen notes in Chapter 3, statistics are perishable. We need new ideas and new approaches to capture what is going on in rural areas and the implications of such conditions for rural and urban policy. Our information system should be sensitive to the conditions of all Americans, not just those living in urban America.

4

Multiple-Level Data Sets

Glenn L. Nelson

Rural problems are set within a system of hierarchical units of analysis which vary over space and time. The principal elements of the hierarchy consist of individuals who are grouped into households as well as into productive organizations such as firms and public agencies; individuals, households, and firms join together into groups to promote shared interests (e.g., a shared position with regard to legislation); households, firms, and public agencies are grouped into communities; and communities are grouped into regions, regions into states, and states into the nation.

While each unit in the hierarchy can be considered merely as the sum of its constituent parts, each level of units also contributes attributes difficult to attain in other levels. The following discussion reviews the dimensions of each level of units that concern us as we reach conclusions regarding well-being.

Units of Analysis

Individuals

Individuals are citizens with rights and responsibilities and are an important unit of analysis for monitoring the state of basic liberties, such as freedom from arbitrary seizure and imprisonment and freedom to associate with those of one's choosing. Individuals are also important, and ultimately the most important, inputs to productive processes. Individuals embody human capital and supply labor. They also allocate the physical capital under their control. In addition, individuals make decisions about institutional forms that govern resource allocation. Individuals are thus an important unit of analysis when examining the productive capacity of a society.

Households

In the United States, the household is usually the unit that makes consumption decisions. This makes the household the relevant unit for analyses based on consumption, such as the adequacy of the basic necessities available to people. Most government programs dealing with people's access to goods and services recognize this by using household variables as indicators of need. For example, poverty is defined with respect to households rather than individuals.

Households are also important as productive organizations. Much of human capital is produced in households. Within households, the adult members share the responsibilities for educating and training members to be productive workers and citizens, for providing adequate nutrition, for securing health care, and for choosing and inculcating values. Transferring information and care from adults to children is an especially important function of a successful household. In addition, physical capital is often the joint property of two or more household members and is managed as a household rather than an individual asset. Finally, successful households supply close interpersonal relationships and mutual support to their members.

Firms and Similar Productive Organizations

The primary role of firms and other productive organizations, such as cooperatives, is to produce goods and services that are subsequently consumed by people. This is an important role, but it is a means to an end rather than an end in itself. Thus, firms are viewed primarily as intermediate variables in the social system; that is, they are units neither closely associated with goals nor directly responsible for policy changes.

A major caveat to this point emphasizes that firms often produce human capital through experience and training; that is, firms often offer "good jobs" rather than "dead-end jobs." This function is so basic to continued economic prosperity that it can be considered as a goal in itself.

Communities

Communities are important in at least three major respects. First, they supply many publicly provided goods and services (e.g., education and physical infrastructure) that affect the well-being of people and they are appropriately included among measures of welfare. Stinson's work (1982) on local government expenditures relative to national norms exemplifies this type of analysis.

Second, communities supply the immediate social environment. This environment sometimes includes members of the extended family and can either embody sharing among, or ignoring of, individuals and households in difficult or good times.

Third, communities play a significant role in designing and implementing policies that affect individual well-being. Communities are thus important units of analysis because they help formulate policy instruments as well as directly provide goods and services that affect individual well-being.

Interest Groups

Interest groups, which are defined in this context as organizations of individuals, households, or firms, whose purpose is to promote the common interests of the members, are important because of their political influence. These groups provide information, albeit often biased, to their members and to the general public as a means to influence public policy. These groups also provide access to decision makers in governments. As with firms, these groups are intermediate actors in the system whose attributes are neither measures of final goals nor policy initiatives. An interest group representing the needs and desires of rural America could be an important actor in rural development policy, but no such group exists (see Cornman and Kincaid, 1984).

Substate Regions

The substate region, a very important unit of analysis, includes much of the work, residential, and purchasing activity of a group of rural people. Policymakers use this regional unit of analysis to gain insight into communities that would otherwise be excluded if these communities were considered in isolation.

Substate regions can be the underlying basis for interest groups that have an important influence on the political process. Such groups are especially easy to form in a system based on geographic representation such as the U.S. system. But the region itself typically does not have a governmental structure that formulates and implements policy—and thus is relevant as an analytic unit for the study of policy instruments. Rather, the interest groups representing the region work in the context of state governments or the federal government that encompasses a broader territory than the substate region.

Substate regions may, and probably should, become more important with respect to measures of goal attainment. The interrelationships among communities are often so intricate that the region is a better focus for work on defining and solving problems. The major deterrents to this approach are that governmental units are often more reflective of rural communities than are regions and that people tend to identify with communities rather than regions. However, analysts must realize the potential gains from cooperation within the substate region or they might lose opportunities for rural development.

State and Federal Governments

State and federal governments, as units of analysis, are very important as wielders of policy instruments but are unimportant as units whose characteristics are direct measures of individual, household, and community well-being. That is, these units are a means rather than an ends. Their important functions include the provision of publicly supplied goods and services and of investments in research and development with broad externalities.

Summary

The choice of goals and associated proxy measures that policymakers emphasize, in part, determines the primary unit of analysis from which outcomes are assessed. Households are the most important unit for consumption-related measures, including but not limited to basic necessities. Individuals are the most prominent unit for measuring basic liberties and productive capacities. Communities are the most important unit for measuring publicly provided goods and services, especially "public goods" with significant externalities.

Proxy measures for policy instruments are usually chosen from the attributes of communities, state governments, and the federal government; more instruments at the scale of the substate region are desirable. One or more of these units are essential in any study of the formation and implementation of rural policy. Households, firms, communities, interest groups, and substate regions are all important intervening units of analysis that affect measures of well-being.

Linkages Among Units of Analysis

Each unit of analysis is associated with a unique role. However, a better understanding of the relationships among the units of analysis often yields insights into the nature of problems, likely implementation problems, and possible solutions. This is especially true in the case of rural development, which entails complex interactions among individual, household, firm, interest group, governmental, community, regional, state, and national factors.

In particular, the behavior of any unit in the hierarchy depends on its setting in the hierarchy as well as on its own characteristics. For example, the prospects of a newborn child depend on the household, community, and state as well as on his or her inherent intelligence and biological fitness. Indeed, when we try to improve a child's prospects through public policy, we focus on the household (e.g., Aid to Families with Dependent Children and Food Stamp programs) and the community (e.g., Head Start and school lunch programs). As another example, the outcome of an entrepreneurial venture depends on the surrounding regional economy as well as on the characteristics of the entrepreneur and the venture.

To illustrate these concepts, three linkages (household formation, commuting, and migration) among units of analysis that affect the evolution of the units over time are discussed.

Household Formation

Individuals join together into households. While many households exist that are not formed as a result of marriages, most of the research has focused on the characteristics of spouses. Schirm (1986:1) found "that assortative mating is possibly a predominant force determining the extent of both intra- and intergenerational inequality." Sweet and Bumpass (1987) found that, in general, people marry people of similar socioeconomic status and this strong tendency perpetuates the pattern of inequality from one generation to the next. This finding also "has important implications for marital stability . . . , human capital investment and family labor supply . . . , and fertility" (Schirm, 1986:1).

A brief literature search did not reveal differences between rural and urban people in this respect or of the role of institutions subject to public policy manipulation (e.g., use of public schools and neighborhood integration). Such studies would be useful in assessing whether smaller scale settlements yield greater mixing of socioeconomic classes in marriage and whether public policy can affect this mixing to any appreciable degree.

Commuting

Individuals, households, firms, and other entities join together into communities. In many cases, an individual is associated with two communities—working in one and residing in another. Improved automobiles and roads in nonmetropolitan areas have made commuting a much more viable option today than at the turn of the century. Commuting is attractive to many rural residents because they have invested in the physical and social infrastructure of their residential communities.

Because commuting is a viable option for rural residents, communities do not need to provide all the economic functions. Practitioners and analysts should recognize this when developing options. As noted, the substate region encompassing the communities takes on great importance for analyzing and facilitating the options of communities. Just as cities have found it desirable to integrate many of the financing and service provisions across neighborhoods, communities in rural areas will need to move in this direction. For example, property taxes on places of employment must be pooled, to some extent, with the taxes on workers' residences if the residential community is to be viable. If not, individuals will have an incentive to locate in the same jurisdiction as industrial facilities for reasons associated with governmental institutions unrelated to the underlying economic costs.

Migration

Households move from one community to another. Thus, the composition of communities with respect to individuals and households is a dynamic matter (Garkovich, 1989).

Although analysts dispute some of the determinants of migration, many points of agreement emerge (Greenwood, 1975; Grosse and Nelson, 1988). Rates of migration tend to be lower when the distance between the origin and the destination is great; this appears to be a result of psychic and informational costs rather than transportation costs. Younger and more educated people are more likely to migrate than older and less-well-educated people. For people with more education, the rate of migration decreases less with greater distance between the origin and destination. Those who have moved once are more likely to move again.

Although economic conditions are known to affect the choice of destination of migrants, analysts dispute their importance as a cause of out-migration. Evidence from a study in Minnesota supports the view that local economic conditions are not significant factors in explaining out-migration (Grosse and Nelson, 1988). Greenwood (1975) reviews the claims that economic conditions significantly affect out-migration as well as in-migration.

The consequences of migration are not as well understood as are the determinants of migration.[1] The complexity of the consequences is in part a result of individuals ignoring social benefits and costs; that is, individuals consider only private benefits and costs. Because migration imposes costs and benefits on those not migrating, a full accounting of the consequences of migration must include the private benefits and costs to individuals and society.

The hypothesis of individual rationality and the results of empirical studies support the notion that private benefits of migration outweigh private costs. While some migrants undoubtedly find themselves worse off in their new location than they were in their old, most migrants find that their economic situation improves.

Migration affects the remaining population in the place of origin in both positive and negative ways. Remaining residents face less competition for employment and thus may find jobs easier or receive higher wages. If out-migrants take less nonhuman capital with them than that possessed by the average nonmigrant, as is assumed in neoclassical formulations and seems reasonable based on the age-profile of the migrants, the remaining capital is spread over a smaller number of people and productivity will rise because of the rise in the capital/labor ratio. This further reinforces the tendency of remaining residents to receive higher wages; owners of capital will find the rate of return to immobile capital under downward pressure. For example, migration out of farming has resulted in more capital per farmer, higher returns to farmers' labor, and downward pressure on the returns to farmland.

A number of factors reduce the well-being of the remaining residents in regions of out-migration. The loss of population may reduce local purchases and cause further losses of jobs and income in the retail and service sectors. If young people, entrepreneurs, and those with more human capital are disproportionately represented among those who leave, future growth will be constrained.

The economics of providing local public services may further worsen the well-being of residents in the jurisdiction of origin. The adverse effect of the loss of educated young people is reinforced by the importance of local taxes in financing primary and secondary education. A jurisdiction or substate region under economic stress finds itself exporting its wealth in the form of human capital and, thus, is under continuing economic stress. In addition, the fall in the local tax base may exceed the decline in the costs of providing public services. The remaining residents face the choice of paying more per capita for the existing level of public services or accepting a decline in the quantity or quality of these services.

When the net effect of out-migration reduces the quality of life for the remaining residents, the incentives for further out-migration increase. Rather than being the equilibrating force between regional economies that some theorists and practitioners hypothesize, migration becomes a force with cumulative effects that leads to downward spirals in some regional economies once set in motion. The potential for such spirals is increased by the local financing of education. As noted, the out-migration of the young and educated is a drain on local wealth. Observing such a drain, the local residents may invest less in education. This reduces the viability of the substate region and increases the net outflow of residents, probably because of little or no in-migration, not because of markedly greater rates of out-migration.

Migration has similarly complex effects on the destination areas. The increased numbers of people will increase the ratio of labor to capital, assuming the in-migrants bring less capital per person than the average person in the destination area. The increased labor/capital ratio will result in higher returns to the owners of capital and, therefore, encourage further capital investments and economic growth.

People other than capitalists in the destination areas are not likely to fare as well. The migrants increase the supply of labor and the competition for jobs and, thereby, decrease the likelihood of wage increases. The migrants may crowd the existing urban poor out of low-skill, entry-level jobs; opportunities and incomes for the existing urban poor may suffer as a result. The migrants may also crowd the existing urban poor out of public assistance programs. This is especially likely if these programs "cream" the potential recipients, that is, systematically concentrate on the easiest cases in order to report the maximum number of success stories.

Finally, in-migration raises the costs of providing public services and may require additional public infrastructure in the destination area. The nature of these costs depends on the number and characteristics of the in-migrants and on excess capacity, if any, in the public sector. For example, the migration of families with children increases the burden on primary and secondary schools, whereas the migration of high school graduates who are single does not entail such a burden. Similarly, in-migrants raise local revenues by increasing the tax base and by increasing the factors used in intergovernmental funding formulas. The increase in local revenues depends on the number and characteristics of the in-migrants and on the structure of taxes and intergovernmental aids. The net effect of in-migration on taxes and public services is impossible to deduce without quantitative analysis of the particular class of cases to which an area belongs. Such analyses should be given high priority.

The social benefits and costs of migration are based on anecdotal evidence, not empirical studies. The discussion of the consequences of migration demonstrates that the problem is not a lack of interesting and exciting hypotheses. The first priority must be to construct a database to adequately test the hypotheses. The gap in our knowledge concerning the social benefits and costs of migration is a key factor leading U.S. analysts and policymakers to tentative, lukewarm statements about the appropriate role for explicit spatial policies.

Gaps in the Database

Analysts do not understand many of the relationships between the units of analysis. For scholars engaged in increasing understanding of social, political, and economic systems, the gaps in understanding are both problems and opportunities. Filling gaps in knowledge is a time-honored and challenging task.

For people engaged in making policy decisions, the gaps in knowledge are only a problem. These decision makers seek to attain goals by manipulating the policy levers at their disposal. A lack of clarity as to the linkages between policy levers and goals leads to mistaken actions and missed opportunities. The prospects for filling these gaps in understanding are poor despite the enthusiasm of scholars and the desires of policy-makers. The database is sorely wanting.

Desired Data

The problems of multiple units of analysis that both appear in hierarchical systems and have important relationships over space and time require a correspondingly complex database for solution. The database should identify the location of the units in the hierarchy.[2] For example, individuals should not only have their own identifying code but also a code corresponding to their household, place of work, and community from which region and state can be easily derived. The database would include provisions for the attributes unique to each level of units—rather than take the naive position that a higher order unit is merely the simple aggregate of the lower order units. For example, a place of work is appropriately recognized as a cooperative, corporation, or owner-managed organization as well as an aggregate of the individuals associated with the place of work. As another example, a community supplies public goods that are available to all, but these goods are not divisible to the level of individual citizens. More specifically, the local public radio signal has the same total costs whether the local area loses or gains 500 people.

The database should include combined time-series and cross-sectional observations; that is, it should include "panel data." The time-series observations allow analysts to study how changes in units affect subsequent changes in these and other units, for example, how an individual's education affects other members of the household as well as decisions about where to live. The cross-sectional observations allow analysts to assess the relative needs of different people and local areas for programs and also to assess the long-term consequences of policy actions. As an example of the latter, the observed behavior of two different households of similar composition but different incomes may help to anticipate the long-term consequences for investment in children by adding to the income of the lower income household.

Major Existing Panel Surveys

The two most important panel studies of broad scope currently available are the Panel Study of Income Dynamics (PSID) and the Survey of Income and Program Participation (SIPP). For more detailed information, see Chapter 5 and Tables 5-1 and 5-2.

The PSID is a combined time-series and cross-sectional annual survey that began with about 5,000 families in 1968 and now includes about 7,000 families (Duncan and Morgan, 1983; Institute for Social Research, 1985). About 2,700 of the households reside in nonmetropolitan areas (Institute for Social Research, 1985). As individuals leave households originally in the sample, the survey attempts to include the new households containing these individuals. The survey collects a lot of information on housing, employment, housework, food consumption, income, family composition, and geographic mobility; it collects less information on other topics. The information from the household survey is supplemented with county-level information on labor market conditions from state Employment Security officials. With the financial support of the Aspen Institute, the Survey Research Center, which manages the PSID, is now adding geographic identifiers to each case in the PSID to facilitate analysis of the spatial dimension of issues (Duncan, 1989). Studies based on the PSID have greatly influenced our understanding of important socioeconomic issues (e.g., Duncan, 1984).

The SIPP is also a combined time-series and cross-sectional survey (Kasprzyk et al., 1987). SIPP has considerably more detail with respect to time than PSID; items are recorded monthly in interviews conducted every four months. Begun in 1984, the samples for the 1984, 1985, and 1986 panels consisted of the individuals residing in approximately 20,000, 14,500 and 12,100 households, respectively, at the time of the first interview. The survey collects extensive data on income, employment, participation in public programs, and many other socioeconomic variables. The sample size is sufficient for much work at the national level but is insufficient for work on subnational nonmetropolitan regions. The SIPP promises to be an important resource to better understand socioeconomic phenomena.

Gaps Between the Desired and Actual Panel Data

The users of the PSID and SIPP encounter two major problems when attempting to analyze problems with a spatial dimension and, especially, the problems of rural people. First, because the data sets include information almost exclusively on individuals and households, they only provide a better understanding of those units. Similar attention to their relationships with firms, substate regions, and other units is needed.

Second, the sample sizes are too small to support work that recognizes the diversity of nonmetropolitan areas (Bender et al., 1985). Scholars and analysts would benefit from an annual survey that obtained data from the four census regions.

Strategies for Filling Data Gaps

The strategies for filling these gaps can be grouped into two camps: brute force and methodological. Within the brute force category, larger surveys and more identifiers are considered.

Brute Force Methods

Analysts of rural social systems would benefit from a larger sample size that included nonmetropolitan areas. The Panel on Statistics for Rural Development Policy convened by the National Research Council supported an expansion of the rural portion of SIPP.[3] The tradeoff is that surveys are very expensive. In early 1988, Kasprzyk, of the Bureau of the Census, indicated the cost of an additional one year's data on one individual in SIPP would be about $300. While scholars and program analysts can justifiably argue that the resulting costs are well worth the gain in understanding, the budgetary climate does not support more money for large surveys.

Research on the relationships between the units of analysis would be facilitated by increasing the number of identifiers. But when information from multiple files is merged, even more massive files are generated. The potential problems resulting from this merger are probably manageable within the current system. However, the resulting files could not be made publicly available because the detail of the data would raise inevitable disclosure problems. (*See* Conclusion at the end of this chapter.)

Synthetic Estimates

The combination of information from multiple surveys can produce estimates that no one survey can support with adequate precision (Nelson, 1989; Platek et al., 1987). This technique, "synthetic estimation," can potentially substitute for an increase of sample size; however, it does not address the issue of obtaining information on additional units of analysis. Synthetic estimation begins with identifying variables of interest that cannot be directly estimated for small areas but whose values are estimated for a larger area. Movement into and out of poverty, migration from one place to another, and movement into and out of public assistance programs are examples of such variables. The PSID and the SIPP are prime places to look for such variables.

The next step in creating synthetic estimates is to build a model, using findings from the social sciences and survey data for the larger area. The model consists of relationships believed to be stable between the variables of interest and other variables, "auxiliary variables," that are available for the larger area and also available for the smaller area of interest. In looking for auxiliary variables, the Current Population Survey (CPS) should be a prime candidate (Gilford, Nelson, and Ingram, 1981). The subject matter of the CPS overlaps with that of the PSID and SIPP which is important because the auxiliary variables must be found in both samples. CPS is a much larger sample of about 59,500 households each month (Ryscavage and Feldman-Harkins, 1988). This sample size is sufficiently large to yield direct estimates of monthly labor force, employment, and unemployment in the 11 largest states and in 2 large metropolitan areas and of the annual averages for the corresponding variables in the other 39 states (Cronkhite, 1987). The CPS has the potential to yield estimates for much smaller areas than the SIPP, but the CPS has less detail than SIPP in several topical areas. Other sources, such as the Census of Population and administrative records, should also be explored for useful auxiliary variables.

Once the model is in hand, relevant values from the larger sample (e.g., CPS) are substituted into the auxiliary variables to generate estimates for the smaller area of interest. The precision of these estimates depends critically on the sampling design of the surveys used, the validity of the model, and the correspondence between the definitions of the auxiliary variables. The cooperation of statisticians and social scientists is essential to the success of this effort. Because errors inevitably occur in computing synthetic estimates, the final phase of the estimation process should be an evaluation of the quality of the estimates (Kalton, 1987).

Recommendations

The recommendations fall into three categories. First, the characteristics of additional units of analysis, such as substate regions, should be added to existing longitudinal files. Second, the use of synthetic estimates as a means to more fully exploit existing survey data should be explored. Third, the benefits in terms of greater precision of estimates resulting from augmenting the rural portion of the PSID and SIPP surveys should be calculated.

Adding Units of Analysis to Existing Longitudinal Files

The data file needed to address the important issues raised in this chapter must contain information on multiple units of analysis. The least expensive, although still expensive, route is to add information on additional units of analysis to existing files, specifically the PSID and the SIPP. The problem, as noted earlier, is that adding more identifiers and more information inevitably creates a file that violates disclosure laws.

To ensure that data are not disclosed improperly, the data file must be centrally held with very tight controls on access. The organization controlling access must have impeccable ethical and statistical credentials. The individuals described in the file must be fully confident that their records are not available to people who would use them for political gain or for program decisions with respect to individuals.

Researchers would have three means of access to these data files. First, they could become permanent employees of the organization managing the file with the understanding that they would not divulge information in a manner that violated disclosure regulations. These people would be comparable to federal scientists currently working with the internal files of the Bureau of the Census.

Second, researchers could join the organization on a temporary basis, such as a sabbatical leave, and work with the same opportunities and restrictions as permanent employees. These people would be comparable to "Census Fellows" now in residence in Washington, D.C.

Third, researchers could design statistical procedures to be run on the file by organizational employees with access to the file. The researcher would receive the statistical output, for example, a print-out of regression results; inferences concerning individual people or households would be impossible based on this output. This procedure would be facilitated by the release of a "dummy file" with the characteristics of the actual file. Researchers could write and debug the needed computer programs using the dummy file.

The main elements of this procedure are in place in many respects, although not for reasons of managing disclosure. Because many social scientists lack the technical expertise to manipulate large data files, they turn to others for the actual computation of statistical parameters. The development of these large data files with restricted access would tend to centralize social science research. The debates about how much to invest in these central, very expensive data resources would be intense.

Synthetic Estimates

The increased precision yielded by synthetic estimates should be explored. To the degree these prove helpful, the technique would allow analysts to more fully exploit existing survey data and avoid the costs of increasing sample size.

Augmenting the Rural Portion of Existing Surveys

The gains in precision of estimates to be realized by augmenting the rural portion of existing surveys, and especially the PSID and SIPP, should be estimated. This work should have a two-pronged approach. One path should assume no gains from synthetic estimates and calculate gains in the context of the individual surveys. The second path should be a component of the work on synthetic estimates. This path would identify the sample observations most likely to further increase the precision of the synthetic estimates. This recommendation closely parallels that of Bonnen (1989) for developing "a comprehensive survey universe and sampling capability."

Notes

The Social Science Research Center, Mississippi State University; the Economic Research Service, U.S. Department of Agriculture; the Northwest Area Foundation, St. Paul, Minnesota; and the Minnesota Agricultural Experiment Station, St. Paul, Minnesota, provided financial support for this work.

1. This section relies heavily on Greenwood (1975) and on ideas generated in discussions with Margaret Dewar and Thomas Stinson.
2. Conversations with scholars in other fields indicate that a substantial literature on hierarchical data systems exists. Exploring these systems would be a useful precursor to more detailed work on the design of an improved data system for socioeconomic studies.
3. The Panel on Statistics for Rural Development Policy, convened by the National Research Council, supported an expansion of the rural portion of SIPP (Gilford, Nelson, and Ingram, 1981:183–184).

References

Bender, Lloyd D., Bernal L. Green, Thomas F. Hady, John A. Kuehn, Marlys K. Nelson, Len S. Perkinson, and Peggy J. Ross. 1985. *The Diverse Social and Economic Structure of Nonmetropolitan America*. RDRR-4. Washington, D.C.: U.S. Department of Agriculture, Economic Research Service.

Bonnen, James T. 1989. The statistical database for rural America. Pp. 25–34 (Senate print 101-50) in *Towards Rural Development Policy for the 1990s: Enhancing Income Employment Opportunities*. Washington, D.C.: U.S. Congressional Research Service and Joint Economic Committee of Congress.

Cornman, John N., and Barbara K. Kincaid. 1984. *Lessons from Rural America*. Cabin John, Md.: Seven Locks Press.

Cronkhite, F. R. 1987. Use of regression techniques for developing state and area employment and unemployment estimates. Pp. 160–174 in R. Platek, J. N. K. Rao, C. E. Sarndal, and M. P. Singh, eds., *Small Area Statistics: An International Symposium*. New York: John Wiley.

Duncan, Cynthia M. 1989. Discussion. Pp. 23–24 (Senate print 101-50) in *Towards Rural Development Policy for the 1990s: Enhancing Income*

Employment Opportunities. Washington, D.C.: U.S. Congressional Research Service and Joint Economic Committee of Congress.

Duncan, Greg J. 1984. *Years of Poverty, Years of Plenty*. Ann Arbor: University of Michigan, Institute for Social Research, Survey Research Center.

Duncan, Greg J., and James N. Morgan. 1983. The Panel Study of Income Dynamics: A summary of its design and major results. Unpublished paper, Survey Research Center, University of Michigan, Ann Arbor.

Garkovich, Lorraine. 1989. *Population and Community in Rural America*. New York: Praeger.

Gilford, Dorothy M., Glenn L. Nelson, and Linda Ingram, eds. 1981. *Rural America in Passage: Statistics for Policy*. Washington, D.C.: National Academy of Sciences.

Greenwood, Michael J. 1975. Research on internal migration in the United States: A survey. *Journal of Economic Literature* 13:397–433.

Grosse, Michael, and Glenn Nelson. 1988. Regional labor markets: Econometric analysis. Working Paper 88-03. University of Minnesota, State and Regional Research Center, St. Paul, October.

Institute for Social Research, Survey Research Center. 1985. *A Panel Study of Income Dynamics: Procedures and Tape Codes, 1983 Interviewing Year*, Wave XVI. A Supplement. Ann Arbor: The University of Michigan.

Kalton, G. Discussion. 1987. Pp. 264–266 in R. Platek, J. N. K. Rao, C. E. Sarndal, and M. P. Singh, eds., *Small Area Statistics: An International Symposium*. New York: John Wiley.

Kasprzyk, Daniel, Pat Doyle, Arnold Goldstein, Patricia Kelly, and David B. McMillen. 1987. *Survey of Income and Program Participation Users' Guide*. Washington, D.C.: U.S. Department of Commerce, Bureau of the Census.

Nelson, Glenn L. 1989. The statistical and analytical base for rural development policy. Pp. 101–107 (Senate print 101-50) in *Towards Rural Development Policy for the 1990s: Enhancing Income Employment Opportunities*. Washington, D.C.: U.S. Congressional Research Service and Joint Economic Committee of Congress.

Platek, R., J. N. K. Rao, C. E. Sarndal, and M. P. Singh, eds. 1987. *Small Area Statistics: An International Symposium*. New York: John Wiley.

Ryscavage, Paul, and Angela Feldman-Harkins. 1988. A comparison of gross changes in labor force status from SIPP and CPS. Survey of Income and Program Participation Working Paper No. 8816. Washington, D.C.: U.S. Department of Commerce, Bureau of the Census.

Schirm, Allen L. 1986. Assortive mating: An economic analysis of who marries whom. Ph.D. Dissertation. University of Pennsylvania.

Stinson, Thomas F. 1982. Public services in rural areas. Pp. 591–604 in *Proceedings of the 1983 Agricultural Outlook Conference*. Washington, D.C.: U.S. Department of Agriculture.

Sweet, James A., and Larry L. Bumpass. 1987. *American Families and Households*. New York: Russell Sage Foundation.

5

Longitudinal Data Sets for Rural Poverty Research

Ann R. Tickamyer and Melissa Latimer

Research on rural and economic development has been hampered both by lack of data on rural residents and lack of interest in the regional and residential dimensions of poverty and employment. The need for social indicators to adequately assess rural labor market performance, economic development, and quality of life has been recognized for some time and has been the subject of numerous conferences, projects, and publications (cf. Gilford, Nelson, and Ingram, 1981; Killian et al., 1986). Until very recently, there has been less attention to data on individual labor force and market status, household composition, and income-generating activities which differentiate between urban and rural strategies and between different types of rural residents. Despite new research initiatives, major gaps still exist. Most noticeably absent are longitudinal analyses which follow the economic fortunes of individuals in rural places over time.

Research on rural poverty is important for several reasons. First, rural areas have a disproportionate share of poor people. During the 1980s only a fifth of the U.S. population lived in rural areas compared to a third of the nation's poor (Deavers and Hoppe, 1991). For much of this period rural poverty rates were comparable to those of depressed inner cities. Second, not only is rural poverty widespread and persistent, but fundamental changes in the national economy over the last decade portend continued economic distress in rural areas (cf. *Rural Economic Development in the 1980s*). Finally, differences in the ecology, resources, and infrastructure of rural areas mandate different policies and programs to deal with rural poverty (Tickamyer and Duncan, 1991). Without good research on rural poverty, it is not possible to design efficient and effective intervention strategies suited to the particular problems of rural residents.

Research generalizable to national and urban populations has made major contributions to answering questions about who is poor, for how long, and for what reasons by following individuals and households over time. Using panel data, misconceptions about the sources and persistence of poverty, as well as the long-term implications for children from poor households, have been addressed in ways not possible with either aggregated social indicators or one-time cross-sectional data. For example, using the Panel Study of Income Dynamics (PSID), a longitudinal panel study following household members, Bane and Ellwood (1986) found far fewer persistently poor persons than individuals and families who have spells of poverty lasting a relatively short time. Using the same data, several researchers have shown there is a fairly low incidence of intergenerational transmission of poverty status and welfare dependency (McLanahan, 1985; Duncan, Hill, and Hoffman, 1988). Most children who grow up in poor homes do not join the welfare roles upon reaching adulthood.

This kind of research is extremely important for untangling myth and reality about poverty and providing a sound foundation for designing effective social welfare policy (Tickamyer and Duncan, 1991). Since very little of this past work has been concerned with regional or residential variation, it is not currently possible to draw firm conclusions about the similarities and differences of these processes for rural poverty populations. To some extent this is an oversight in the use of existing data; to some extent it reflects limits on what is possible with existing data.

This chapter examines the usefulness of major longitudinal data sets for conducting research on rural poverty. We review, compare, and evaluate sample, design, and measurement properties of the three leading panel studies most widely used for socioeconomic research. While many of the advantages and disadvantages of the data described are generic to longitudinal designs (Boruch and Pearson, 1985), this review focuses on rural poverty. The results should inform researchers, decision makers, policy analysts, and action groups on what is available and what is possible with current longitudinal data. It also provides the foundation for assessing future data needs and how to fulfill them.

Overview of Longitudinal Data

Thee major national longitudinal data sets are widely used that are ongoing, have panel designs, and provide detailed economic information for individuals, households, and families. These are the National Longitudinal Surveys (NLS), the Panel Study of Income Dynamics (PSID), and the Survey of Income and Program Participation (SIPP). The major features of each of these will be described in turn, drawing from a variety of sources including handbooks, codebooks, and secondary sources cited in the references. Note 1 lists these sources for each data set. Tables 5-1 and 5-2 summarize the information which follows. Table 5-1 summarizes characteristics of each data set and Table 5-2 compares their usefulness for rural poverty research.

National Longitudinal Surveys (NLS): Labor Market Experience

NLS data consist of five separate age-sex cohorts surveyed periodically since the mid-1960s by the Center for Human Resources Research of the Ohio State University under contract from the U.S. Department of Labor. The surveys were designed to evaluate different types of labor market experiences specific to different segments of the population. The five cohorts are samples of mature men, mature women, young men, young women, and a more recently initiated mixed-sex youth sample.

Sampling design and implementation for the original four cohorts were conducted by the Census Bureau. Each of the four samples consists of a multi-stage probability sample representing the entire noninstitutional civilian population of the United States. Black households were oversampled at a rate of three to four times that of white households. The goal was a sample of approximately 3,500 whites and 1,500 blacks for each cohort. These procedures produced the following four cohorts:

- Mature men, aged 45–59 in 1966 (5,020 original cases);
- Mature women, aged 30–44 in 1967 (5,083 original cases);
- Young men, aged 14–24 in 1966 (5,225 original cases); and
- Young women, aged 14–24 in 1968 (5,159 original cases).

All individuals were sampled from 13,582 households. Therefore, in many cases, more than one respondent comes from the same household, both within and across cohorts. It is possible to link household members for the purpose of examining specific types of relationships. These include husband-wife, parent-child, and brother-sister relationships in large enough numbers to perform multivariate analyses.

The youth cohort survey was added to the NLS in 1979. The sample was designed and conducted by the National Opinion Research Center to

Table 5–1. Characteristics of Three Longitudinal Data Sets

Data Set	Purpose	Time of Initiation	Survey Framework	Group Managing the Survey	Sample	Oversampled Groups
NLS	To examine the labor market experience of different segments of the population	Mid-1960s	1. Longitudinal 2. Individuals surveyed at 1–2-year intervals since inception	Center for Human Resources of the Ohio State University under contract to the U.S. Dept. of Labor	*Mature men:* aged 45–59 in 1966 (5,020 original cases) *Mature women:* aged 30–44 in 1967 (5,083 original cases) *Young men:* aged 14–24 in 1966 (5,225 original cases) *Young women:* aged 14–24 in 1968 (5,159 original cases) *Young cohort:* aged 14–21 in 1979 (12,686 cases)	Black households were oversampled in groups 1–4. Disadvantaged youth were oversampled in group 5 (10 categories)
PSID	To provide longitudinal data on determinants and consequences of family income	1968	1. Longitudinal 2. Surveys are conducted annually	Survey Research Center of the University of Michigan	1. 3,00 representative households of the coterminous U.S. population 2. 2,000 households with income less than twice the poverty level selected from the survey of economic opportunity	Low income household heads under 60 from SMSAs and non-SMSAs in the South were oversampled
SIPP	To provide detailed data on individuals' income, program participation, and factors affecting both	1983	1. Short-term (2½ yr) rotating longitudinal panel study 2. New panel (sample) initiated each year 3. Interviews are conducted every 4 months	U.S. Census Bureau	1. 20,000 households representative of U.S. and metropolitan areas within the U.S. in 1983 and 1984 2. Slightly over 13,000 households representative of U.S. and metropolitan areas within the U.S. in 1985	None

Table 5–1. Characteristics of Three Longitudinal Data Sets *(continued)*

Data Set	Current Status	Subject of Interview/ Source of Information	Family/Household Information
NLS	1. Ongoing for (a) mature women, (b) young women, and (c) youth cohort 2. Discontinued for (a) mature men, and (b) young men	1. Mature men 2. Mature women 3. Young men 4. Young women 5. Youth 6. Face-to-face and telephone interviews	1. Multiple respondents from the same household can be linked to examine specific types of relationships 2. Provides household and labor market status of specific age-sex cohorts 3. Detailed household and members and relationships to respondent available for many (but not all) survey years
PSID	Ongoing for 5,000 families sampled	1. Household head (defined as male when male is present) is primary source of data 2. Information about wives and children are filtered through interview with husband/father 3. Face-to-face 1968–1972 (primarily); telephone 1973 and later	1. Detailed information on income sources for every current family member is available 2. Children born to sampled families become part of the sample and are followed 3. Family members "added" to household are part of the family as long as they reside within the household 4. Characteristics of a household are ascribed to each individual within a family
SIPP		1. Personal interviews with individuals 15 years old or older 2. Two-thirds are self-administered interviews 3. One-third are proxy interviews	1. Changes in household composition are identified on a monthly basis. 2. Income information is asked for each person in the household (15 years old and older) 3. Nonsample members are dropped from the sample once they leave the household 4. Households in the sample that move within 100 miles of any SIPP PSU are followed 5. Individuals are defined in their relationship to a reference person 6. Information on relationships between nonreference persons is limited

Table 5–2. Advantages/Disadvantages of Three Longitudinal Data Sets

Data Set	Advantages	Disadvantages
NLS	1. Provides detail on household and labor market status of specific age-sex cohorts. 2. Can link household members across cohorts 3. Oversamples blacks and disadvantaged youths 4. Low attrition 5. Support from NLS clearinghouse	1. Size, complexity 2. Inconsistencies in question format and coding procedures 3. Incomplete labor force and household histories 4. Limited income and program use data 5. Attrition and nonresponse (low but less detailed investigation than other surveys) 6. Some cohorts discontinued
PSID	1. Extensive data set which is updated yearly 2. Reliable subpopulation analysis 3. Extensive investigation of data's weaknesses/strengths 4. Detailed information on household income, expenditures, and employment 5. Oversamples low-income families 6. Length of study permits intergenerational analysis 7. Neighborhood identification (e.g., census tract or enumeration district) is available on specially constructed files	1. Size, complexity 2. Bias from using household head as the primary data source 3. Wives' activities are filtered through the husband
SIPP	1. Provides monthly data on income-generating and other household activities 2. Provides weekly data on labor force participation 3. Short-term data collection: (a) improves understanding of time-ordered events, (b) improves subject recall, and (c) reduces under-reporting 4. Provides detailed information on participation in programs not covered by other data sets 5. SIPP Access Center was established by NSF to provide services that enhance user access to data	1. Size, cohort 2. Short-term longitudinal (2½ yrs). Shorter period than NLS or PSID 3. Cannot examine long-term life events or intergenerational processes and change 4. Funding problems have reduced sample size and data collection 5. Strict Census Bureau confidentiality rules limit place identifiers

Table 5-2. *(continued)*

Usefulness for Poverty Research	Usefulness for Rural Poverty Research
1. Information on household income and income-generating strategies is sketchy. 2. Youth sample has more information on economic circumstances but limited numbers of waves have been completed.	*Original Cohort* 1. Has limited regional and residential identifiers 2. Impossible to specify anything beyond urban-rural or metro-nonmetro residence *Youth Cohort* 1. Detailed geographic detail available 2. Small rural subsample
1. Low-income families are oversampled 2. Has detailed information on household composition, activities, employment, expenditures, and income over time 3. Family and neighborhood effects can be studied	1. Extensive analysis of local labor market conditions is possible using county identifiers 2. Number of observations sufficient for studying poverty in rural and nonmetro, small towns (combined)
1. Best data set for studying poverty and its relationship to the socioeconomic backgrounds and activities of household members 2. Cannot be reliably used for subnational estimates	1. Virtually impossible to get rural estimates because metro/nonmetro defined ambiguously

represent ten groups of youth between the ages of 14 and 21 in 1979. The ten groups targeted were Hispanic males and females; black males and females; economically disadvantaged nonblack, non-Hispanic males and females; nonblack, non-Hispanic males and females; and male and female military personnel. The final sample included 12,686 cases.

Each of the five cohorts has been surveyed at intervals varying from one to two years since their inception. Initially the surveys were to end after a five-year period; but the amount of the interest they generated and the low attrition rates resulted in the extension of the original four cohorts as well as the addition of the youth cohort. Surveys of the two male cohorts were discontinued in 1981 for the young men and in 1983 for the mature men, although there has been a one-time follow-up for the mature men. Surveys of both female cohorts and the youth cohort continue at this time. Surveys vary widely in comprehensiveness and specific items asked.

Table 5–2 lists major advantages and disadvantages of the NLS (as well of the PSID and SIPP). Many of the problems with the NLS are generic to panel designs (although gaps and changes in data and question format are particularly troublesome). There are more serious limits for the study of rural poverty. The original four cohorts have very limited regional and residential identifiers, making it impossible to specify anything beyond urban-rural or metro-nonmetro residence. Furthermore, although there is a great deal of information on labor force status, economic information is not easy to use and is inconsistent across years, making detailed analysis and information on household income and income-generating strategies somewhat problematic. The youth survey is better suited both to identifying region and residence (including migration) and economic circumstances. The oversampling of disadvantaged youth makes this a particularly useful sample. However, the youthfulness of the cohort (14 to 21 in 1979, therefore still in early adulthood at the beginning of the 1990s) and the limited number of waves completed curtail its current utility for analyzing poverty longitudinally.

Panel Study of Income Dynamics (PSID)

PSID is a complex multistage, stratified sample begun in 1968 by the Survey Research Center at the University of Michigan. The initial study combined two separate samples: approximately 3,000 households representing the population of the coterminous (48 states and the District of Columbia) United States; and a subsample of slightly under 2,000 households from the Survey of Economic Opportunity, originally conducted by the Census Bureau for the Office of Economic Opportunity. This component of the survey provided an oversample of low-income household heads under 60 from standard metropolitan statistical areas (SMSAs) and non-SMSAs in the South. Household heads have been interviewed annually since the initial survey. Information is also available on all members of the initial sampled families and children born into these families. To a more limited extent, information is available on household members who were not part of the original sample. Each new wave is added to the previous waves, making sample size and composition variable. In the mid-1980s there were over 20,000 individuals in the sample and just under 6,000 families. Numbers of cases are smaller for data spanning the duration of the study.

The purpose of the PSID was and remains to provide longitudinal data on determinants and consequences of family income. For each wave of the study, detailed information is available on income sources for every current family member. (Individuals who were not part of the original sample who join a household are studied for as long as they remain in the household. Children born to sampled families become permanent members of the sample.) Similarly detailed information is available on employment and unemployment, household work, expenditures, family composition, and educational background and attainment. Also, miscellaneous information is available on sociodemographic background variables and attitudes relating to economic status and behavior. A limited amount of information describing local labor market conditions has also been added to files.

The PSID was specifically designed to study poverty. Low-income households were oversampled, and detailed information on household composition, activities, employment, expenditures, and income permit highly sophisticated analysis of the relationships among these factors over time. A vast amount of literature devoted to this task has emerged from the PSID. However, there is currently very little analysis specifically examining rural poverty or rural-urban differences, although some studies include metro-nonmetro and regional differences (see Adams and Duncan, 1991). On the other hand, it is quite possible to do more extensive analysis. For example, in 1980 over a quarter of the sample resided in nonmetro areas. Slightly under 4 percent resided in completely rural areas, and another 10 percent lived in urban areas of less than 20,000 residents not adjacent to a metro area. Without the last group, the numbers are too small to do extensive subgroup analysis, but large enough for exploratory purposes (there are approximately 400 completely rural cases and another

1,500 who reside in small nonmetro towns). In addition, the recent addition of more detailed measures of urban-rural locations and the separately obtainable county and census tract identifiers allow more extensive analysis of local labor market conditions.

Survey of Income and Program Participation (SIPP)

SIPP is a rotating panel survey in which a new panel (sample) is initiated each year. SIPP data have the most detailed records of income and household income-generating activities in longitudinal form, but the data are collected for shorter time periods. SIPP also has the most complex and specialized design. The need for the SIPP was policy driven, arising from questions about income measurement, program use, and effects of changes in eligibility rules and regulations. These issues emerged with the expansion of social welfare programs in the 1960s and could not be addressed by the cross-sectional design of the March Income Supplement of the Current Population Survey (CPS).

SIPP grew out of the Income Survey Development Program (ISDP), a 1975 effort to improve data collection procedures for subannual income data. Its early history was marked by uncertain funding and authority. In 1983, however, the Census Bureau received funds for the project and the first data were collected late in the year. The Census Bureau has continued to manage SIPP since 1983.

The study design for SIPP has multiple, rotated waves in an overlapping set of panels, each designed to last approximately two and one-half years. Multistage stratified sampling was used to select a panel of approximately 20,000 households, and interviews were conducted with household members. Personal interviews are conducted with individuals 15 years old and older. Self-administered interviews constitute roughly two-thirds of the interviews, and proxy interviews constitute the remaining one-third of the interviews. Each interview covered household activities for the previous four months. Rotation groups consisting of one-fourth of the households were followed and reinterviewed once every four months over two and one-half years for a total of nine interviews in the first panel (but fewer in subsequent panels). If household members move, they are followed and interviewed. If the household dissolves and reforms, new households are added, which include both the original members and the new ones (for as long as they are members of original participants' households).

SIPP was designed to have new panels begin every year, and therefore overlaps with the interview cycles of the previous years' panels. It is difficult to keep up with the current availability of the data. Interested users should check Census Bureau publications for the most recent status reports. Due to budget cutbacks, reductions were made in the number of households in each rotation group for the first panel and in subsequent panels as well. It is possible to combine data collected from two different panels conducted within the same time period to increase the sample size. The 1985 panel interviewed slightly over 13,000 households.

There is undoubtedly no better data source than the SIPP for studying poverty and its relationship to the socioeconomic activities of household members. While much of the information already generated by using SIPP data is technical or deals with specific narrow populations or problems (e.g., alternative definitions of longitudinal households, comparisons of SIPP, ISDP, and CPS estimates of income and poverty), a great deal of information will be forthcoming. However, two problems limit the usefulness of SIPP. First, SIPP data are well suited to generating detail on short-term change in household economic activity. SIPP provides monthly data on sources of income (i.e., income from jobs, interest and dividends, and income maintenance programs) and weekly data on labor force participation. It is not able to look at long-term, life-course change (except in aggregate terms similar to those used in cross-sectional designs) nor at intergenerational processes and change.

The more serious drawback is that SIPP was designed to be representative of the United States as a whole and of metropolitan areas within the United States. It cannot be reliably used for many subnational estimates, and it is virtually impossible to get rural estimates from it. Forty-five metropolitan statistical areas are "self-representing"; that is, they can be identified and reliable estimates can be made. However, nonmetro status is problematic. In fact, the label "nonmetro" does not appear on the SIPP files. Instead, the label is "residual" and it represents a combination of both metro and nonmetro households not in the metro subsample. Most states have enough cases for exploratory analysis, but should not be used for reliable population estimates. Some states were combined for sampling purposes (e.g., Mississippi and West Virginia and some small-population western states), making even state and regional analysis problematic. Data permitting rural or nonmetro estimates are available to the Census Bureau but are suppressed in the publicly available data to meet confidentiality requirements (although there are possibilities for negotiating use of internal SIPP files for researchers working at the Census Bureau (cf. Hoppe, 1988). In short, information on rural households forms a major gap in the publicly available SIPP data.

Applications to Rural Poverty Research

Three types of information are necessary to study rural poverty. Economic measures provide the means for measuring poverty, income, and income-generating activity. Family and household structure are crucial because economic circumstances are closely tied to family and household composition and characteristics. Spatial measures are necessary for comparison of opportunities available in different locations. The three data sets vary widely in availability, detail, and consistency of the information. For this review however, we focus on assessing spatial measures, since these are among the most problematic aspects of these data.

Spatial and Areal Measures

Although it is widely recognized among all the social and policy sciences that spatial location is a primary determinant and indicator of individual opportunity and collective economic organization, measures locating individuals spacially are often crude and infrequently systematically studied. They often combine or confuse different conceptual approaches to ecological characteristics. For example, both size and economic organization are confused in commonly used measures of "urban-rural" or "metro-nonmetro." Similarly, geographic location is sometimes conflated with socioeconomic factors as when regional designations (e.g., "South-non-South") are employed. In both examples, the important features may be population size, population density, economic structure, or economic diversity, but there is no way of distinguishing among them.

The degree of specific identification of place varies widely. For some data sets, it is impossible to obtain specific information on locale because of confidentiality constraints. In others, detail down to the county or even the zip code is possible. The greater the detail available on specific location, the greater the ability of the researcher to define and investigate salient areal characteristics.

The most commonly used measures do not identify the actual location, but indicate aggregate characteristics based on size and place. These measures include: (1) *urban-rural*—measured with varying degrees of detail from a simple dichotomy to multiple categories based on size and proximity to metropolitan areas; (2) *metro-nonmetro*—similar to urban-rural, except the distinction is based on residence in an MSA (metropolitan statistical area, formerly standard metropolitan statistical area, or SMSA) or proximity to one. Because it is possible to live in a rural area in an

MSA or an urban area which is not in an MSA, the most commonly used distinction between metro and nonmetro residence can be quite misleading if used alone; (3) *region*—based on location of state, usually measured as a dichotomy (South–non-South) or as a four-category variable corresponding to North, South, East, and West census regions; and (4) *farm-nonfarm*—specifies residence on a farm, but often ignores other approaches to farm living including farm occupations and farm ownership.

A problem with collecting data to be representative of the entire U.S. population is that the predominance of urban and metro residence means that unless specific oversampling for rural residence is used, the approximately 20 percent of the population living in rural areas will not be well represented, and confidentiality problems will ensue. None of the samples in question oversample rural residents and, in at least one case, there is a bias toward metro residence.

Two other types of spatial measures are sometimes used. The first consists of contextual measures giving information about characteristics of the place without specifically locating it (e.g., population size, labor force size and its components, unemployment rate, and type of industry). The second indicates movement. These vary from merely indicating whether current residence differs from previous residence to specifying the direction of movement (urban-rural, metro-nonmetro) to actual location of movement (identified by county or metro area).

The three longitudinal data sets differ in the extent of spatial measures available, and the amount of detail varies by subsample. A summary of available measures for each of the three data sets follows.

NLS. All cohorts of the NLS specify South–non-South and metro residence. Detailed urban-rural categories are available, with rural broken down to include places less than 2,500 inside and outside metro areas. In addition, information on whether the respondent has moved since the previous survey and whether a move out of the state or out of the county/metro area is included. A limited number of local labor market characteristics are provided, including size of labor force and unemployment rate.

The youth cohort includes the same information as the original four cohorts, but in addition has potential for far more detailed investigation of environmental factors and mobility. Supplemental tapes are available which provide detailed geographic information on respondents' location (state, county, and metro area) for each survey period and link this to existing data on the characteristics of these areas. Special licensing arrangements are necessary to obtain the data which are maintained in separate files because of potential confidentiality problems. Details of necessary procedures are outlined in the NLS Handbook which describes the data and is obtainable from the Center for Human Resources of the Ohio State University.

PSID. This data set includes region, size of place, size and distance to nearest metro area, and intra- and intercounty mobility. Each record in the file includes data on state and county of residence, where the household head grew up (rural vs. urban, state and county), all states the head has lived in, and whether the head has ever moved to take a job. In addition, interview information has been supplemented with county-level data on unemployment rates, wage rates for unskilled workers, and labor market demand conditions. Under special arrangements with the Survey Research Center, researchers can obtain identifiers that locate the census tract or enumeration district in which respondents have lived in each year they participated in the survey.

The Survey Research Center has added Beale codes to PSID data files from the 1985–1987 panels. These codes classify six groups of nonmetro counties based on how urban (or rural) their population is and how close they are to metro areas. At one end of the spectrum are "urbanized adjacent" counties that have an urbanized population of at least 20,000 and are adjacent to a metro area. At the other end are "totally rural nonadjacent" counties that have no urban population (that is, no place with a population of at least 2,500) and are not adjacent to a metro area. Interested researchers can add Beale codes to earlier files by using the FIPS code contained in each record.

SIPP. Currently SIPP data can be broken down into metro residence of one million or more, less than a million, and nonmetro. Individual states can be identified with some exceptions which have been aggregated (i.e., Mississippi and West Virginia and Idaho, New Mexico, South Dakota and Wyoming). A large number of metropolitan statistical areas are identifiable, permitting information on the socioeconomic characteristics of these areas to be merged with individual and household data. Information on rural residence is not available, and analysis of specifically rural issues is not possible by researchers working outside the Census Bureau.

Rural Poverty Research

A review of research using the three socioeconomic longitudinal databases reveals almost no work which specifically deals with rural poverty and, surprisingly, few studies which examine the relationship between any sort of spatial or areal measure and poverty. Studies using each of the three data sets were reviewed for their relevance to issues of rural poverty. A brief overview of the literature follows. For a detailed review of NLS, PSID, and SIPP research organized by type of spatial measure and data set, see *National Longitudinal Surveys: A Guide for Rural Poverty Analysts* (Tickamyer and Latimer, 1991).

NLS. Researchers utilizing the NLS data have rarely examined either poverty or rural variables in their analysis. No NLS studies were found that deal with rural poverty per se, and only four articles were found that utilize rural variables in their analysis. Only one of these articles can be used to indirectly measure rural poverty. A number of NLS studies employ various spatial and areal measures in their analysis, but do not examine rural poverty. These studies are important in showing the types of location variables possible with NLS data and, thus, what can be done in terms of rural poverty with this data set. The spatial and areal measures employed in these studies include indicators of urban and regional residence.

PSID. Of the three data sets, the PSID has been used the most extensively for research on rural poverty. The spatial/areal measures used in this research include two categories: those that reflect current residence and those that reflect residential background. A number of PSID studies also employ various spatial and areal measures but do not examine rural poverty. These studies are worth noting because they reveal what can be done in terms of rural poverty with this data set. The spatial and areal measures in these studies can be categorized into four types of residential variables: proxy residence variables, specific residence variables, regional residence variables, and residential background variables.

SIPP. As stated, the SIPP was designed to be representative of the total United States or its metropolitan areas. Thus, it is virtually impossible to use this data set to investigate rural poverty. Currently, many of the articles on SIPP deal mainly with either methodological or technical aspects of the data set and focus on SIPP's potential rather than actual applications of the data to poverty issues.

Conclusion

In 1981, the Panel on Statistics for Rural Development Policy of the National Research Council published an assessment of data needs for rural development policy (Gilford, Nelson, and Ingram, 1981). This panel pointed to the vast changes occurring in rural America, the problems of specifying these changes, and the need for more and better data to address these issues. They made a number of recommendations to improve the quality and quantity of data available for rural areas which could inform researchers and decision makers about rural issues. Unfortunately, many of the recommendations remain to be implemented, while the need for information continues to grow.

The panel did not look at the longitudinal databases discussed in this paper (with the exception of recommendations for extending the SIPP). It is our contention that some of the needs for rural data could and should be met by greater use of existing longitudinal data, which present a high-quality, efficient, and cost effective way of studying socioeconomic change for individuals, households, and to a lesser extent, communities. The review of rural poverty research shows the extent to which it is currently possible and what has already been done. It also points to serious obstacles to greater utilization of these data for research on rural issues.

All of the databases reviewed have the potential for more extensive and effective application to examine the diversity of poverty populations both within and across rural areas. They differ in the extent to which they can be used immediately or require modification of measurement and sample design. Especially attractive features of these data sets are their utility for studying inter- and intragenerational aspects of poverty, employment, and income generation. The most disappointing result of this review is the limited utility for using the data most specifically aimed at the study of poverty to understand rural poverty. The limited geography that is publicly available on the SIPP at this time prevents using it for research on rural problems. Despite limitations, there is far greater need and potential for longitudinal research on rural poverty using these data sources than currently has taken place.[2]

Ways to make these data more usable include the following suggestions. First, access to information that is embedded in the data on rural areas can be extended. This means adding spatial identifiers to files where possible (as with the PSID). It also means finding ways to negotiate access to data when confidentiality restrictions based on law prevent use of feasible identifiers (as with SIPP). Suggestions for allowing researchers access to suppressed data without violating disclosure rules are discussed by Nelson (1989).

Second, spatial and ecological measures can be constructed, which can be included in files even when there are reasons to suppress actual location. This would entail demographic, economic, and sociopolitical constructs that could be used to describe locales. Similarly, measures of rural areas along the lines of MSAs can be developed, which can be used to provide contextual measures for rural populations and which routinely can be provided in data files regardless of how much other geography is suppressed. One effort in this direction is exemplified by PUMS-D, the last version of the 1980 public use microdata sample. PUMS-D sampled on empirically defined local labor market areas defined by commuting patterns. Labor market areas aggregate counties connected by commuter flows without restriction by state lines or by any requirement for an urban center. The result is a set of rural local labor markets similar to urban MSAs (cf. Tolbert and Killian, 1987). Standard construction and use of such categories would facilitate the study of rural areas.

Finally, rural populations can be oversampled when new data initiatives are undertaken. Minorities, low-income, and other statistically infrequent groups are oversampled routinely for policy purposes. The same approach needs to be taken for rural populations. The problems facing rural America, the complex interconnections between rural and urban areas, and the need for policy and programs to address these problems in ways that recognize this complexity require more attention to rural data needs.

Notes

Originally prepared for and supported by MACED and the Rural Economic Policy Program of the Aspen Institute and the Ford Foundation. Portions of this chapter were presented at the Rural Data Needs Conference in Lexington, Kentucky, in March 1989 and were adapted from A. Tickamyer and M. Latimer, *National Longitudinal Surveys: A Guide for Rural Poverty Analysts*, The Aspen Institute, Rural Economic Policy Program, Washington, D.C., July 1991. The authors thank Cynthia Duncan, Greg Duncan, Robert Hoppe, Daniel Kasprzyk, Priscilla Salant, Susan Sechler, and Anita Waller for comments and assistance.

1. National Longitudinal Surveys (NLS) include: Bielby, Hawley, and Bills, 1978; Bilsborrow and Aking, 1982; Borus, 1982; Daymont and Andrisani, 1983; Duncan and D. H. Hill, 1985; Duncan and M. S. Hill, 1985; Duncan, Hill, and Hoffman, 1988; Leigh, 1982; Mott, 1979; *The NLS Handbook, 1987*; Parnes, 1972, 1975, 1981; Peterson, 1979, 1980; Saunders, 1973; Sproat, 1979; Stafford, 1986; U.S. Department of Labor, 1980.

Panel Study of Income Dynamics (PSID) include: Becketti et al., 1983; Duncan, 1983; Duncan and Morgan, 1982; Morgan, 1972, 1981; Survey Research Center, 1984.

Survey of Income and Program Participation (SIPP) include: Bane and Welsh, 1985; Bell, 1985; Borus, 1982; Center for Research and Retrieval of Data from the SIPP and ISDP, 1985; Coder and Feldman, 1985; Dahmann, 1985; *Data User News*, 1985; David, 1985*a*, 1985*b*, 1985*c*; David and Fitzgerald, 1987; David, Robbin, and Rockwell, 1985; David et al., 1985; Duncan, 1983, 1985*a*, 1985*b*; Duncan and Morgan, 1985; Ernst, Hubble, and Judkins, 1984; Espenshade and Wolf, 1985; Farley, 1985; Fields and Jakubson, 1985; Haber, 1985; Haber et al., 1985; Herriot and Kasprzyk, 1985; *Focus*, 1985, 1987–1988; Hoppe, 1988; Huang, 1984; Jean and McArthur, 1984; *Journal of Economic and Social Measurement*, 1985; Kalton and Lepkowski, 1985; Lamas and McNeil, 1985; Latest Report from Survey of Income and Program Participation, 1985; McMillen and Herriot, 1984, 1985; McMillen, Nelson, and Kasprzyk, 1986; McNiel and Salvo, 1985; Microdata File with Data from the Survey of Income and Program Participation, 1984; Nestel, 1981; News from the Survey of Income and Program Participation, 1985*a*, 1985*b*; Olneck, 1985; Roman and O'Brien, 1984; Ryscavage, 1985; SIPP and SIPP Access, 1987–88; Smeeding, 1985; Smith, 1985; *Survey of Income and Program Participation and Related Longitudinal Surveys*, 1984, 1985; Symposium on SIPP, 1985; U.S. Bureau of Labor Statistics, 1982; U.S. Department of Commerce, Bureau of the Census, *Current Population Report* Series 19; U.S. National Commission on Employment and Unemployment Statistics, 1979; Watts, 1985; What is SIPP, 1985; Wilensky, 1985; Ycas and Lininger, 1982.

2. There are additional problems with these standard data sets not discussed here. These problems include inadequate measures of the relationship between reproduction and production, household structure and dynamics, and the importance of the informal labor market in economic activities. For further discussion of these and related topics, see Tickamyer et al. (1993).

References

Adams, T., and G. Duncan. 1991. Long-term poverty in rural areas. Pp. 63–93 in Cynthia M. Duncan, ed., *Rural Poverty in America*. New York: Auburn House.

Bane, M. J., and D. T. Ellwood. 1986. Slipping into and out of poverty: The dynamics of spells. *Journal of Human Resources* 21(Winter):1–23.

Bane, M. J., and W. Welsh. 1985. SIPP's potential contributions to policy research on children. *Journal of Economic and Social Measurement* 13:273–279.

Becketti, S., L. Gould, L. Lillard, and F. Welch. 1983. *Attrition from the PSID*. Santa Monica, Calif.: Unicon.

Bell, C. S. 1985. SIPP and the female condition. *Journal of Economic and Social Measurement* 13:263–271.

Bielby, W. T., C. B. Hawley, and D. Bills. 1978. Research uses of the national longitudinal surveys. *A Research Agenda for the National Longitudinal Surveys of Labor Market Experience: Report on the Social Science Research Council's Conference on the National Longitudinal Surveys*. October 1977, Part V. Washington, D.C.: Social Science Research Council.

Bilsborrow, R. E., and J. S. Aking. 1982. Data availability versus data needs for analyzing the determinants and consequences of internal migration. *Review of Public Data* 10:261–284.

Boruch, R. F., and R. W. Pearson. 1985. *The Comparative Evaluation of Longitudinal Surveys*. New York: Social Science Research Council.

Borus, M. E. 1982. An inventory of longitudinal data sets of interest to economists. *Review of Public Data Use* 10:113–126.

Center for Research and Retrieval of Data from the SIPP and ISDP. 1985. *Focus* 8(1):18–19. University of Wisconsin-Madison Institute for Research on Poverty.

Coder, J. F., and A. M. Feldman. 1985. Early indications of item nonresponse on the SIPP. Pp. 109–114 in *Survey of Income and Program Participation and Related Longitudinal Surveys: 1984*. Washington, D.C.: Department of Commerce, Bureau of the Census, Population Division.

Dahmann, D. C. 1985. Panel surveys as a source of migration data. Pp. 57–62 in *Survey of Income and Program Participation and Related Longitudinal Surveys: 1984*. Washington, D.C.: Department of Commerce, Bureau of the Census, Population Division.

David, M. 1985*a*. Comments. Pp. 75–78 in *Survey of Income and Program Participation and Related Longitudinal Surveys: 1984*. Washington, D. C.: Department of Commerce, Bureau of the Census, Population Division.

______. 1985*b*. The distribution of income in the United States: Implications for the design of the SIPP panel. *Journal of Economic and Social Measurement* 13:305–317.

______. 1985*c*. Introduction: The design and development of SIPP. *Journal of Economic and Social Measurement* 13:215–224.

David, M., and J. Fitzgerald. 1987. Measuring poverty and crises: A comparison of annual and subannual accounting periods using the Survey of Income and Program Participation. Institute for Research on Poverty, Discussion Paper no. 843-87, University of Wisconsin-Madison.

David, M., A. Robbin, and R. C. Rockwell. 1985. Summary and recommendations: Second SSRC symposium on the scientific and research potential of SIPP—June 28–29, 1985. *Journal of Economic and Social Measurement* 13:385–392.

David, M., R. C. Rockwell, A. Robbin, and F. W. Monfort. 1985. Summary of the SIPP conference and recommendations of the conferees. *Journal of Economic and Social Measurement* 13:77–83.

Daymont, T., and P. Andrisani. 1983. The research uses of the national longitudinal surveys: An update. *Review of Public Data Use* 11:203–310.

Deavers, K., and R. A. Hoppe. 1991. Policy options for the rural poor in the 1990s: The past is prologue. Pp. 85–101 in C. B. Flora and J. A. Christenson, eds., *Rural Policies for the 1990s*.

Duncan, G. J. 1983. *Years of Poverty Years of Plenty*. Ann Arbor: Michigan Institute for Social Research, University of Michigan.

______. 1985*a*. Discussion. Pp. 153–156 in *Survey of Income and Program Participation and Related Longitudinal Surveys: 1984*. Washington, D.C.: Department of Commerce, Bureau of the Census, Population Division.

______. 1985*b*. A framework for tracking family relationships over time. *Journal of Economic and Social Measurement* 13:237–243.

Duncan, G. J., and D. H. Hill. 1985. An investigation of the extent and consequences of measurement error in labor—Economic survey data. *Journal of Labor Economics*. 3(4):508–532.

Duncan, G. J., and M. S. Hill. 1985. Conceptions of longitudinal households: Fertile or futile? *Journal of Economic and Social Measurement* 13:361–375.

Duncan, G. J., and J. N. Morgan. 1982. Longitudinal lessons from the Panel Study of Income Dynamics. *Review of Public Data Use* 10:179–184.

Duncan, G. J., M. S. Hill, and S. D. Hoffman. 1988. Welfare dependence within and across generations. *Science* 239:467–471.

Ernst, L. R., D. L. Hubble, and D. R. Judkins. 1984. Longitudinal family and household estimation in SIPP. SIPP Working Paper Series No. 8406. Washington, D.C.: U.S. Bureau of the Census.

Espenshade, T. J., and D. A. Wolf. 1985. SIPP Data on Marriage, Separation, Divorce, and Remarriage: Problems, Opportunities, and Recommendations. *Journal of Economic and Social Measurement* 13:229–236.

Farley, R. 1985. Understanding racial differences and trends: How SIPP can assist. *Journal of Economic and Social Measurement* 13:245–261.

Fields, G. S., and G. H. Jakubson. 1985. Labor market analysis using SIPP. *Journal of Economic and Social Measurement* 13:281–286.

Gilford, D., G. Nelson, and L. Ingram, eds. 1981. *Rural America in Passage*. Washington, D.C.: National Academy Press.

Haber, S. E. 1985. A perspective on linking SIPP to administrative and statistical records *Journal of Economic and Social Measurement* 13:331–340.

Haber, S. E., P. Ryscavage, D. Sater, and V. Valdisera. 1985. Matching economic data to SIPP: A pilot study. Pp. 69–74 in *Survey of Income and Program Participation and Related Longitudinal Surveys: 1984*. Washington, D.C.: Department of Commerce, Bureau of the Census, Population Division.

Herriot, R., and D. Kasprzyk. 1985. The Survey of Income and Program Participation. Pp. 161–170 in *Survey of Income and Program Participation and Related Longitudinal Surveys: 1984*. Washington, D.C.: Department of Commerce, Bureau of the Census, Population Division.

Hoppe, Robert A. 1988. Defining and measuring nonmetro poverty: Results from the Survey of Income and Program Participation. Paper presented at the annual meeting of the Rural Sociological Society, Athens, Georgia.

Huang, H. 1984. Obtaining cross-sectional estimates from a longitudinal survey: Experiences of the Income Survey Development Program. SIPP Working Paper Series No. 8406. Washington, D.C.: U.S. Bureau of the Census.

Jean, A. C., and E. K. McArthur. 1984. Some data collection issues for panel surveys with applications to the SIPP. SIPP Working Paper Series No. 8407. Washington, D.C.: U.S. Bureau of the Census.

Kalton, G., and J. Lepkowski. 1985. Following rules in SIPP. *Journal of Economic and Social Measurement* 13:319–329.

Killian, M., L. Bloomquist, S. Pendleton, and D. McGranaham. 1986. *Symposium on Rural Labor Markets Research Issues*. Economic Research Service Staff Report No. AGES860721. Washington, D.C.: U.S. Department of Agriculture.

Lamas, E., and J. M. McNeil. 1985. The measurement of household wealth in the SIPP. Pp. 15–24 in *Survey of Income and Program Participation and Related Longitudinal Surveys: 1984*. Washington, D.C.: Department of Commerce, Bureau of the Census, Population Division.

Latest Report from Survey of Income and Program Participation (SIPP). 1985. *Data User News* 20(5):9. (Bureau of the Census)

Leigh, D. E. 1982. The national longitudinal surveys: A selective survey of recent evidence. *Review of Public Data Use* 10:185–201.

McLanahan, S. 1985. Family structure and the reproduction of poverty. *American Journal of Sociology* 90:873–901.

McMillen, D. B., and R. H. Herriot. 1984. Toward a longitudinal definition of households. SIPP Working Paper No. 8402. Washington, D.C.: U.S. Bureau of the Census.

______. 1985. Conceptions of longitudinal definition of households. *Journal of Economic and Social Measurement* 13:349–360.

McMillen, D., D. Nelson, and D. Kasprzyk. 1986. The Survey of Income and Program Participation (SIPP): A new Census Bureau data source. Pp. 1–3 in the *ICPSR Bulletin*. Ann Arbor, Michigan, October.

McNeil, J. M., and J. J. Salvo. 1985. Lifetime work experience and its effects on earnings: data from ISDP. Pp. 47–56 in *Survey of Income and Program Participation and Related Longitudinal Surveys: 1984*. Washington, D.C.: Department of Commerce, Bureau of the Census, Population Division.

Microdata File with Data from the Survey of Income and Program Participation (SIPP). 1984. *Data User News* 20(2):4. (Bureau of the Census)

Morgan, J. N. 1972. *A Panel Study of Income Dynamics*. Ann Arbor: Institute for Social Research, University of Michigan.

______. 1981. *A Panel Study of Income Dynamics: Procedure and Tape Codes, 1980 Interviewing Year: Wave XIII*. A supplement.

Mott, F. L. 1979. *The Socioeconomic Circumstances of Households Headed by Women: Results from the National Longitudinal Surveys*. Monograph No. 72. Washington, D.C.: Employment and Training Administration, U.S. Department of Labor.

The NLS Handbook. 1987. Columbus: Center for Human Resource Research, The Ohio State University.

Nelson, G. L. 1989. Longitudinal data sets: Revealing the limitations for rural information systems. Paper presented at the Rural Data Needs Conference, Lexington, Ky.

Nestel, G. 1981. A longitudinal study of labor market behavior—Advantages and some methodological problems in analysis. Pp. 122–125 in *Proceedings of the Social Statistics Section of the American Statistical Association*.

News from the Survey of Income and Program Participation (SIPP). 1985*a*. *Data User News* 20(6):6. (Bureau of the Census)

News from the Survey of Income and Program Participation (SIPP). 1985*b*. *Data User News* 20(12):1–2. (Bureau of the Census)

Olneck, M. R. 1985. Critique of questions pertaining to education in SIPP. *Journal of Economic and Social Measurement* 13:299–304.

Parnes, H. S. 1972. Longitudinal surveys: Prospects and problems. *Monthly Labor Review* 95(February):11–15.

______. 1975. The national longitudinal surveys: New vistas for labor market research. *American Economic Review* (May):244–249.

______. 1981. An overview of results from the national longitudinal surveys. *Review of Public Data Use* 9:31–38.

Peterson, J. L. 1979. Work and socioeconomic life cycles: An agenda for longitudinal research. *Monthly Labor Review* 102(February):23–27.

______. 1980. An agenda for socioeconomic life cycle research. *Journal of Economics and Business* 32(Winter):95–110.

Roman, A. M., and D. V. O'Brien. 1984. The student follow-up investigation of the 1979 Income Survey Development Program. SIPP Working Paper No. 8407. Washington, D.C.: U.S. Bureau of the Census.

Ryscavage, P. 1985. SIPP and CPS labor force concepts: A comparison. Pp. 63–68 in *Survey of Income and Program Participation and Related Longitudinal Surveys: 1984*. Department of Commerce, Bureau of the Census, Population Division.

Saunders, D. N. 1973. Labor force behavior: A longitudinal perspective. *Review of Public Data Use* 1(July):7–13.

SIPP and SIPP Access: Initial Findings from a New Data Base. 1987–88. *Focus* 10(4):18–19. (Institute for Research on Poverty, University of Wisconsin-Madison)

Smeeding, T. M. 1985. The scientific potential of SIPP: Its content and methods regarding fringe benefits, noncash income, and the value of government services. *Journal of Economic and Social Measurement* 13:287–294.

Smith, J. D. 1985. A little SIPP: Old wine in new bottles—Let's recask it. *Journal of Economic and Social Measurement* 13:341–347.

Sproat, K. 1979. Using national longitudinal surveys to track young workers. *Monthly Labor Review* 102(October):28–33.

Stafford, F. 1986. Forestalling the demise of empirical economics: The role of microdata in labor economics research. Pp. 387–423 in O. Ashenfelter and R. Layard, eds., *Handbook of Labor Economics*, Vol. 1. New York: Elsevier Science Publishers.

Survey Research Center. 1984. User guide: Panel Study of Income Dynamics. Ann Arbor: Survey Research Center, University of Michigan.

Symposium on SIPP. 1985. *Data User News* 20(2):5. (Bureau of the Census)

Tickamyer, A. R., and C. M. Duncan. 1991. Work and poverty in rural America. Pp. 102–113 in C. B. Flora and J. A. Christenson, eds., *Rural Policies for the 1990s*. Boulder, Colo.: Westview Press.

Tickamyer, A. R., and M. Latimer. 1991. *National Longitudinal Surveys: A Guide for Rural Poverty Analysts* Washington, D.C.: The Aspen Institute, Rural Economic Policy Program.

Tickamyer, A., J. Bokemeier, S. Feldman, R. Harris, J. P. Jones, and D. Wenk. 1993. Women and persistent rural poverty. In Rural Sociological Society Task Force on Persistent Rural Poverty, eds., *Persistent Poverty in Rural America*. Boulder, Colo.: Westview Press.

Tolbert, C., and M. Killian. 1987. *Labor Market Areas for the United States*. Technical report for Agricultural and Rural Economics Division. Washington, D.C.: Economic Research Service, U.S. Department of Agriculture.

U.S. Bureau of Labor Statistics. 1982. *Labor Force Statistics Derived from the Current Population Survey: A Databook*. Bulletin 2096, Washington, D.C.: U.S. Government Printing Office.

U.S. Department of Commerce, Bureau of the Census. *Current Population Reports Series P-70*. Washington, D.C.: Bureau of the Census.

U.S. Department of Labor. 1980. *The Socioeconomic Status of Households Headed by Women*. R&D Monograph 72, February 14.

U.S. National Commission on Employment and Unemployment Statistics. 1979. *Counting the Labor Force*. Washington, D.C.: U.S. Government Printing Office.

Watts, H. W. 1985. The scientific potential of SIPP for analysis of living arrangements for families and households. *Journal of Economic and Social Measurement* 13:225–227.

What is SIPP? 1985. *Data User News* 20(2):4. (Bureau of the Census)

Wilensky, G. R. 1985. SIPP and health care issues. *Journal of Economic and Social Measurement* 13:295–298.

Ycas, M. A., and C. A. Lininger. 1982. The Income Survey Development Program: Design features and initial findings—Paper 1. Presented at the Social Science Research Council Conference, Washington, D.C., October.

6

Rural Family Studies: Multiple Wave, Multiple Indicator Data

Frederick O. Lorenz and Rand D. Conger

Rural policymakers need information that accurately describes and explains how structural changes in agriculture are affecting rural institutions. Of particular importance among these institutions is the family. For years, families living in rural areas and small towns have had to adapt to the economic pressure and social distress associated with the cumulative structural changes in agriculture, changes which accelerated with devastating consequences during the "farm crisis" of the mid-1980s (Murdock and Leistritz, 1988). These fundamental changes have both increased the likelihood of psychological distress and decreased the capability of individuals and families to help one another. Recent increases in spouse abuse, divorce, suicide, and depression have been dramatic. Among rural youth, drug abuse and delinquency are on the rise (Davidson, 1989; Rosenblatt, 1990).

Humane policy responses to these conditions require information that not only describes change at a macro level but also leads to a deeper understanding of how social change is linked to specific family and individual experiences. From a policy perspective, interactions between family members have proven to be a pivotal mechanism for either exacerbating or diminishing the negative mental and physical health effects of socioeconomic disorganization. Compared with urbanites, rural people are far more likely to turn to nuclear or extended family members to meet their social, economic, emotional, and physical health needs (Conger et al., 1990). However, families are tightly interlocked social units, and the methods required to accurately describe how changes are affecting their members are more complex than can be captured by single-respondent, cross-sectional surveys.

The purpose of this chapter is to describe research strategies that will help us to better decipher these complex relationships and to provide more accurate information for policy development. These strategies emphasize (1) the use of panel studies of families to better monitor change as it occurs, and (2) the use of multiple measurement methods such as interviewing and videotaping family members so that we can obtain richer detail about family interactions. The value of this approach lies in its potential to create more sensitive, comprehensive, and valid models of rural life on which to build policy. Such models are also needed to provide insights for counselors and other health-care professionals who are responsible for helping citizens meet their emotional and physical health needs.

To illustrate the advantages of panel data and multiple sources of information as a base from which rural family policy can be established, we draw from our current research, the Iowa Youth and Families Project (IYFP). The purpose of the IYFP is to assess the effects of intervening variables on the relationship between economic hardship and its eventual consequences. In this chapter, we use information from a pretest of 76 families in one county, collected in the spring of 1988, and from a panel study of 451 rural Iowa families, collected in the springs of 1989, 1990, and 1991. To test hypotheses that the consequences of socioeconomic change would be different for different family members, the design included plans to interview a seventh grader, a sibling closest in age to the seventh grader, and both parents. Because of the importance placed on behaviors that reflect family life, data-collection activities included videotaping and coding behaviors of family members as they interacted with one another.

Research Design in Rural Studies

To better monitor social change and its effects on families, research designs that go beyond current survey practices need to be developed. The difficulties in advancing the quality of research have been explored by Blalock (1984), who notes that the tensions created by the competing demands of indirect measurement, multiple causation, and generalizability of results are inherent in a discipline whose subjects are heterogeneous and whose causal laws are both multivariate and indeterministic. In a complementary way, Kish (1987) argues that research design must make tradeoffs between the three R's of randomization, representativeness, and realism. These ideals are not hierarchically ordered; rather, they represent legitimate goals that must be balanced in any design.

Among rural sociologists, the balance has been in favor of representative surveys that provide generalizable results from which to garner evidence for important policy positions (see Chapters 4 and 5). Recent review articles in *Rural Sociology* confirm that sample surveys remain the data-collection method of choice among rural sociologists, while linear models, especially analysis of variance and regression, are the preferred means to analyze returned questionnaires (Stokes and Miller, 1985). This preference for a single method is sometimes viewed critically (Falk and Zhao, 1989; Bealer, 1990). As Bokemeier and Yount point out in Chapter 8, there are many instances in which we need more details about social processes, details that necessitate intensive study of individual exemplars of an issue.

In spite of the inadequacies of survey research, it can be used to improve simultaneously our ability to measure and model multiple causation. Statistical advances have already proven to be important in solving modeling problems. Over the years, mathematicians, econometricians, and psychometricians have developed methods to estimate linear models that take into account problems arising from indirect measurement, especially unreliability and correlated errors. More recently, Bollen (1989) has incorporated many of these advances into a unified account of measurement theory and structural equation modeling that can be read and applied by most sociologists. Although these methods usually assume indicators of concepts are measured on a continuum, parametric procedures for categorical data are rapidly developing and coming into use (Hagenaars, 1990). In a similar manner, social scientists have adapted ideas from life testing and related statistical traditions to develop event history analysis (Tuma and Hannan, 1984; Yamaguchi, 1991), a set of procedures that explicitly incorporates the dynamics of time into the modeling of transition rates from one state to another (e.g., from single to married or from unemployed to employed).

Such recent advances are not a panacea for all our design problems, but they do provide more subtle and precise methods for addressing difficult problems than previously attempted. However, the opportunities these new methods create are not without costs because the data they demand are expensive and require disciplined planning at the design stage. An optimistic note is that current federal policy may provide help. USDA's renewed emphasis on longer term projects, with experiment station support serving as seed money, is encouraging interdisciplinary research with closer ties to theoretical problems funded by other federal agencies (e.g., National Science Foundation and National Institutes of Mental Health) and to practical interventions funded by private endowments (e.g., Kellogg Foundation). These institutional changes can complement attempts to advance research design.

Panel Design and Analysis

The recent statistical advances and changing institutional policies provide new opportunities to move beyond one-shot surveys to more insightful longitudinal studies. Although there are numerous ways to design longitudinal studies (Duncan and Kalton, 1987), panel designs are particularly relevant for the study of family problems. Compared with trend and cohort studies, panel designs are distinguished by observing the same families, and individuals within families, at different points in time.

Although panel designs do not rival well-designed experiments in their ability to make statements about "cause," they do provide advantages over cross-sectional surveys. They allow researchers to actually observe intrafamily or intraindividual change as it unfolds rather than infer change from differences between families or individuals (Nesselroade and Baltes, 1979). Given an agreed-upon ordering of predictor variables in a regression or path framework, panel designs allow researchers to model change more effectively, to examine reciprocal and lagged effects of one variable on another and, under certain conditions, to test for spurious effects (Kessler and Greenberg, 1981).

Panel studies are not easy to conduct. They are certainly more costly than one-time, cross-sectional surveys, and issues of data quality and data management multiply with each additional wave. One lesson veterans of panel research have learned is that maintaining focused objectives is difficult. Because panels require the long-term commitments of time and resources, investigators are tempted to pack the study with many agendas. In recent years, considerable time and research talent has gone into the design and execution of numerous national panel studies, including the Continuous Work History Sample, the Survey of Income and Program Participation, the National Crime Survey, and the Panel of Income Dynamics (see Chapter 5).

The design of these large-scale studies has been informed by two separate traditions: the child development movement of the early part of the century, in which the goal of research was the normative description of growth and development, and the market research efforts of Lazersfeld, which had strong quasi-experimental overtones. These two traditions often make competing demands on how data are collected, and attempts to blend the two goals in large-scale studies have sometimes failed to satisfactorily achieve either goal (Campbell, 1988).

Some Design Considerations

One lesson we learned from the "theory construction" movement of the early 1970s is that linking design decisions to substantive theory is a sensitive process that cannot be reduced to a formula (Cohen, 1989). Like any other design, the value of a panel study depends on how well it builds a compelling scenario or explicates competing theories so that the resulting data can help rule out one argument relative to another (Kessler and Greenberg, 1981; Kasprzyk et al., 1989). The first question to ask is whether one's research objectives can be achieved by less expensive means. If not, there remain several ways in which to collect panel data. The most common procedure is a prospective sample in which respondents in the initial wave of data collection are recontacted at specific intervals. In implementing this approach, researchers must make decisions about the appropriate sample size, timing of data-collection activities, interval between contacts, and number of waves of data required to properly identify important models. Additional decisions must also be made about sample retention, tracking nonrespondents, and imputing missing data (Kasprzyk et al., 1989). Often these decisions are dictated by specific concerns about the identification and estimation of key theoretical models. But some decisions are arbitrary. In the IYFP, families are contacted once every year; longer intervals could miss important events as they unfold but shorter intervals would be logistically impossible to implement.

There are less expensive and less time-consuming alternatives to prospective panels, such as using archival data and retrospective sampling methods. One method is to select a cross section of subjects and then reconstruct previous events in their lives either by asking them about those events or by gaining access to archival data about them (*follow-back designs*). However, the problems with telescoping and selective recall that are associated with asking people about past events are well documented with follow-back designs. A second approach is to identify a sample from a previous study and then locate those people for a follow-up (*catch-up designs*). Both of these retrospective methods often suffer from the problem of "selecting on the dependent variable"; that is, some people are systematically excluded from the study because the event of interest has not happened to them.

Analysis Strategies

An important dimension of research design is to relate study goals to analysis strategies. The most frequently used approaches to analyzing panel data include single-equation regression or multivariate analysis of variance, event history analysis, structural equations, and latent class/latent trait models. Each of these approaches makes different assumptions about the data and addresses different research questions. For example, if the goal of a study is to understand how one's status or position at a particular point in time is related to prior statuses and events, then the outcome can be modeled as a single ordinary least squares or a logistic regression equation. Ollenburger, Grana, and Moore (1989) used this approach to explain changes in women's labor force participation as a function of marital status, whether they lived on farms, and other predictor variables. They used prospective data from the Nebraska Annual Social Indicators Survey to monitor the timing and rates of entrance of women into the Nebraska labor force. Likewise, Dorfman et al. (1988) interviewed 149 elderly Iowa couples to monitor changes in their retirement satisfaction, and Moore (1989) used a panel of Wisconsin farm couples to study changes in family identification with farm and land.

In contrast to traditional regression approaches, if the goal of a study is to explain the dynamics of social change, and to explain why some individuals or families make transitions from one state to another faster than others, then event history models are particularly appropriate. Event history analysis is distinctive in that the rate of change from one state to another is itself the outcome variable. One complication of this approach is censoring; that is, the observation period often ends before all the consequences of a certain process have completely unfolded.

To implement an event history analysis, researchers must obtain accurate details about when specific events, such as marriages or job changes, actually occurred. Data can be obtained retrospectively or prospectively through interviews, self-administered questionnaires, or archival sources. As an example in rural sociology, Heaton, Lichter, and Amoateng (1989) used a variant of event history analysis to examine rural/urban differences in the timing of first intercourse, first marriage, and birth of the first child among young women. The data are censored because some of the women had not yet experienced these events at the end of the observation period.

Structural Equations for Panel Data

Part of our research on rural families is directed toward understanding how economic conditions and life events are affecting families, and how interactions among family members mediate the effects of these conditions and events on individual well-being. Among the intervening variables reported in the literature are the concepts of individual resilience and vulnerability as well as family and social support. Most of these cognitive, affective, and behavioral concepts do not have fixed transition states into which participants can be classified; instead, they must be measured by pencil-and-paper instruments or observed at particular points in time.

These features of our research program and data are particularly congruent with structural equation modeling which, when coupled with panel designs, can help provide insight into ongoing processes as they unfold, change as it occurs, and developmental trajectories (Bollen, 1989; McArtle and Aber, 1990). To model these data using structural equations, the issues of specification and identification must be addressed. *Specification* refers to whether a proposed model includes all the appropriate variables, whether the variables are in their correct temporal order within the model, and whether they are validly and reliably measured. *Identification* refers to whether a proposed model has a unique solution for each parameter being estimated.

To illustrate, Figure 6–1*a* proposes an ongoing stress process in which economic pressure is related to subsequent depression, both directly and indirectly through spouse support and respondent sense of mastery. Researchers familiar with path analysis know that, although this model is identified, it is convincing only to the extent that it is properly specified. In our IYFP, *economic pressure* is defined in terms of the adjustments family members have had to make and their feelings about those adjustments when they experience loss of income, reduced assets relative to debts, and unstable work (Conger et al., 1990). For wives in our study, a husband's support was measured by asking her whether he "let me know he appreciates my ideas or the things I do," "was loving and affectionate toward me," "let me know he really cares about me," and "was supportive and understanding toward me." Mastery was measured from Pearlin's well-known Mastery scale (Pearlin et al., 1981), and depression was operationalized by the number of depressive symptoms reported by the wives (Derogatis, 1983). Our results indicate that economic pressure, measured in 1989, is significantly related to both wives' sense of support ($\beta_{21} = -0.15$) and mastery ($\beta_{31} = -0.35$) in 1990. Subsequent depressive symptoms in 1991 are directly related to support ($\beta_{42} = -0.15$) and

(a) A three-wave model of the stress process.

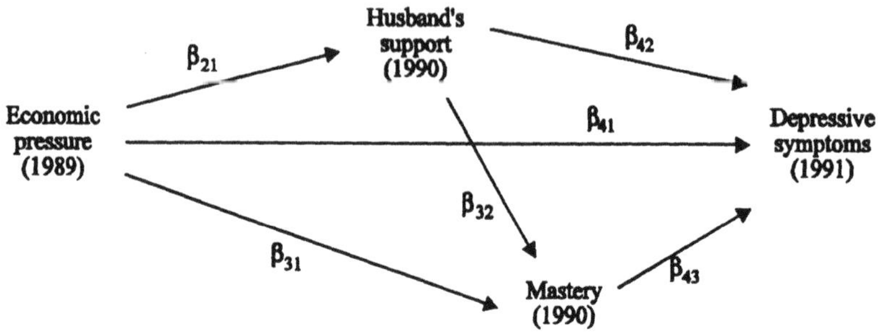

(b) A two-wave, two-variable panel model.

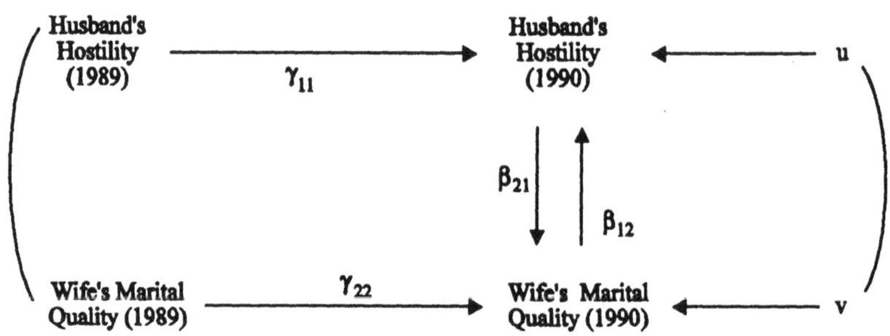

(c) Simple latent growth curve model.

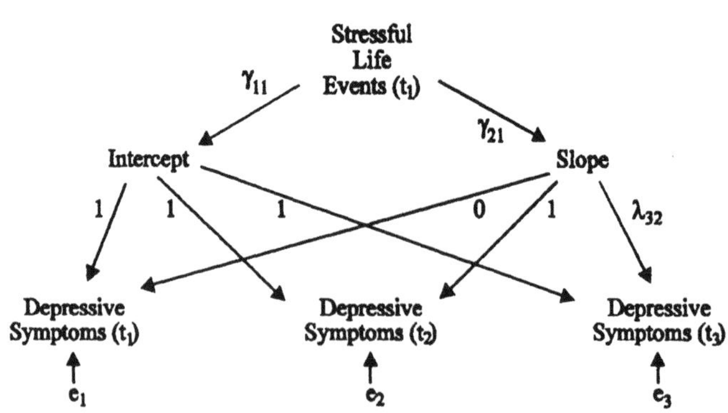

Figure 6-1. Some simple panel models.

mastery ($\beta_{43} = -0.47$), but not directly related to economic pressure ($\beta_{41} = 0.08$). A more detailed analysis showed that the relationship between mastery and depressive symptoms was especially strong (−0.82) when the husbands' support was below the median reported by women (Lorenz et al., 1993).

Although the model captures important aspects of the stress process as it unfolds by temporally ordering variables, it remains that the causal order must be established a priori. Furthermore, it does not assess change. The simple autoregressive model in Figure 6–1*b* attempts to examine the relative effects of change in husbands' hostility on change in wives' marital quality, and vice versa. But one important issue in estimating this model is identification. This model is "just identified" because the number of parameters being estimated exactly equals the number of normal equations generated by the model (see Duncan, 1975). In Figure 6–1*b*, husbands' hostility appears to have a stronger effect on wives' marital quality ($\beta_{21} = -0.26$) than does wives' marital quality on husbands' hostility ($\beta_{12} = -0.17$), largely because the stability coefficient linking husbands' hostility at times 1 and 2 ($\gamma_{11} = 0.65$) is greater than that linking wives' marital quality at times 1 and 2 ($\gamma_{22} = 0.50$). In this model, the wife's report of her husband's hostility was measured by asking her whether, in the past few weeks, her husband "got angry at me," "criticized or made fun of my ideas," "shouted or yelled at me because he was mad at me," and "threatened to do something that would upset me if I didn't do what he wanted." Marital quality was measured by asking her how happy and satisfied she was with their marriage.

The model in Figure 6–1*b* is a simple one, and its merits ultimately rest on the specification of a more complete model. In general, two-wave, two-variable autoregressive models, such as this one, are often used as heuristic devices or as starting points to examine more elaborate processes. Expanding it to include more variables or more waves of data allows one to identify the model with less restrictive assumptions (Kessler and Greenberg, 1981:28–46). However, most autoregressive models use information about the covariances among variables only and provide little information about how developmental processes unfold over time.

Figure 6–1*c* sketches a model in which information about mean scores across time is incorporated with information about covariances to provide insight into actual trajectories of change (McArtle and Aber, 1990). For example, an untimely negative event (e.g., loss of parent or unwanted pregnancy) in an adolesecent's life may not only affect her report of depressive symptoms at a point in time, but it may actually initiate a process sending her on a trajectory of increasing depression over time. In Figure 6–1*c*, the paths linking "intercept" and "slope" to depressive symptoms at three points in time imply that information about the means and variances of each depressive symptom, along with the covariances between them, can be transformed into a developmental trajectory, with each respondent having his or her own unique trajectory. The paths linking negative life events to the intercept (γ_{11}) and slope (γ_{21}) imply that the events not only affect the contemporaneous level of distress but may initiate a process sending her on a trajectory of increasing depression over time. With three or more waves of data, the slopes may be quadratic or represent an even more complicated process. In a more elaborate model, the intercept and shape of the curve can be explained by both time invariant variables (e.g., age and socioeconomic status) and time-varying variables (e.g., social support). In a work in progress, Ge et al. (1993) demonstrate that the growth in depressive symptoms observed in girls as they pass through adolescence can be explained in large part by a parallel growth in stressful life events that are associated with learning adolescent and adult roles.

Multiple Indicators and Measurement Error

Although panel data allow researchers to examine more critically assumed causal ordering and more creatively map developmental trajectories than do cross-sectional data, these models are still affected by measurement error. Erroneous assumptions about the structure of measurement errors can lead to biased coefficient estimates and substantive misinterpretations. Thus, one of the most important questions confronting family research is how to get accurate (reliable) and appropriate (valid) measures of important attitudes and behaviors. For years, researchers routinely used multiple questionnaire items to tap important domains of indirectly observed concepts and to achieve an acceptable level of internal consistency. But only with the more recent technical advances in confirmatory factor analysis and structural equation modeling have researchers become more sensitive to the implications of measurement strategies for the relationships among concepts. As a result, some rural sociologists are now using the redundancy associated with multiple indicators to evaluate the structural clarity of their concepts (Farmer, Ilvento, and Luloff, 1989) and to separate the effects of measurement error from the relationship of one substantive concept to another (Sapp and Harrod, 1989).

The Role of Multiple Indicators

When researchers have only a single indicator of a concept, they are implicitly assuming their items are measured without error. However, with multiple indicators of the same concept, one can draw on "true score" theory from psychology to actually estimate the measurement error and correct for its attenuating effects. In addition, panel models have been used to separate stability and reliability when a concept is measured with only a single indicator (Wiley and Wiley, 1985), and multiple indicators have come to play an important role in panel analysis in obtaining estimates of the stability of a concept and the reliability of its indicators.

The simple model in Figure 6–2 shows how panel data can be used from two points in time to estimate the stability and reliability of husband's hostility. In this figure, the latent construct, husband's hostility, is measured at two points in time using the same five indicators each time. Measures of husband's hostility were obtained by asking husbands how often in the past week they had been bothered by "temper outbursts that you could not control," "having urges to beat, injure, or harm someone," "having urges to break or smash things," "getting into frequent arguments," and "shouting or throwing things" (Derogatis, 1983). These items are numbered 1 through 5, respectively, at both times 1 and 2. As in factor analysis, the variance of each indicator can be partitioned into common and unique variance. The coefficient of 0.80 linking the latent concept of husband's hostility at time 1 to item 1 (referring to "temper outbursts") is a factor weight which, when squared (0.64), represents the proportion of variance in the item that is explained by the common factor of hostility and can be used as a measure of the reliability of the item relative to the concept it is measuring (Bollen, 1989:220–221). For item 1 at time 1, the unique variance is the portion of variance not explained by the common factor (variance $\{e_1\} = 1 - 0.64 = 0.36$). This unique variance is composed of two parts: random error and item-specific error, or the error that is unique to the item but not to the latent factor. The correlation of 0.06 between e_1 at time 1 and e_1 at time 2 reflects the presence of a relatively insignificant amount of item-specific error that is carried from time 1 to time 2; the similar correlation linking e_2 from time 1 to time 2 is significant. The coefficient of 0.64 linking the latent construct of hostility at times 1 and 2 reflects the strength of the correlation between the two constructs at two points in time. In the language of psychometric theory, this stability coefficient is "corrected for attenuation"; that is, it reflects the true correlation between constructs after factoring out the biasing effects of measurement error.

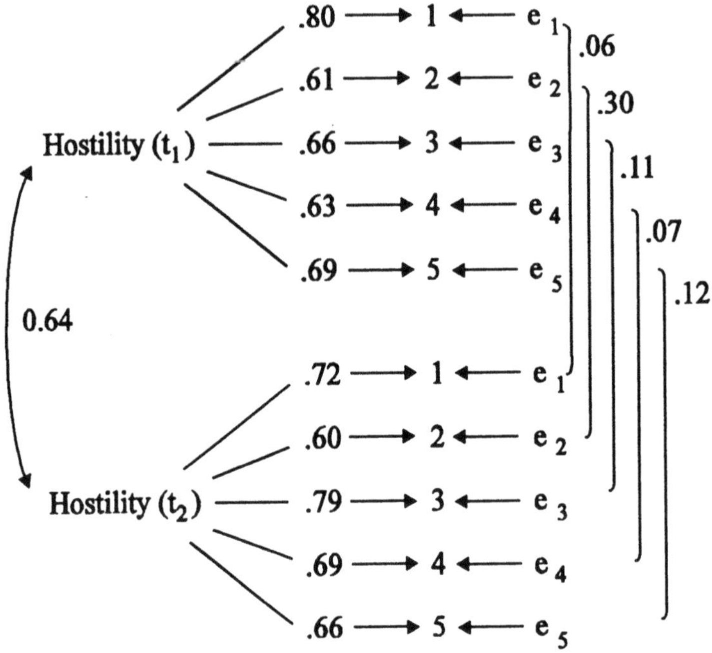

Items from the SCL-90-R (Derogatis, 1983). Have you been bothered by:

1. Temper outbursts that you could not control.
2. Having urges to beat, injure, or harm someone.
3. Having urges to break or smash things.
4. Getting into frequent arguments.
5. Shouting or throwing things.

Figure 6-2. Model of husband's self-reported hostility at time 1 and time 2 (n = 426).

The Role of Multiple Informants

For most research, multiple indicators of constructs are obtained from a single respondent. If the purpose of the study is to describe populations or monitor trends, then single-respondent methods are adequate. But when the purpose is to model complex phenomena such as the effects of structural changes in agriculture on relationships among family members, then the richness and insight gained from multiple sources of information become an important aspect of the modeling process.

We can illustrate the complexity of detail that is hidden from a researcher when data are collected from a single source. From numerous social psychological studies, we know that individuals may be unable to conceptually distinguish attitudes they have about aspects of their lives or other family members from their own overarching dispositions, traits, or attributional styles. In such situations, correlations and path coefficients linking one concept to another may appear large simply because the indicators are from a single source. This phenomenon, an important aspect of the more general "method variance" problem, has been shown to threaten the credibility of previous family studies (Lorenz et al., 1991).

To illustrate the implications of method variance, two alternative parameterizations of the same model are shown in Figure 6–3, which examines the relationship between economic pressure and wives' marital quality, using husbands' hostility and supportiveness as intervening variables. In Figure 6–3*a*, economic pressure was based on both the husbands' and wives' reports. A husband's hostility and supportiveness were measured using both his wife's report and an observer's report. Observer ratings were obtained when trained coders recorded selected behaviors from videotapes. A husband's observed hostility toward his wife was defined as critical, disapproving, and rejecting behavior and as control attempts that used hostile, threatening, or blaming behavior. Observed supportiveness included a husband's expressions of interest, care, concern, support, and encouragement, and attentiveness to the verbalizations of actions of his wife. All ratings were on a five-point scale. Using data from the sample of 451 families, the results in Figure 6–3*a* imply a strong link between economic pressure and husbands' hostility (0.30; $t = 3.7$) and between economic pressure and supportiveness (-0.23; $t = -3.5$), while the effect of husbands' supportiveness on wives' marital quality is very large (0.76; $t = 4.4$). In Figure 6–3*b*, wives' reports of their husbands' hostility and supportiveness are included as indicators of their own marital quality. In this version, the effects of economic pressure on husbands' hostility (0.11; $t = 2.1$) and supportiveness (-0.14; $t = -2.5$) were still significant, although more modest than in Figure 6–3*a*. In turn, the coefficients linking wives' marital quality to their husbands' hostility (−0.08; t = −1.6) and supportiveness (0.38; t = 7.5), although smaller, actually had larger t-values (essentially the same results are obtained when a parallel model is applied to husbands' marital quality).

Empirically, we have several reasons to doubt that the wives in our study were able to separate feelings about their marriage from assessments of their husbands' behaviors. First, in Figure 6–3*b*, the factor weights linking marital quality to the wives' reports of their husbands' hostility (−0.67) and supportiveness (0.75) are almost as strong as those linking marital quality to their reports of happiness (0.88) and satisfaction (0.88) with the marriage. Second, when the wives' reports of their husbands' hostility and supportiveness are modeled as we intended them, in Figure 6–3*a*, the result is a set of characteristics symptomatic of multicollinearity. That is, the coefficients linking marital quality to hostility (−0.16) and supportiveness (0.76) are actually larger than those in Figure 6–3*b*, but the associated t-tests are smaller, implying that the standard errors are inflated. Furthermore, the correlation of the residuals between the husbands' hostility and warmth, not shown in the figures, is −0.70 for Figure 6–3*a*, compared with a more modest −0.35 for Figure 6–3*b*. Substantively, the models in Figure 6–3 do suggest that monomethod models provide only a small glimpse of reality. Obtaining information from multiple sources will not make our job easier; in fact, it may represent a certain "loss of innocence." Currently, those of us in the IYFP and colleagues in like-minded research centers are attempting to devise modeling strategies that effectively incorporate multiple-respondent viewpoints in a single coherent model. In the long run, grappling with issues like the method variance problem will lead social scientists to a more three-dimensional and textured view of our social world, a view that we believe will provide more mature and subtle scenarios about the ways in which social change affects individuals and their families.

Recommendations for Data Collection and Policy

In this chapter, we have argued, along with others (e.g., Murdock and Leistritz, 1988:180–181), for expanding typical survey methods to include more panel studies, which places greater emphasis on multiple indicators of concepts. Panel studies allow researchers to better observe social change and its consequences as they occur; multiple indicators, especially indicators from several sources, allow researchers to triangulate on

(a) Wife's report as a measure of husband's hostility and supportiveness.

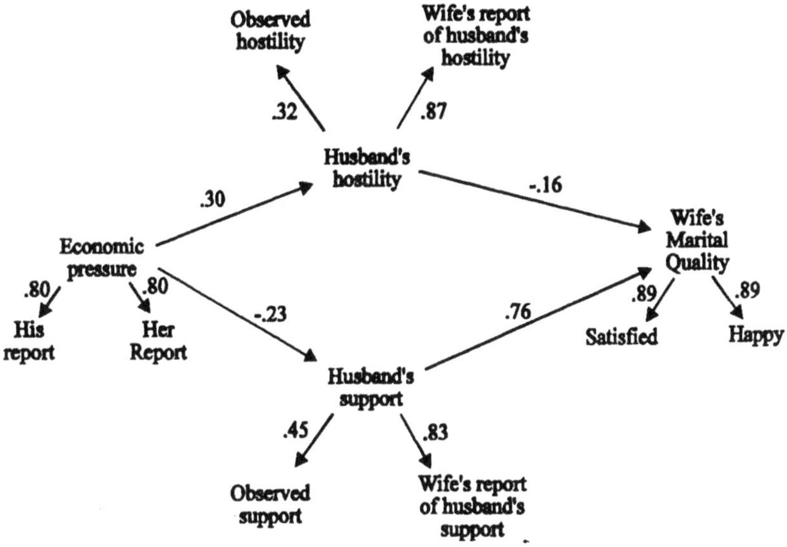

(b) Wife's report as a measure of her marital quality.

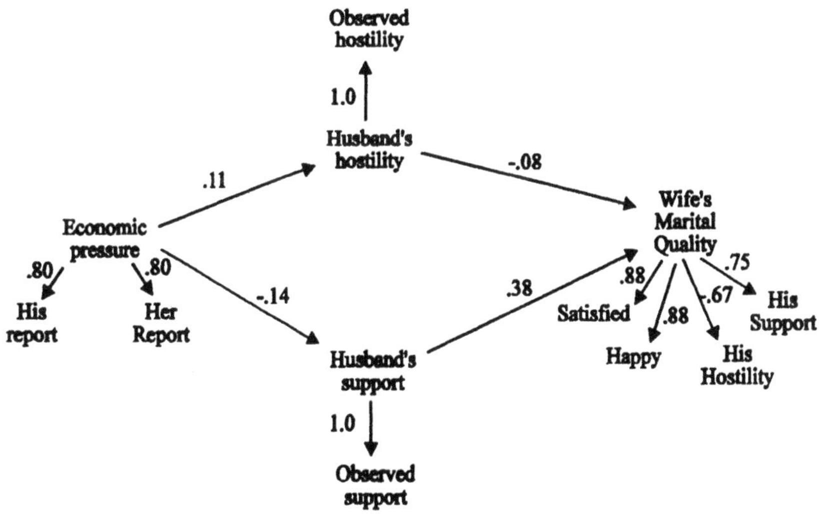

Figure 6-3. Is a wife's report of her husband's behavior a measure of his behavior (pretest data; n = 451)?

measurement error and examine the biasing effects of method variance. In general, our research on rural Iowa families suggests that modeling data from a single source can lead to biased results, primarily because of the effects of method variance. Conversely, our experience with observational data leads us to recommend it whenever information about objective behaviors and family interactions is needed to understand basic relationships. Family members may share meanings that others do not understand, but observers have the advantage of being trained to judge actions by comparing them to wider social norms or accepted definitions. Family members may not see their abusive behaviors as problematic but, relative to other families, their hostile acts may have social consequences for the community in which they reside.

We argue for collecting data from multiple sources while recognizing their effects on research designs: they will be more expensive and time consuming to initiate and maintain than single-respondent studies; they will typically have less coverage than nationally sponsored sample surveys because they are more labor intensive and require more careful management at the data-collection stage. Furthermore, observational data are not without problems. Our results so far suggest that some behaviors, such as acts of hostility, are more reliably rated by observers than are others. Acts of hostility may be discrete, and observers usually agree about their occurrence, while acts of warmth and support may be more difficult to isolate and document because they are embedded in the nuances of daily life. We encourage other researchers to use observational data so that a critical mass can begin to work closely together to develop standardized protocols. Refining and standardizing observational tasks and rating procedures can have the same advantages as standardized pencil-and-paper indices have in advancing scientific boundaries.

Cost and procedural concerns about collecting multiple waves of data from multiple respondents are valid and should be addressed within the larger framework of the role of research in policy decisions. Thinking back to the observations of Blalock (1984) and Kish (1987), there are times when generalizability is of paramount importance because we need reliable national samples to establish policy guidelines or adjust existing programs to changing trends. If information is needed to identify precisely what proportion of rural residents live under the poverty level, and how poverty conditions correlate with specific attitudes toward other salient features of social life, then there is no substitute for self-reports from known populations. Many policy questions are of this nature, and establishing national data banks, as Nelson has called for in Chapter 4, is one way to assure the quality and comparability of data.

On the other hand, panel data with multiple indicators of concepts and multiple sources of information become important when we want to move beyond the description of trends. In the case of rural farm and family policies, debates are not only about trends, but about the consequences of the trends. When the debate moves into an arena requiring more complete explanations about the mediating processes and moderating conditions that link social and economic changes to the mental, physical, and behavioral outcomes of rural residents, then it becomes important for scholars to provide interpretations that are informed by empirically tested, middle-range models of family processes. In many instances, the kind of data scholars need to help them interpret the effects of social change on family processes and outcomes must be more detailed and more sensitive than can be garnered from large-scale sample surveys. But unless one is blessed with an unlimited budget, the drive for greater realism in measurement and the expedience of proper model specification require one to sacrifice immediate generalizability and representativeness; one simply cannot manage data-collection activities from multiple respondents on the same scale as a NORC opinion survey, especially if the data include videotaping family members as they interact with each other.

Still, there are several ways that results from more intensive, community-based studies can be generalized. First, nearly all community studies collect paper-and-pencil indices of important concepts, just as national sample surveys do, and these common indices provide important moments in the research process where national surveys intersect with community samples. When important indices from national surveys are used in more localized community studies, they provide a means to compare results and speculate about the generalizability of the intensive study. Common indices also permit one to speculate about the effects of method variance bias on national samples and to provide insight into the interpretation and meaning of relationships found in national studies.

Second, models that identify and operationalize important family processes can be generalized through replication across sites. Replication across research sites enhances the research community's confidence that the mechanisms identified in a model operate in a variety of environments. IYFP investigators' early attempts to exchange models of adolescent behavior with scientists at another site, the Oregon Social Learning Center, are promising.

From the larger perspective of a national policy toward research, longer-term projects that place greater emphasis on managing multiple causation and measurement error improve our chances of building policy on the dynamic interplay between theory, research, and program evaluation. This interplay is encouraged when specific research projects are seen as part of a program of research or when the evaluation of a program is grounded in rigorous methodologies designed to ask whether theory-based mechanisms are working.

Government agencies, in turn, are beginning to encourage this broader perspective by funding programs of research rather than isolated projects and by devising procedures to better coordinate research between agencies. While the USDA is encouraging longer term experiment station projects that provide seed money for larger competitive grants, other agencies have made explicit attempts to fund research associated with rural problems. Several sessions at the 1992 Rural Sociological Society annual meeting were devoted to new funding sources within the USDA. Most notably, one session was sponsored by the National Institute of Mental Health (NIMH) Office of Rural Mental Health Research, during which time specific programs linking NIMH's interest in basic research to rural problems were discussed. In November 1992, a workshop sponsored by the Office of Rural Mental Health Research had as its expressed goal "to stimulate promising investigators to pursue research on rural mental health" to "increase the number of investigators actively engaged in research in this area." The research NIMH is interested in funding includes not only basic science, but also demonstrations and evaluations of delivery of services to rural areas. Increased communication and coordination between agencies could provide the seeds upon which the next generation of research studies are based, studies that go beyond large-scale surveys and begin to dig deeper into persistent and troubling problems of rural America.

Notes

This paper is based on collaborative research involving the Iowa Youth and Families Project at Iowa State University, Ames, and the Social Change Project at University of North Carolina, Chapel Hill. The combined research is supported by the National Institute of Mental Health (MH3270, MH48165), the National Institute on Drug Abuse (DA05347), the John D. and Catherine T. MacArthur Foundation Program for Successful Adolescent Development among Youth in High-Risk Settings, a Research Scientist Award (MH00567), and the Iowa Agriculture and Home Economics Experiment Station. Journal paper 15091 of the Iowa Agricultural and Home Economics Experiment Station, Ames, Iowa, Project No. 2931. Correspondence should be addressed to Frederick O. Lorenz, Department of Sociology, 310 East Hall, Iowa State University, Ames, IA 50010.

References

Bealer, Bob. 1990. Paradigms, theories, and methods in contemporary rural sociology: A critical reaction to critical questions. *Rural Sociology* 55:91–100.

Blalock, Hubert H., Jr. 1984. *Basic Dilemmas in the Social Sciences.* Beverly Hills, Calif.: Sage.

Bollen, Kenneth A. 1989. Structural Equations with Latent Variables. New York: John Wiley and Sons.

Campbell, R. T. 1988. Integrating conceptualization, design, and analysis in panel studies of the life course. Pp. 43–69 in K. W. Schaie, R. T. Campbell, W. Meredith, and S. C. Rawlings, eds., *Methodological Issues in Aging Research.* New York: Springer.

Cohen, Bernard P. 1989. *Developing Sociological Knowledge* (2nd ed.). Chicago: Nelson-Hall.

Conger, Rand D., G. H. Elder, Jr., F. O. Lorenz, K. J. Conger, R. L. Simons, L. B. Whitbeck, S. Huck, and J. N. Melby. 1990. Linking economic hardship to marital quality and instability. *Journal of Marriage and the Family* 52:643–656.

Davidson, O. G. 1989. *Broken Heartland: The Rise of America's Rural Ghetto.* New York: Anchor Books.

Derogatis, L. R. 1983. SCL-90-R: *Administration, Scoring, and Procedures Manual-II* (2nd ed.). Towson, K/D: Clinical Psychometric Research.

Dorfman, Lorraine T., D. A. Heckert, E. A. Hill, and F. J. Kohout. 1988. Retirement satisfaction in rural husbands and wives. *Rural Sociology* 53:25–39.

Duncan, O. D. 1975. *Introduction to Structural Equation Models.* New York: Academic Press.

Duncan, Greg, and G. Kalton. 1987. Issues of design and analysis of surveys across time. *International Statistical Review* 55:97–17.

Falk, William W., and S. Zhao. 1989. Paradigms, theories and methods in contemporary rural sociology: A partial replication and extension. *Rural Sociology* 54:587–600.

Farmer, Frank L, T. W. Ilvento, and A. E. Luloff. 1989. Rural Community poverty: A LISREL measurement model. *Rural Sociology* 54:491–508.

Ge, Xiaojia, F. O. Lorenz, R. D. Conger, G. H. Elder, Jr., and R. L. Simons. 1993. Trajectories of stressful life events and depressive symptoms during adolescence. *Developmental Psychology* (in press).

Hagenaars, J. A. 1990. *Categorical Longitudinal Data*. Newbury Park, Calif.: Sage Publications.

Heaton, T. B., D. T. Lichter, and A. Amoateng. 1989. The timing of family formation: Rural-urban differentials in first intercourse, childbirth, and marriage. *Rural Sociology* 54:1–16.

Kasprzyk, D., G. Duncan, G. Kalton, and M. P. Singh, eds. 1989. *Panel Surveys*. New York: Wiley Interscience.

Kessler, Ronald C., and D. F. Greenberg. 1981. *Linear Panel Analysis: Models of Quantitative Change*. New York: Academic Press.

Kish, Leslie. 1987. *Statistical Design for Research*. New York: John Wiley and Sons.

Lorenz, F. O., R. D. Conger, R. B. Montague, and K. A. S. Wickrama. 1993. Economic conditions, spouse support, and psychological distress among rural husbands and wives. *Rural Sociology* (in press).

Lorenz, F. O., R. D. Conger, R. L. Simons, L. B. Whitbeck, and G. H. Elder, Jr. 1991. Economic pressure and marital quality: An illustration of the method variance problem in the causal modeling of family processes. *Journal of Marriage and the Family* 53:375–388.

McArtle, J. J., and M. S. Aber. 1990. Patterns of change within latent variable structural equation models. Pp. 151–224 in A. von Eye, ed., *Statistical Methods in Longitudinal Research*, Vol. 1. New York: Academic Press.

Moore, Keith M. 1989. Agrarian or nonagrarian identities in farm spouses. *Rural Sociology* 54:74–82.

Murdock, Steve H., and F. L. Leistritz. 1988. *The Farm Financial Crisis: Socioeconomic Dimension and Implications for Producers and Rural Areas*. Boulder, Colo.: Westview Press.

Nesselroade, J. R., and P. B. Baltes, eds. 1979. *Longitudinal Research in the Study of Behavior and Development*. New York: Academic Press.

Ollenburger, Jane C., S. J. Grana, and H. A. Moore. 1989. Labor force participation of rural farm, rural nonfarm, and urban women: A panel update. *Rural Sociology* 54:533–550.

Pearlin, L. I., M. A. Lieberman, E. G. Menaghan, and J. T. Mullan. 1981. The stress process. *Journal of Health and Social Behavior* 22:337–356.

Rosenblatt, P. C. 1990. *Farming Is in Our Blood: Farm Families in Economic Crisis*. Ames: Iowa State University Press.

Sapp, Stephen G., and W. J. Harrod. 1989. Social acceptability and intentions to eat beef: An expansion of the Fishbein-Ajzen model using Reference Group Theory. *Rural Sociology* 54:420–438.

Stokes, C. Shannon, and M. K. Miller. 1985. A methodological review of fifty years of research in rural sociology. *Rural Sociology* 50:539–560.

Tuma, Nancy B., and M. T. Hannan. 1984. *Social Dynamics: Models and Methods*. New York: Academic Press.

Yamaguchi, K. 1991. *Event History Analysis*. Newbury Park, Calif.: Sage.

Wiley, D. E., and J. A. Wiley. 1985. The estimation of measurement error in panel data. Pp. 133–144 in H. H. Blalock, ed., *Causal Models in Panel and Experimental Designs*. Chicago: Aldine.

7

Sampling Frames for Rural Household Surveys

Robert D. Tortora

A *universe* or target population consists of all the people, firms, housing units, and so on that a researcher wants to study. For example, it could be all the households in the United States outside metropolitan statistical areas (MSAs) with a population of 50,000 or more; or all the households without farm income outside MSAs with a population of 250,000 or more; or all the children under age 14 living outside the city boundaries of Louisville, Kentucky, but in Jefferson County.

The universe of study is defined long before the survey is conducted, when the researcher develops a scientific approach. This approach includes a theoretical orientation, hypothesis development, and an analysis scheme with output tables and tabulation plans. The tabulation plan includes cross tabulations for the descriptive statistics, including desired sampling errors; statements of hypothesis to be tested; and proposed methods of testing.

The *sampling frame* is a means of access to the universe. Ideally, it should provide access to the entire universe, or at least enough of the universe to make the research worthwhile. Without a frame that provides reasonable access to the target population, the researcher cannot use probability sampling techniques and cannot make statistically correct inferences to the target population.

There are other important factors in survey design such as non-sampling errors that can occur at each stage of the survey process, from planning through publication of the results, that are not associated with a sampling frame. The magnitude of these errors can seriously reduce the quality of the survey data. See the *Journal of Official Statistics* Special Issue on Nonsampling Errors (1987) for more information on this topic.

Evaluation Factors for Sampling Frames

When developing or evaluating a sampling frame for the universe of study and the research analysis, several factors are very important to consider for the sampling frame. These factors include coverage of the universe and coverage bias for variables in the tabulation plan, efficiency or accuracy of the sample considering the purpose of the sample, and cost of the sampling frame.

Coverage and Coverage Bias

Coverage refers to the frame's ability to provide access to the elements in the target population. A frame provides complete coverage if all the elements in the target population can be accessed. If not, coverage bias exists for the variables in the tabulation plan. *Coverage bias* is defined as the difference between the expected value for a variable of interest given the incomplete frame and the expected value for a variable of interest given a complete frame. Differential coverage bias can also occur if the frame is incomplete. Here, coverage varies for different social, demographic, and economic subpopulations. These types of coverage errors usually cause a negative bias, but coverage errors can also produce a positive bias.

Undercoverage occurs if population units are missing from the frame. This error can be of major concern since inferences are often made that include these missing units for which no data are available. For example, a frame based on registered voters in a county does not represent the county population for inference purposes.

Another error that can cause coverage bias is the omission of household members for surveys requiring household roster data. Here, the target population includes individual household members, say all males over the age of 14. If these members of the target population are consistently missed, particularly in important subpopulations, the differential coverage bias can be large. This error usually occurs during the listing of the household roster (Maklan and Waksberg, 1988; Groves and Kahn, 1979; Bailar, 1986), that is, when the sampling frame for the household members is made.

Another type of frame error is when nonpopulation (blank or foreign) elements are included in the frame; this causes *overcoverage* if the elements are not removed or detected during data collection. These types of frame elements provide access to units that are not a part of the target population. For example, if a list of agricultural producers also contains names of landlords who do not operate any land, there is the potential for the landlords to report data for the operator too.

Clusters of elements can be together on the frame. Instead of a frame unit accessing one unit of the target population, it accesses many units. When these elements are unrecognized, they can also produce overcoverage. For example, a multifamily household, if not detected during frame construction or data collection, can cause overcoverage.

Finally, frames can also contain duplicate elements because generally there are multiple ways to access or reach an element in the universe of study. For example, a frame of directory names and addresses may contain a separate listing for each spouse. If these duplicate listings are not eliminated from the frame or detected during data collection, they are a source of overcoverage.

Table 7-1 summarizes these sources of error and shows whether the bias is positive or negative. The first error, missing units, usually causes the most serious coverage bias; unlike other frame errors, it cannot be eliminated during data collection. The magnitude of this bias depends on the rate of the coverage and the differential coverage by subpopulation. If it is small, its effect can be ignored. If it is large, an alternative strategy must be used, either a statistically sound adjustment procedure or another sampling frame or design, such as dual frame methods, to compensate for the bias. Unfortunately, the last three errors also increase sampling error if they are not eliminated during frame construction but are detected instead during data collection.

Table 7-1. Source of Coverage Error and Sign of Bias

Source of Error	Sign of Bias
Units missing from frame	–
Units within households missing[a]	–
Blanks and foreign units[b]	+
Clusters of units[b]	+
Duplicate units[b]	+

[a]Occurs when within household rosters do not reflect all household members that are in the target population.

[b]Occurs when not removed from frame and data-collection procedures do not screen out units outside target population.

Sampling Efficiency

The choice of a sampling frame affects the efficiency of the sample design. Blanks and foreign units cause, at a minimum, increased sampling error. The existence of auxiliary variables for stratification (the process of grouping units of like size or type) for most frame units can reduce sampling error for a fixed sample size. However, incorrect auxiliary information can negate some part of this reduction in sampling error. For a rare population, auxiliary information can be very important. If it can group the rare population into strata, and the rare population represents a relatively large proportion of these strata, the frame can provide acceptable sampling errors. When units appear in clusters on the frame, sampling errors can also increase when compared with a fixed-size sample of unclustered units. The increase in sampling error is caused by a positive intracluster correlation coefficient. In short, the efficiency of design can be greatly affected by the choice of the sampling frame. Table 7-2 displays the impact on sampling efficiency for various frame problems and the effect of auxiliary information for stratification on efficiency.

Besides decreasing sampling efficiency the first three errors in Table 7-2 are potential sources of other nonsampling errors and also increased cost. The procedure to detect these errors complicates and lengthens each interview.

Table 7-2. Sources of Error and Effect on Sampling Efficiency

Source of Error	Effect on Sampling Efficiency[a]
Blanks and foreign units[b]	–
Clusters of units	–
Duplicate units[b]	–
Auxiliary information	
Correlated for stratification	+
Absent	–
Unavailable for subpopulations	–

[a]A minus sign indicates the sampling efficiency decreases; that is, the sampling error increases.

[b]Occurs when not removed from the frame even though data-collection screening eliminates units for interview.

Cost

Finally, the total survey cost is related to selecting and developing a sampling frame. Total survey cost is a function of the costs of planning a survey, including sampling frame selection; required sample size; mode of data collection; length of interview; and analysis and summary, including all adjustments. These costs are not independent and many are affected by the choice of the frame.

For example, the frame often dictates the mode of data collection. Face-to-face interviewing is more expensive than mail or telephone interviewing. When interviewers are used, the cost of training also needs to be included in the total survey cost. The sources of cost associated with the frame type are described in Table 7-3.

List Sampling Frames for Rural Household Surveys

Sampling frames for rural household surveys include residential and commercial directories of addresses and telephone numbers and directories of all possible telephone numbers.

Directory of Commercial Telephone Numbers

A directory of commercial listings provides frames for mail, telephone, and face-to-face surveys. The frame of all possible telephone numbers provides a frame for telephone surveys.

All these frames are incomplete in terms of coverage errors. The magnitude of the incompleteness for directories of commercial listings varies by the type of frame, the sources used for constructing the frame, and the age of the frame. For example, Groves and Lepkowski (1986) indicate that for a survey of telephone households in rural areas, a frame based on telephone directories may have a considerably higher coverage rate since more telephone numbers are listed than for a comparable frame for urban areas. However, coverage rates can vary across subpopulations, resulting in differential coverage bias. Even though a master address list is continually revised within six to eight weeks of directory publication (Donnelley Marketing, 1986), Mohadjer (1988) reports that for national samples, this frame adequately represents black and Hispanic populations; however, it does not provide effective coverage for Asian-Americans. It is also possible to miss directories when building these frames, especially in remote rural areas, which further reduces coverage.

Table 7-3. Survey Costs Associated with the Frame

Source of Cost	Description of Work
Frame evaluation	Determining whether the frame will allow the researcher to complete the tabulation plan. This may also require a pilot survey to be able to make a complete evaluation.
Frame procurement	The cost of buying the frame or access to a sample frame.
Sample size	Frames of clustered units may increase required sample sizes when compared to frames of unclustered units. Frames with auxiliary data for stratification may reduce required sample sizes.
Mode of data collection	The choice of frame may decide the mode of interview; for example, an area sampling frame may require face-to-face interviewing. Include interviewer training costs for telephone or face-to-face surveys.
Length of interview	The frame may increase data-collection costs if it requires additional screening to detect frame problems.
Analysis	A frame that causes a multistage clustered sample design increases costs for analysis since this complex survey design has to be correctly accounted for in the analysis.
Coverage bias adjustments	If required by the frame, methods of coverage bias adjustments must be developed and implemented.

Frames based on directory or commercial listings also have overcoverage. A household may have two different telephone number listings or two address listings. Of course, if this potential duplication is not eliminated during frame construction, it must be detected and eliminated during data collection.

Address listings usually have geographic information and may have other characteristics such as household size and income associated with each sampling unit. This information may be useful in developing more efficient sample designs. If the target population is rare and the auxiliary information is used to group the rare population into strata, then these strata have a high proportion of the population and are likely to result in efficient designs.

Address lists also have differential coverage bias. Childers (1993) reports on missed housing units by type of place in the 1990 Decennial Census of Population and Housing. As population size decreases, missed housing units increases. For large urban areas (population of 250,000 or more) the estimate of occupied housing units was not significantly different from zero (based on a 95 percent confidence interval). However, for other urban and rural areas, the estimates of undercoverage for occupied housing units were both significantly different from zero (0.81 percent and 1.67 percent, respectively), but not different from each other. This work also illustrates that data-collection costs can increase if the address list contains out-of-scope units. For the 1990 census, the estimate of vacant housing units in rural areas was 10.21 percent (standard error of 2.13 percent). The cost to identify these vacant units can be a substantial part of the total data collection.

Finally, the costs of obtaining and using these frames need to be carefully considered. For surveys of large populations, such as all rural households in the United States, the cost of obtaining a commercial list may be very large because costs are directly proportional to the size of the list or the number of units that need to be processed. In this latter case, even if a firm can select samples according to the specified survey design, it may not significantly reduce costs (Groves and Lepkowski, 1986). In both cases, acquisition costs are large.

These frames can contain a large number of blanks, foreign elements, or insufficient auxiliary information for stratification, depending on the target population and tabulation plan. Clearly, adjustments for coverage bias must be made. So when choosing a directory or commercial list frame, care must be taken in evaluating each cost component.

All Possible Telephone Numbers

The sampling frame of all possible telephone numbers is built by adding four digit suffixes to a list of three digit area codes and three digit prefixes obtained from Bell Communications Research (BCR). The BCR list includes exchange name, geographic coordinates of the center of the exchange, time zone, and new area-code-prefix combinations three months before they are added to the telephone system.

Thornberry and Massey (1988) have studied detailed trends in the proportion of households in the United States with telephones. By 1985/1986, 7.2 percent of households in the United States were without telephones. By region, the Northeast has the fewest households without phones (4.5 percent), followed by the North Central/Midwest (5.3 percent), the West (6.9 percent), and the South with the largest proportion without telephones (10.4 percent). For rural areas, 4.5 percent of the farm households are without telephones and 9.4 percent of rural nonfarm households are without telephones. For rural areas outside of MSAs, 11.0 percent of households are without telephones. The Northeast has the fewest with 4.2 percent and the West the largest with 17.5 percent of the households without telephones.

Thornberry and Massey also show that, when considering the percent of persons in nontelephone households, there is considerable variation by family income. They also show that in nontelephone households there are more persons with low family income, particularly in the South, more persons below the poverty level, more blacks, more separated persons, and more persons where the highest education level of adults is less than 11 years. In short, there can be a considerable undercoverage for various subpopulations of the frame of households with telephones.

Survey researchers have developed a technique called *random digit dialing* (RDD) to sample the frame of all telephone numbers. RDD provides coverage of listed and unlisted telephone numbers. By using an up-to-date BCR list of area code-prefix combinations, coverage of new telephone numbers can be maximized. RDD also reduces the cost of finding telephone numbers for the target population. However, over three-fourths of the BCR list numbers are not assigned to telephone households (Groves and Kahn, 1979).

Mitofsky (1970), Waksberg (1978), Sudman (1973), and Potthoff (1987) have proposed two-stage RDD sample designs to reduce the number of calls needed to find residences because residential telephone numbers are clustered within banks of telephone numbers. A prefix area is selected within an area code at random and with replacement, and then a telephone number within the prefix area is selected at random and dialed. If the selected number is eligible, the prefix area is selected for subsampling at the second stage; otherwise, it is eliminated from the first stage. Within selected prefix areas, a set of k–1 additional numbers are generated at random and without replacement. These numbers are dialed and if any are not eligible they are replaced by another number in the prefix area until the eligible numbers are identified in the prefix area. Lepkowski (1988) describes these procedures in detail.

As indicated, the cost of acquiring this frame is relatively low. However, the cost of collecting data using RDD methods can be relatively high. For household surveys, the large proportion of ineligible numbers increases interviewer costs. RDD samples also result in more wrong connections, fast busy signals, silence, or strange noises. Careful records of each call must be maintained to effectively manage the data-collection effort by keeping track of the result of each call and redialing numbers, often over several days. This careful record keeping also increases data-collection costs. Lepkowski (1988) notes that these costs are even higher for surveys of rural populations because these areas have more problem numbers when compared with urban areas.

In rural areas, there are also more ineligible numbers, banks of numbers assigned in groups of 1,000, and prefixes not specifically assigned for business use. In addition, nonworking numbers in rural areas may continue to ring. Data-collection costs may rise further because prefix codes do not match political boundaries. Thus, the interviewer must spend additional time identifying the location of the answered number (also risking that the location will be identified incorrectly and another nonsampling error will be added to the survey). Finally, post-data-collection costs can rise for surveys of rural populations because weighting adjustment procedures are necessary.

Area Frame Sampling

While none of the list sampling frames gives complete coverage of the rural population, the area frame used by the National Agricultural Statistics Service (NASS) for the farm population provides complete coverage for the rural population (Fecso, Tortora, and Vogel, 1986).

This NASS area frame covers the entire land area of the United States, and thus each rural household (also each farm, business, urban household, etc.) is in the sampling frame. This area frame is stratified by land use; typical strata are defined by intensively cultivated land, cultivated land, minimally cultivated land and rangeland, agricultural urban areas, urban areas, and nonagricultural land.

While this frame is complete, it does not guarantee zero coverage bias. Inaccurate screening of sampling units, called *segments*, could result in missed households, particularly in more densely populated areas. Matthews (1988) describes this problem for farms. Duplicate households should not be a major source of error. Foreign or blank elements also do not present major problems, especially if the rural population is defined along county boundaries because the NASS frame is constructed (but not sampled) county by county.

Coverage bias using the NASS area frame should also be small. Any bias that occurs would probably come from faulty screening procedures, not frame defects. For farms, Matthews (1988) found a coverage bias four times the sampling error, which was caused by the screening process.

Nealon (1988*a*, 1988*b*) evaluated the area frame for estimating rural households and found that the sample design is suboptional when estimating rural households. For example, if the definition of the rural population excluded all MSAs of population 1,000,000 or more, the current sample design provides a coefficient of variation of 2.8 percent for total rural households. The optimum design would provide a coefficient of variation of 1.3 percent. To increase the efficiency of the NASS area frame, Nealon recommended adding additional geographic substrata in the agricultural urban strata, increasing the U.S. sample size by about 1,000 segments, and developing improved outlier adjustment procedures.

In summary, although the current area frame design can be inefficient for rural household surveys, when compared to the optimal design, the modifications are relatively modest to reach the optimal. However, for rare items, say single parent households, other techniques such as multiplicity sampling (Steiner, 1981) or dual frame sampling need to be used. This latter technique will be discussed later.

The final item of consideration for the area frame is cost. Building an area frame for a state can be very expensive. Considerable resources are needed just to obtain mapping and photographic materials, over and above staff costs for actually building the frame. The cost of selecting the sample from an area frame is also relatively more expensive than the cost of selecting a sample from a list frame. Data-collection costs can also be high because area frame surveys usually require face-to-face interviewing. This cost can be too high for a given survey budget, so techniques such as dual frame sampling may be used to provide acceptable levels of sampling error for a given cost. Since the coverage bias associated with this area frame is relatively small, post-data-collection costs associated with these errors should also be small.

For the four factors for evaluating sampling frames—coverage, coverage bias, sampling efficiency, and cost—each type of frame has strengths and weaknesses. To take advantage of the strengths and reduce the weaknesses of a particular frame, a methodology that combines frames called "multiple frame sampling" is used (Hartley, 1962). Multiple frame sampling is usually implemented as dual frame sampling.

Dual Frame Sampling

One way to eliminate the coverage bias of the list frame of all possible telephone numbers is to combine this frame with the area frame of all households. An optimum allocation between the two frames may produce output tables with acceptable levels of precision and cost without coverage bias. NASS uses this methodology for its surveys of U.S. agricultural producers.

One frame is a list of producers built and maintained by NASS. The list contains about 55 percent of the U.S. farms but covers much larger proportions for cattle, hogs, grain in storage, and so on. The other frame is the NASS area frame described above.

Others have studied these methods for different frames and different populations and found them to improve on the one frame approach. One frame would be an area frame and the other would be the frame of all possible telephone numbers. Groves and Lepkowski (1986) studied this methodology when one frame is the frame of all telephone numbers and the other frame is the frame of listed numbers.

Dual frame methods offer increased strengths when evaluated against the four factors—coverage, coverage bias, sampling efficiency, and cost. However, improvements are not free. Dual frame methods increase administrative costs and also introduce new sources of error. These errors arise because this methodology requires that the frame membership for each sampling unit be accurately determined.

Note

The expressions and opinions expressed in this paper are those of the author and do not reflect the policies of either the National Agricultural Statistics Service or the U.S. Bureau of the Census.

References

Bailar, B. A. 1986. Information needs, surveys, and measurement methods. Paper presented at the Conference on Panel Surveys. Washington, D.C.

Childers, D. R. 1993. Memorandum: Dual System Estimates of Housing Coverage. Washington, D.C.: U.S. Census Bureau.

Donnelley Marketing. 1986. *Donnelley Marketing Advantages*. Stamford, Conn.: R. H. Donnelley Corporation.

Fecso, R., R. D. Tortora, and F. A. Vogel. 1986. Sampling frames for agriculture in the United States. *Journal of Official Statistics* 2(3):279–292.

Groves, R. M., and J. M. Lepkowski. 1986. An experimental implementation of a dual frame telephone sample design. Pp. 340–345 in *Proceedings of the Section on Survey Research Methods*, American Statistical Association.

Groves, R. M. and R. L. Kahn. 1979. *Surveys by Telephone: A National Comparison with Personal Interviews*. New York: Academic Press.

Hartley, H. O. 1962. Multiple frame surveys. Pp. 203–206 in the *Proceedings of the Social Statistics Section*. American Statistical Association.

Lepkowski, J. M. 1988. Telephone sampling methods in the United States. Pp. 51–98 in R. M. Groves et al., eds., *Telephone Survey Methods*. New York: John Wiley and Sons.

Journal of Official Statistics. 1987. Special issue on nonsampling errors. *Journal of Official Statistics* 3(4):321–475.

Maklan, D., and J. Waksberg. 1988. Within-household coverage in RDD surveys. Pp. 143–160 in R. M. Groves et al., *Telephone Survey Methods*. New York: John Wiley and Sons.

Matthews, R. V. 1988. *Screening Residential Tracts for Agricultural Activity*. National Agricultural Statistics Service Staff Report No. SSB-88-05. Washington, D.C.: NASS.

Mitofsky, W. 1970. Sampling of telephone households. Unpublished CBS memorandum.

Mohadjer, L. 1988. Stratification of prefix areas for sampling rare populations. Pp. 161–174 in R. M. Groves et al., eds., *Telephone Survey Methodology*. New York: John Wiley and Sons.

Nealon, J. 1988*a*. *Alternative Population Definitions for Rural Household Surveys*. National Agricultural Statistics Service Staff Report No. SMB-88-05. Washington, D.C.: NASS.

______. 1988*b*. *Prospects for Conducting Household Surveys with an Agricultural Area Frame*. National Agricultural Statistics Service Staff Report No. SSB-88-06. Washington, D.C.: NASS.

Potthoff, R. F. 1987. Some generalization of the Mitosky-Waksberg technique for random digit dialing. *Journal of the American Statistical Association* 82(398):409–418.

Steiner, M. A. 1981. The use of network sampling in agricultural surveys. Pp. 496–499 in *Proceeding of the Section on Survey Research Methods.* Washington, D.C.: American Statistical Association.

Sudman, S. 1973. The uses of telephone directories for survey sampling. *Journal of Marketing Research* 10(2):204–207.

Thornberry, Jr., O. T., and J. T. Massey. 1988. Trends in United States telephone coverage across time and subgroups. Pp. 25–50 in R. M. Groves et al., eds., *Telephone Survey Methodology.* New York: John Wiley and Sons.

Waksberg, J. 1978. Sampling methods for random digit dialing. *Journal of the American Statistical Association* 73(361):40–46.

8

Qualitative Insights to Enhance National Information Systems

Janet L. Bokemeier and Kristen R. Yount

Traditionally, land-grant universities have been characterized by efforts to conduct applied research geared to formulating policies that improve the lives of rural residents. However, rural America is perhaps best characterized by economic and cultural heterogeneity among geographic areas and by rapid change associated with industrial, agricultural, and demographic transitions. Thus, pressing needs in one area may not exist in another; policies effective in one region may not apply elsewhere. National policies have failed to take into account unique rural needs and resources (Flora and Christenson, 1991). Farmers mock farm policies and government agencies because they find the policies and implementation procedures to be absurd or costly considering their particular situation and community context. How, then, can we come to understand the needs of specific rural areas and develop policies that are practical and effective? Data must be available that inform us about the diversity within rural America and the critical differences between rural and urban areas.

Recent reviews of the literature emphasize that many rural social scientists have relied primarily on the administration of surveys to accomplish applied research objectives (Falk and Gilbert, 1985; Stokes and Miller, 1985). However, as these authors and others emphasize, there is growing recognition that exclusive reliance on a positivistic approach inhibits researchers' abilities to comprehend social complexity and change. Survey research typically relies on survey methodology, quantitative secondary data, and individuals as units of analyses. For the most part, survey researchers turn to the existing theories and pursue leads provided by previously collected survey data. On the basis of this information, they pose both the questions and the response options with the basic presumption that they know the critical questions and answers that indicate alternatives for social action.

While we have become increasingly precise and sophisticated in survey techniques of measurement and analyses, we are still limited in the scope of phenomena examined (Stokes and Miller, 1985). Thus, these strategies emphasize the researcher's knowledge and assumptions. They may therefore limit the policy relevance of the research because of their inability to discover the emerging problems and experiences of rural residents and to appreciate the complexity of rural life. One problem with this approach is timing; researchers may have keen insights into past issues but not into newly emerging concerns. Another problem with this approach is that it is quite possible that few people who have developed the perspectives on which surveys are based have gone directly to rural residents to systematically obtain community members' perspectives and opinions. Thus, critical factors bearing on the feasibility of policy options may be overlooked.

When social scientists rely too much on survey data, they fail to challenge and critique the status quo or to identify policy alternatives that challenge what currently exists (Falk and Gilbert, 1985). Thus, social scientists are perceived as timid and conservative. Furthermore, social science data are essentially irrelevant for policy without some ideological sensitivity and advocacy that is better served by data that build on a crucial human touch. Also, to communicate effectively within the policy areas, personal accounts of relevant experiences are essential to illustrate and sensitize leaders to public needs. It is time to ask "what [is] not being done and to suggest new directions" (Falk and Gilbert, 1985:571).

This chapter presents a triangulated research design for conducting policy-oriented studies in rural communities. The design includes the collection of survey data and also incorporates field research intended to position the researcher within the natural setting and to give rural residents a more active role in the research process. We highlight the ways in which field and survey methods can be integrated to help overcome the shortcomings of each approach and discuss the ways in which field research data can help to effectively communicate policy recommendations stemming from the research.

Rural people respond to social policies in a processual and interpretive fashion at the local level, that is, the community or neighborhood. Qualitative research differs from survey research in that it positions research closer to the natural setting, granting a more active role to respondents in the research process and focusing on discovery. Qualitative field research is appropriate for investigating dynamic situations and those in which the subjects' interpretations of events and activities are the focus of study. However, qualitative research has certain limitations as well. For example, researchers cannot generalize to a known population from qualitative data. Nor can they draw conclusions regarding the distribution of phenomena of interest. Qualitative researchers must address concerns regarding the credibility of informants and the impact of interviewer bias on conclusions.

Thus, reliance on either approach is inadequate for policy research involving both understanding of problems to be addressed by public policy and evaluating implemented policies. A preferred policy research approach integrates the flexibility of qualitative research to study dynamic situations about which there is limited knowledge of expected outcomes and the descriptive power of quantitative studies to detail phenomena in large, heterogeneous populations.

The current debate over poverty policy and research well illustrates these assertions. The ever-increasing levels of unemployment, homelessness, hardship, and inequality show that previous welfare programs have been ineffective. Some argue that welfare programs have failed because they encourage welfare dependency and are disincentives to employment. Others claim the problem lies with inadequate funding and failure to address structural constraints that contribute to poverty. In such policy polarizations, social scientists only contribute to the stalemate by clinging to old typologies and analytical strategies (Duncan and Tickamyer, 1988, 1990). Negative stereotypes of the poor as culturally deficient promote the assumption that either culture, family, or welfare policies are the villain in persistent poverty.

Quantitative studies have contributed much to our understanding of poverty, for example, the rural-urban comparison of those in poverty, the distinction between individual episodes of poverty and geographic areas of persistent poverty, the challenge of the negative stereotypes depicting the poor as urban, unemployed, black, unwed mothers. But new policy alternatives must consider adaptive strategies currently relied on and must examine the cultural response to persistent economic hardship.

Qualitative studies will inform policy as to effective points of entry for survival support as well as the diversity of policies required to address a complex problem. In a recent study, Rank and Hirschl (1987) employed quantitative methods to discover that the rural poor are less likely to participate in welfare programs; they then used qualitative methods to find out why. Such combinations of techniques are more effective than single techniques in addressing policy concerns.

Overview of the Research Design

The methodological approach we present here stems from our research experiences and also draws from the model of triangulation originally suggested by Sieber (1973) and exemplified by others (e.g., Madey, 1982).[1] This approach is both sequential and interactive in that findings from field and survey research complement each other.[2] Neither methodology assumes a secondary or supplementary role in the research process.

The research process begins with preliminary ethnographic or field research that provides the basic conceptual foundation of the survey. Here, the research team enters the rural setting to observe, interact with, and interview rural residents to identify relevant variables and generate hypotheses to be assessed on the survey. The team then withdraws from the community to analyze the fieldwork data and to construct the survey based on this analysis. After the survey data have been collected, researchers integrate the analyses from both types of data and specify gaps in understanding, discrepancies between the survey and fieldwork conclusions, and other puzzles raised but unanswered. Finally, to "round out" the analysis, the team returns to the rural setting to conduct further ethnographic work to investigate these issues and to complete the formulation of policy alternatives.

Because few researchers are adequately trained in both methodologies, we suggest that the field research and survey components of the study each be directed by an individual with a strong background in one of the two approaches. However, involving all research team members in the entire research process will help them gain insight into and understand the epistemological limitations of each method of investigation. Collaboration in all phases will minimize proprietary feelings and resulting tensions over one source of data or the other.

Initial Field Research

The distinguishing characteristic of ethnographic fieldwork is that researchers enter the daily world of community members in order to gain, to the fullest extent possible, an intimate familiarity with their lives. Fieldworkers seek to learn firsthand about how the people live, to identify their problems, to comprehend their perspectives on these problems, and to assess the values and assumptions that guide their behavior. In short, positioning the researcher within the natural setting leads to a richer understanding of the meanings that activities have for those involved. In contrast to survey work designed to test a priori theories, the primary purpose of fieldwork is to generate empirically grounded concepts and tenable hypotheses.[3]

In their capacity as researchers, fieldworkers temporarily become peripheral members of the rural community. They attend various community events (e.g., church services, county extension programs, and county fairs) and observe the daily activities of members (e.g., the work day of a farm manager on a dairy operation). During this time, they interact with people, engage in conversational interviews, and maintain extensive field notes with the goal of being open to all sources of information and clues to understanding. Relevant field documents should also be collected for analysis (e.g., personal diaries, folklore, and reports on population, economic, and agricultural changes). In a recent study of farm communities, we found the county historical society to be a valuable source of data.

In most studies, however, the primary source of fieldwork data consists of in-depth, semistructured interviews. In general, interview questions are purposely broad and nondirective. Interviewers use probes to encourage interviewees to discuss topics in detail, to point to factors they believe to be important, and to minimize the extent to which the interviewer frames their answers (Spradley, 1979). Descriptive and comparative questions are often used: "Can you tell me what you did when they started the drought-relief program?" "What are the differences between the farmers who used the program and those who didn't?" "What are some common misperceptions that town people have about farmers?" The ethnographer's attitude toward interviewees as well as all community members is very important; that is, the investigator should conceive of and interact with residents not as subjects to be studied, but as teachers of the social life under investigation. Soliciting advice from interviewees (e.g.,"What advice would you give to people who are running the farm program?") is a good way to explore their attitudes and policy options while conveying the message that they are viewed as instructors and active participants in the research process.

Focus groups are particularly useful in terms of expediting data collection (Morgan, 1988). Here, researchers assemble a group of individuals, raise a set of topics related to the research problem in a very general way, and allow participants to discuss them. One advantage of employing this technique is that investigators can elicit the opinions of several people in a short time. The comments of others also spark consideration of relevant factors pertaining to policy issues that may not occur to people in individual interviews. For example, a focus group of hired laborers may have had few opportunities to reflect on their shared experiences and economical employment expectations. Moreover, because the sessions stimulate discussion and debate, researchers are able to assess the ways in which conflicting interests and positions are justified and to determine attitudes as they are reflected by interactions among community members. While focus groups help to draw out the residents' points of view, the presence of other community members also inhibits their expression of certain opinions and attitudes. Therefore, individual interviews should also be conducted.

Because one research purpose of fieldwork is to generate explanations and understanding of underlying processes, researchers must continually analyze incoming data to make decisions regarding future data collection. This means that, first, researchers must constantly revise interview questions to develop the emerging analytical framework. This process involves dropping questions that are continually answered in the same way and adding questions that explore newly identified issues. Second, the task of developing theory mandates that sampling procedures are highly flexible. Initial sampling decisions may certainly be made before data are collected. Investigators should interview some members of each group of stakeholders, or those they expect to be advantaged or disadvantaged by policy decision (e.g., farmers or labor unions) to obtain their concerns, opinions, and suggestions. It is also essential to involve and consult policymakers throughout the research process (Majchrzak, 1984; Weiss, 1984).

However, unlike survey research techniques, sampling decisions are not finalized prior to data collection but are modified as new discoveries are made. For example, in the course of interviews with farm operators, if hired laborers were found to determine farm strategies in response to changing economic situations and agricultural markets, then tenants and hired laborers would be added to the sample. Thus, decisions regarding specific community members to be interviewed are made as a study progresses. Because researchers cannot anticipate all the relevant groups and individuals whose perspectives should be considered, the sampling process involves the conscious construction of comparison groups as the study proceeds. During the initial interviews of a study of agriculturally dependent counties in rural Kentucky, Bokemeier and Garkovich (1987) discovered that a substantial number of farmers were "back-to-landers" who had moved into the area ten to twenty years ago. The farm practices, lifestyles, and political orientations of these farmers differed significantly from other farmers in the county and made traditional farmers more cognizant of their own practices and successful alternatives. This constant and rigorous search for negative or qualifying instances helps investigators develop hypotheses that "fit" the empirical world and that "work" or provide relevant explanations and predictions (Glaser and Strauss, 1967).

Initial fieldwork provides insights regarding critical variables of study and, thus, gives the underlying structure of a survey. The Bokemeier and Garkovich (1987) field research examined the ways that families were responding to major changes in their farm situation during a drought period in which emergency relief programs were put in place. The investigation produced accounts of the significance of intergenerational family interactions, concerns about government supports, and descriptions of the ways in which farmers manipulated existing policies to accommodate emerging problems. Farm couples explained how their plans would differ depending on the way relief programs were implemented. The fieldwork allowed the team to identify key factors related to program utilization and to identify emerging areas of concern including the availability, quality, and cost of hired labor and the availability and cost of family labor as situated in the off-farm employment option.

Based on the accounts of farm families, the researchers were able to determine several action areas that were appropriate for state-level policy consideration. For example, with regard to hired-labor incentives, they specified policy alternatives including state-sponsored health insurance pools, extension of the Job Training Partnership Act (JTPA) to farm labor, and modification of assistance programs to eliminate disincentives to work. The relevant point here is that many of these issues and options were not reflected in the research team's preconceived notions of farm families' concerns and would have been omitted on a survey constructed prior to the field research. In addition, investigators may also draw on their sociological expertise to construct a survey that may incorporate standardized scales and indices that would allow analyses of these variables and comparison across populations. Researchers must make parsimonious and difficult choices, selecting only the most pertinent of these measures to allow space on the survey for area-specific variables indicated as relevant by community members.

One of the primary benefits of field research is that it highlights important variables not recognized in the literature or anticipated by investigators. For example, in a study of the social impact of energy development in rural Colorado towns (Lillydahl et al., 1982), the research team was interested in assessing a variety of issues, including sources of distress and patterns of affiliation among community members. Existing life stressor inventories, however, did not include references to "cabin fever" or irritability stemming from confinement in a house during the winter months. Nor did the social impact literature refer to the importance of occupational status in determining social support networks among newcomers and longtimers. These factors, however, were found to be critical during the field research (Yount, 1986*b*).

Preliminary ethnographic research allows investigators to assess the concerns, beliefs, knowledge, and viewpoints of those who hold a stake in policy issues and helps to frame the research problem. Fieldwork in a rural community also elicits creative suggestions regarding policy options and provides insights into the feasibility of implementing these options by allowing researchers to identify competing interests, values, and norms bearing on the reception of policy alternatives. By allowing the respondents to shape the research, the investigator identifies new and critical areas of study that may have been neglected by authorities who lack concrete experience in the field of study.

Other benefits of this initial phase should be noted. Ethnographic work is instrumental in determining the ways in which samples should be stratified to reflect subgroups of the population most relevant to accepting or rejecting policy programs. For example, investigators may determine a need to oversample a segment of the community found to be critical to policy implementation. In addition, participant observation work is highly useful for alerting researchers to the need to more clearly specify empirically ambiguous categories that may have been taken for granted beforehand (e.g., "farmer"). Finally, fieldwork familiarizes investigators with language usage in a particular rural area so that surveys can be worded in ways meaningful to respondents. For example, sociologists would be ill-advised to use the term "ignorant" on a questionnaire in rural Colorado if they intend to imply lacking knowledge because residents also use the term to refer to a hostile attitude.

Analysis and Fieldwork Following Survey Administration

Survey administration and analysis techniques will not be discussed at length here. (See Chapters 9 and 10 for more information.) It should be noted, however, that fieldwork may benefit subsequent survey work in two ways. First, pretesting a survey instrument is critical. Field research helps to identify community members who will cooperate in answering a preliminary survey and discuss the shortcomings and merits of the instrument's items and instructions. These sessions may be conducted either individually or as focus groups and should be recorded and used both as survey critiques and as important sources of data. Second, personal relationships developed during the field research period and the visibility of researchers at community events generate interest in the study and facilitate good response rates for the survey.

Our primary focus in this section concerns the ways in which survey and ethnographic data mutually inform each other. One way in which this may occur is corroboration. If findings from both sets of data coincide, confidence in the analysis is increased. Convergent validity is one important purpose of employing a between-method research design. Basing the survey on the initial fieldwork enhances the probability of validity; that is, survey results should be more credible because the items were based on empirical data. In addition to corroboration, two other outcomes generally occur; namely, aspects of the two sets of data elaborate each other and provide new insights that initiate further investigation (Rossman and Wilson, 1985).

Mutual Elaboration

Assessing the Representativeness of Fieldwork Data. While skilled ethnographers conscientiously and constantly strive to seek opposing or alternate viewpoints, one risk they run is overexposure to the relatively small number of people with whom they have spent time. Ethnographers tend to inappropriately generalize the perspectives of these people to large segments of the community. Standardized measures and sampling procedures employed with surveys enhance the original ethnographic research by providing a statistical basis for assessing how representative the fieldwork conclusions are.

Interpreting Survey Data. The utility of ethnographic data in terms of interpreting and elaborating relationships found on surveys has been acknowledged for some time. Correlations uncovered through statistical analysis do not constitute a theory. Rather, a theoretical explanation must include the mechanisms or processes that generate relationships. Space and time constraints, however, prohibit the measurement of all theoretically relevant variables on survey instruments. Field research allows important insights with respect to causal relationships and offers the analyst a rich, detailed explanation of the complexity of these relationships, the contextual factors that affect them, and an understanding of interaction processes through which events and attitudes are shaped. While surveys provide wide-angle snapshots that assess social reality at one point in time, field research allows the collections of historical information bearing on policy issues that enhance prediction through assessment of the forces and direction of change.

Ethnographic data also help to clarify ambiguous or unexpected survey results. For example, on survey items assessing the gender orientations of rural community members, a research team found that certain subgroups of men were more nurturant than subgroups of women (Yount, 1986*a*). Given the empirical findings of others within the sex and gender literature, these results would have been quite puzzling without an understanding, stemming from fieldwork, of the extend to which the leisure life of men in this sample centered on children and charity work.

Discovering Hidden Data. Both ethnographic and survey methods have potential for cloaking important information from researchers that may be picked up by the other approach. Survey data often draw out information that individuals are reluctant to discuss in a face-to-face situation. During an interview, for example, people may manage to appear confident in the presence of a fieldworker, while inside they are actually experiencing a great deal of emotional distress. They may, however, be willing to admit these feelings on a written questionnaire in the privacy of their own home.

Conversely, while survey research is based on the assumption that respondents are willing and able to provide complete and accurate answers, discrepancies may exist between what people do and what they say they do on written instruments (Deutscher, 1973). Living in a community, observing people, and talking informally with them helps to provide researchers with a validity check on survey results. For example, while rural respondents might be reluctant to admit on a survey that they grow and sell marijuana, a fieldworker who has interacted with community members in a variety of leisure settings would at least be able to point to the existence of the practice. The growing involvement in the informal economy through work sharing, personal service-type work, and home-based work is not fully assessed by standard national data sets. Interviews can establish and verify the researcher's thesis of diverse, alternative income strategies by indirect methods that protect respondents from revealing unconventional activities.

Generating Issues for Further Investigation

Just as ethnographic methods provide information that helps to elaborate the "bare bones" of statistical data, survey results also expose theoretically relevant phenomena that were not raised by community members and were not addressed in the preliminary fieldwork. Because fieldwork relies on a relatively small, theoretically derived sample, fieldworkers may have overlooked important sources of variation in the perspectives of community members during the initial stage of the study. In addition, controlling for basic demographic variables (e.g., age) may uncover factors missed by fieldworkers that affect receptivity to a policy option. The inclusion of standardized instruments on the survey frequently offers insights. A good example is provided by the social impact assessment research mentioned earlier in which the research team sought information on community mental health (Lillydahl et al., 1982). Because a person's sense of personal worth is considered, in the literature, to be a critical variable determining the experiences of distress, a self-esteem scale was included on the survey instrument. To our surprise, the self-esteem of women was much lower than the men's in rural Colorado towns, a finding that differed from previous research (Wylie, 1979).

Unexplored areas of investigation and unsolved puzzles may require that the research team return to the field for a relatively short time to fill out and refine the analysis. Survey results provide an important resource for this final stage of the research in that the statistical profiles taken from the instrument serve as a basis for collecting additional ethnographic information.

Communicating Needs and Facilitating Policy Initiatives

Determining the implications of policy research does little good unless researchers are able to effectively communicate them to those empowered to implement new policies or to modify old ones. New policy recommendations often challenge or disrupt the status quo. Moreover, researchers from outside the area must contend with a degree of ethnocentric tension generated by local residents' suspicion of outsiders. Data collected through fieldwork methods can enhance receptivity to policy recommendations (Guba and Lincoln, 1981; Madey, 1982; Majchrzak, 1984). Researchers from urban universities have more credibility if they present themselves as individuals who have talked with and learned from rural people and who are summarizing community opinions and perspectives rather than imposing an outsider's frame of reference on rural life.

Policymakers also are more receptive to inputs by outsiders and are more likely to be receptive to their recommended policy changes if the policymakers have been active participants in and contributors to the research process, that is, if they were included in initial interviews, if they were regarded as experts rather than subjects, if their ideas were addressed on surveys. Initial interviews with policymakers also familiarize researchers with the policymakers' perspectives and values and help investigators frame their presentation in terms that the policymakers will find suitable for policy development. Moreover, researchers who spend considerable time in the field and who develop their skills in interpersonal relationships gain a degree of familiarity, rapport, and friendship with local policymakers and community stakeholders. Also, by identifying unique local concerns, researchers can develop a basis for framing national data sets in a way that highlights the unique local niche.

Another advantage of ethnographic data in facilitating policy implementation lies in audience comprehension and assimilation of the needs and problems addressed in the research report. While survey research terminology and procedures may seem arcane to individuals who are not trained in their use, real-life descriptions are more likely to make sense. Ethnographic accounts that present issues in the audience's everyday language facilitates an understanding of the rationale of recommended policy options because it builds on their tacit knowledge of the rural setting and immediate situation. Moreover, descriptions of case studies and interview excerpts bring to life the problems addressed by policy recommendations. They allow users of the research report to take the role of the other, that is, to place themselves in the position of individuals, to vicariously experience their situation, and to develop empathy for them. In short, ethnographies have an aura of realism not found in statistical evidence which can generate understanding and concern for policy needs.

In summary, many policy decisions rely on national surveys and information systems. Field studies provide local policymakers information on the needs and implementation concerns of their constituency population. Fieldwork can assist policy researchers in designing national surveys by determining important variation at the local and regional levels. Thus, the differential impact and acceptance of national policies can be anticipated.

Notes

Authorship is listed alphabetically; both authors contributed equally to the chapter. The authors wish to acknowledge the helpful comments from Dr. Marilyn Aronoff.

1. Each of the two authors has utilized both survey and field research to study issues of work, the family, and gender in rural America. However, Bokemeier has relied primarily on survey methods while Yount has emphasized ethnographic studies. Our collaboration began with discussions of the advantages and drawbacks of the two approaches.

2. An alternative approach to triangulation involves the use of both fieldwork and survey research teams that investigate a research issue concurrently but work relatively independently from each other. See Trend (1979) and Knapp (1979) for illustrations of problems that may arise in employing this strategy. Other discussions that address triangulation in evaluation and policy research, in particular, are offered by Green and McClintock (1985), Cook and Reichardt (1979b), Rossman and Wilson (1985), and Van Willigan and DeWalt (1985). More general discussions of triangulation and comparisons of positivist and naturalistic epistemological paradigms are provided by Denzin (1970), Duffy (1987), Fielding and Fielding (1986), Hammersley and Atkinson (1983), Jick (1983), Knorr-Cetina and Cicourel (1981), Guba and Lincoln (1981), Cook and Reichardt (1979a), and Webb et al. (1966).

3. There are, of course, different approaches to field research. For some ethnographers, the goal is to produce a rich, detailed, or "thick" description of social life and to interpret the meanings of these data in light of existing cultural norms and values (e.g., Geertz, 1983). Others, most notably, proponents of the "grounded theory" approach (Glaser, 1978; Glaser and Strauss, 1967; Strauss, 1987), emphasize the generation of theoretical propositions from the data to explain the regularities and variations of interactions of perspectives within a setting or culture. Texts that provide a good overview of fieldwork processes include Douglas (1976), Emerson (1983), Hammersley and Atkinson (1983), Johnson (1975), Lofland and Lofland (1984), and Whyte (1984). For discussion of the application of ethnographic methods to evaluation research in particular, see Guba and Lincoln (1981) and Patton (1981, 1987).

References

Bokemeier, Janet, and Lorraine Garkovich. 1987. Assessing the influence of farm women's self-identity on task allocation and decision-making. *Rural Sociology* 52(1):13–16.

Cook, Thomas, and Charles S. Reichardt. 1979a. Beyond qualitative versus quantitative methods. Pp. 7–32 in Thomas D. Cook and Charles S.

Reichardt, eds., *Qualitative and Quantitative Methods in Evaluation Research.* Beverly Hills, Calif.: Sage.

______, eds. 1979b. *Qualitative and Quantitative Methods in Evaluation Research.* Beverly Hills, Calif.: Sage.

Denzin, Norman K. 1970. *The Research Act: A Theoretical Introduction to Sociological Methods.* Chicago: Aldine Publishing.

Deutscher, Irwin. 1973. *What We Say, What We Do: Sentiments and Acts.* Glenview, Ill.: Scott, Foresman and Company.

Douglas, Jack D. 1976. *Investigative Social Research: Individual and Team Field Research.* Beverly Hills, Calif.: Sage.

Duffy, Mary E. 1987. Methodological triangulation: A vehicle for merging quantitative and qualitative research methods. *Image: Journal of Nursing Scholarship.* 19(3):130–133.

Duncan, Cynthia, and Ann R. Tickamyer. 1988. Poverty research and policy for rural America. *American Sociologist* 19(3):243–259.

______. 1990. Poverty and opportunity structure in Rural America. *Annual Review of Sociology* 16:67–88.

Emerson, Robert M. 1983. *Contemporary Field Research: A Collection of Readings.* Boston: Little, Brown and Company.

Falk, William, and Jess Gilbert. 1985. Bringing rural sociology back in. *Rural Sociology* 50(1):561–577.

Fielding, Nigel G., and Jane L. Fielding. 1986. *Linking Data.* Beverly Hills, Calif.: Sage.

Flora, Cornelia B., and James A. Christenson, eds. 1991. *Rural Policies for the 1990s.* Boulder, Colo.: Westview Press.

Geertz, Clifford. 1983. Thick description: Toward an interpretive theory of culture. Pp. 37–59 in Robert Emerson, ed., *Contemporary Field Research: A Collection of Readings.* Boston: Little, Brown and Company.

Glaser, Barney G. 1978. *Theoretical Sensitivity.* Mill Valley, Calif.: The Sociology Press.

Glaser, Barney G., and Anselm L. Strauss. 1967. *The Discovery of Grounded Theory: Strategies for Qualitative Research.* New York: Aldine.

Green, Jennifer, and Charles McClintock. 1985. Triangulation in evaluation: Design and analysis issues. *Evaluation Review* 9(5):523–545.

Guba, Egon G., and Yvonna S. Lincoln. 1981. *Effective Evaluation.* San Francisco: Jossey-Bass.

Hammersley, Martyn, and Paul Atkinson. 1983. *Ethnography: Principles in Practice.* New York: Tavistock.

Jick, Todd D. 1983. Mixing qualitative and quantitative methods: Triangulation in action. Pp. 135–148 in John Van Maanen, ed., *Qualitative Methodology.* Newbury Park, Calif.: Sage.

Johnson, John M. 1975. *Doing Field Research.* New York: The Free Press.

Knapp, Michael S. 1979. Ethnographic contributions to evaluation research: The experimental schools program evaluation and some alternatives. Pp. 118–139 in Thomas D. Cook and Charles S. Reichardt, eds., *Qualitative and Quantitative Methods in Evaluation Research.* Beverly Hills, Calif.: Sage.

Knorr-Cetina K., and A. V. Cicourel. 1981. *Advances in Social Theory and Methodology: Towards an Integration of Micro- and Macro-Sociologies.* London: Routledge and Kegan Paul.

Lillydahl, Jane H., Elizabeth W. Moen, Elise Boulding, Kristen R. Yount, Susan Scott-Stevens, and Illana Gallon. 1982. *Quality of Life, Expectations of Change, and Planning for the Future in an Energy Production Community.* Boulder, Colo.: Institute of Behavioral Science.

Lofland, John, and Lyn H. Lofland. 1984. *Analyzing Social Settings: A Guide to Qualitative Observation and Analysis.* Belmont, Calif.: Wadsworth.

Madey, Doren L. 1982. Benefits of qualitative and quantitative methods in program evaluation, with illustrations. *Educational Evaluation and Policy Analysis* 4(2):223–236.

Majchrzak, Ann. 1984. *Methods for Policy Research.* Newbury Park, Calif.: Sage.

Morgan, David L. 1988. *Focus Groups as Qualitative Research.* Beverly Hills, Calif.: Sage.

Patton, Michael Q. 1981. *Qualitative Evaluation Methods.* Beverly Hills, Calif.: Sage.

______. 1987. *How to Use Qualitative Methods in Evaluation.* Newbury Park, Calif.: Sage.

Rank, Mark R., and Thomas A. Hirschl. 1987. A rural-urban comparison of welfare exists: The importance of population density. *Rural Sociology* 53(2):190–206.

Rossman, Gretchen B., and Bruce L. Wilson. 1985. Numbers and words: Combining quantitative methods in a single large-scale evaluation study. *Evaluation Review* 9(5):627–643.

Sieber, Sam. 1973. The integration of fieldwork and survey methods. *American Journal of Sociology* 78(6):1335–1359.

Spradley, James P. 1979. *The Ethnographic Interview.* New York: Holt, Rinehart, and Winston.

Stokes, C. Shannon, and Michael K. Miller. 1985. A methodological review of fifty years of research in *Rural Sociology. Rural Sociology* 50(1):539–560.

Strauss, Anselm L. 1987. *Qualitative Analysis for Social Scientists.* Cambridge: Cambridge University Press.

Trend, M. G. 1979. On the reconciliation of qualitative and quantitative analyses: A case study. Pp. 68–85 in Thomas D. Cook and Charles S. Reichardt, eds., *Qualitative and Quantitative Methods in Evaluation Research.* Beverly Hills, Calif.: Sage.

Van Willigan, John, and Billie R. DeWalt. 1985. *Training Manual in Policy Ethnography.* Washington, D.C.: American Anthropological Association.

Webb, Eugene J., Donald T. Campbell, Richard D. Schwartz, and Lee Sechrest. 1966. *Unobtrusive Measures: Non-Reactive Research in the Social Sciences.* Chicago: Rand McNally.

Weiss, Carol H. 1984. Increasing the likelihood of influencing decisions. Pp. 159–190 in Leonard Rutman, ed., *Evaluation Research Methods: A Basic Guide.* Beverly Hills, Calif.: Sage.

Whyte, William F. 1984. *Learning From the Field: A Guide From Experience.* Beverly Hills, Calif.: Sage.

Wylie, Ruth. 1979. *The Self-Concept Theory. Theory and Research on Selected Topics.* Vol. 2. Lincoln: University of Nebraska Press.

Yount, Kristen R. 1986*a*. A theory of productive activity: The relationships among self-concept, gender, sex-role stereotypes, and work-emergent traits. *Psychology of Women Quarterly* 10:63–88.

______. 1986*b*. Work-emergent behaviors and traits: The segregation of energy workers in boom towns. Pp. 119–143 in Pamela D. Elkind-Savatsky, ed., *Differential Social Impacts of Rural Resource Development.* Boulder, Colo.: Westview Press.

PART THREE

Technologies for Rural Information Systems

This final section looks at new tools and ideas that foster rural information systems. Dillman outlines how recent advances in survey methodology can supplement, refine, and extend national systems. Carpenter then describes how new software and technology can facilitate this process. Finally, Shultz and MacArthur describe how geographic information systems (GIS) can provide a way to synthesize and summarize rural data for information systems.

9

Surveys and Rural Data Needs

Don A. Dillman

Since the nation's first census in 1790, surveys have provided a powerful tool for assessing the needs of rural Americans. For over 200 years, surveys have been at the core of policy formation because they have accurately ascertained the percentage of people in a population who have a certain characteristic (e.g., those who reside in a particular geographic region, depend on agriculture as their primary source of livelihood, or migrate from one location to another). With the development of probability sampling techniques during the twentieth century, the power of surveys has been greatly strengthened, which has allowed close estimates of population characteristics to be made by surveying only a small fraction of the members of that population.

As we near the twenty-first century, two issues are converging which substantially alter the traditional ways that surveys have been used to meet the nation's rural data needs and to develop rural information systems. The first issue involves changes in the type of survey data that are needed for guiding rural policy. The second concerns changes in who performs and how to conduct valid surveys that are responsive to the current needs for knowledge about rural America.

This chapter examines the following argument. The time between recognizing problems and attempting to solve them continues to shrink. Because American society is in transition from a mass society to an information society, the most efficient efforts for solving problems are those that are targeted at small geographic areas and populations (e.g., growers of particular commodities). Advancements in survey methodology make it possible to conduct targeted surveys that are responsive to these problems. However, it is extremely difficult to modify federal surveys, the traditional source of policy relevant data on rural needs, so that timely, targeted surveys can be accomplished. One solution is to develop an appropriate division of labor between the federal government, on the one hand, and state and local governments and universities, on the other (see Chapter 1). This solution, however, is not without certain risks.

Changes in the Data Needs of Rural America

The dominant rural data need for rural development decisions is no longer agricultural statistics. Data needs have become much broader for several reasons: today fewer than 500 rural counties depend on agriculture, the primary growth in rural employment between 1980 and 1990 was in services, and there has been a growth in economic importance of rural tourism and commuting from one place to another.[1]

Homogeneity has been the philosophical underpinning of rural information systems for decades. During the midtwentieth century, a mass society orientation to economic development prevailed (Dillman and Beck, 1988). At its core was a belief that the most efficient and feasible mode for production and distribution of all goods and services was a model that emphasized sameness. Corporations produced millions of nearly identical products from cars to breakfast cereals. The broadcast and print media produced a limited number of mass-oriented products, from national network news to *Time* and *Life* magazines, and farmers grew commodities that could be blended with products produced by others (Dillman, 1990).

Building giant industries was predicated on developing products that would satisfy most consumers, and mass production efficiently produced these products at affordable prices. This tendency was echoed in the development and distribution of government programs which, for reasons of fairness and limited administrative technology, tended to provide (through formulas) the same programs to all jurisdictions, regardless of need. In a mass society environment, it could be reasonably argued, the nation's rural data needs could best be met by national survey efforts that collected the same data throughout the United States. This tendency blended results across regions rather than focused on differences.

We are now in full-scale ascent toward an information age, which facilitates targeting policy responses to specific issues and small geographic regions. The essence of an information age is to increase the use of information relative to other factors of production (time, labor, energy, and natural resources). The advantage of such a system is a more precise response to the specific, rather than the average, needs of groups of potential employers, employees, and so on. Therefore, a major difference between data needs for a mass society and the information age is to obtain data on specific groups and problems.

A second need is to gather and analyze data quickly. The information age places primacy on quick responses. Policy formation that once took years to accomplish may now be attempted in months, weeks, or even days, as efforts are made to respond intelligently to sudden changes in economic opportunities or disruptions. Such changes range from the threat of plant closings to dealing with erratic shifts in consumer demand (e.g., as in the Alar incident).

In an information age context, the need for quickly conducted, small-area or industry-targeted surveys on a variety of topics for policy purposes can easily be imagined. For example, is rural growth in the commuter fringe around a large city occurring because of longer commuting distance or something else? Is the increased number of welfare households in a rural area being fed by migration due to higher housing costs in cities or to indigenous growth? Is long distance telecommuting and other forms of telework (i.e., productive labor that depends on computer workstations and telecommunication of work inputs and products) contributing to population growth in a destination resort area? Are local services increasing their sales outside the community where they are located? Are producers of value-added forest products increasing the proportion of products sold overseas? Are lentil producers in the Pacific Northwest willing to switch varieties of lentils in order to produce sufficient volume for export to a new market?

During the midtwentieth century, at the height of the mass society, policy information surveys were rarely performed. The generally accepted method for surveying mass society was the face-to-face interview. At that time, neither telephone nor mail surveys were considered reliable and personal surveys were too costly to be done routinely. When doing a survey was justified, it took a long time to design and implement. In addition, the processing methods, by today's standards, were inordinately slow and labor intensive. It is little wonder that doing surveys was reserved for society's most important and enduring problems. Fortunately, this situation has now changed (Dillman, 1992).

Changes in Survey Methodology

Telephone Surveys

Prior to the 1970s, the telephone was rarely used to conduct surveys. Today, some twenty years later, the telephone is augmenting, and in many cases completely replacing, the face-to-face interview for doing important national surveys.

Originally there were two major barriers to conducting telephone surveys. First, many people did not have telephones, and those who did not were different (i.e., they had less education and lower incomes) than those who did have them. Second, the telephone was not considered conducive to asking people about sensitive issues such as their spending habits, political preferences, and income. Further, long-distance rates were expensive, and the telephone was considered a device to be used for short, to-the-point conversations.

Two personal experiences illustrate the suspicion with which the telephone was viewed by survey methodologists. In 1970, I conducted my first telephone survey on university students who, in retrospect, were a very easy group from which to get a response. After asking two pages of questions, we informed the respondents that "since telephone surveys must be short, we would like to send [them] a brief mail questionnaire (four more pages) to get additional information." The response rate for the telephone survey was over 90 percent, and as subsequent research and other experiences showed, all of the questions could easily have been asked without adversely affecting the response rate. Three years later, at a national conference of health survey researchers, which included many eminent survey methodologists, the question of whether telephone surveys on health topics could be done was posed to a mostly skeptical audience. A surprising and major conclusion of the conference was that these types of surveys could not only be done, but that some people could be convinced to stay on the phone for a half hour or more.

Three books published in the mid-1970s (Blankenship, 1977; Dillman, 1978; Groves and Kahn, 1979) argued the case for conducting telephone surveys. Since then, at least 500 publications on aspects of telephone surveys have been published and a major methodological conference solely on telephone surveys has been held (Groves et al., 1989).

The rise of telephone interviewing can be traced in part to developing a sampling method that included unpublished telephone numbers. "Random digit dialing," a term that persists despite the demise of the telephone dial, made it possible to calculate known probabilities for all working telephones that could be included in easy-to-draw national samples. This capability is critical, since more than half of the households with phones in some metropolitan areas (e.g., in California) have unpublished numbers.

An even more important reason for the increase in telephone surveys was the capability of designing, implementing, and reporting results quickly. During the Watergate hearings in 1974, the telephone was first used to conduct overnight surveys on peoples' opinions about President Nixon's possible involvement. Today telephone interviews for conducting overnight surveys during presidential election campaigns are the norm. The ability to conduct and report such surveys is closely tied to the development of computer-assisted telephone interviewing, commonly referred to as "CATI," which puts questionnaires on computer screens and facilitates computerized selection of numbers to call, recording of answers, and compilation of results.

Finally, costs for conducting telephone interviews are substantially lower than are those for conducting face-to-face interviews. When a busy signal is encountered or the phone is not answered, interviewers can quickly recall the number at another time. This method of contacting a household is faster and less expensive than the face-to-face interview, where the interviewer has to drive to the interviewee's home or place of business.

Mail Surveys

A study of all surveys approved by the Office of Management and Budget in 1981 revealed that nearly three-fourths of the nation's federally sponsored surveys relied on mail procedures. Thus, the number of mail surveys that were conducted far outnumbered the combined total of telephone and face-to-face interviews (U.S. Office of Management and Budget, 1984). This finding likely stems from the fact that most surveys are not conducted of the general public, for which inadequate sampling frames exist for contacting households by mail. Also, mail surveys are often performed by sponsoring organizations without turning them over to a survey data collection firm, resulting in lower costs than for telephone surveys, and far lower costs than for face-to-face interviews.

Prior to the 1970s, although widely used, the mail survey was mostly considered a method to be avoided. Response rates of well under 50 percent were often considered acceptable based on the false assumption that higher rates were impossible to achieve. Since 1970, research has demonstrated that response rates from mail surveys can be as high as those from telephone or face-to-face interviews. Collectively, this research has shown that the following elements, when used together, can produce high-response rates with low-item nonresponse: four or five contacts, including a prenotice and a contact sent by special mail (e.g., certified, two-day priority or special delivery); a prepaid financial incentive; a respondent-friendly questionnaire; questions that are salient to the respondents;

stamped return envelopes; personalized correspondence with a message that appeals to the respondents' social responsibility; and careful articulation of all parts of the survey (e.g., timing of follow-ups) so that they mutually support one another (Dillman, 1978, 1991; Herberlein and Baumgartner, 1978; and Fox, Crask, and Kim, 1988). As suggested by Goyder (1985), much of the improvement in mail survey response rates has come from applying concerted and repeated efforts through appropriately varied media, which personal interviewers have traditionally been trained to do.

Research has recently shown that response rates between 65 and 73 percent can even be achieved for mail surveys addressed only to households (Dillman, Clark, and Sinclair, Forthcoming). This finding opens the way to overcoming the sampling barriers that have prevented applying mail survey methods to general public samples. Further, in conducting mail surveys, survey researchers have capitalized on developments in desktop publishing and information-processing equipment which greatly simplify sending, receiving, and processing mail survey data. It has now become possible to survey thousands of people with the same effort that was required to survey hundreds in the past.

Implications of Telephone and Mail Improvements

To understand the far-reaching implications of doing quality mail and telephone surveys, it is essential to describe a fundamental attribute of what makes sample surveys work. That attribute is the ability to estimate the proportion of people in a large population who have a particular characteristic (e.g., are employed full-time) by surveying only a small number of people from the population of interest. More important for our purposes here, the number of people who need to be surveyed in order to estimate that proportion at a given level of confidence does not vary by much, except when the population is quite small.

For example, to estimate, within three percentage points, the percentage of people in Pullman, Washington (population 25,000), who have graduated from high school requires about the same sample size (n = 1,000–1,100) as is needed to develop a similar estimate for the state as a whole (population about 4,900,000) or even the entire nation (about 250,000,000 people). In addition, relatively small sample sizes can achieve fairly accurate results. A sample size of 95 should produce results that are ±10 percent of the population value (19 out of 20 times, assuming all 95 people are interviewed). Reducing this sampling error by half would require a sample approximately four times as large (i.e., 385), and reducing it again in half to ±2 percent would require a sample size of 2,175.

Consequently, accurate surveys of fairly small geographic areas can only be accomplished by surveying about the same numbers of people from those regions as would be required for doing state or national surveys. And if somewhat more sampling error can be tolerated (e.g., being satisfied with estimates of ±5 to 7 percent rather than ±1 to 2 percent), substantially fewer people need to be surveyed.

For surveys that measure the functioning of our nation (e.g., the Current Population Survey, from which unemployment rates are estimated), even estimates with 1 to 2 percent error are too large to accept. For other surveys (e.g., estimating the number of farmers who have home computers in a county), a 5 to 7 percent error may be easily tolerated.

High-quality mail and telephone survey methods have changed the way surveying is performed in the United States. First, they have overcome the problem of geographical dispersion. The costs of doing surveys are only slightly affected by where people live. Second, the reduced costs, in comparison to face-to-face interviews, have made it possible to conduct larger samples than were previously possible. And third, the error requirements for many surveys are substantially less stringent than those needed for many national surveys.

New survey organizations have emerged rapidly within universities and as separate organizations, many of which are capable of doing national as well as regional surveys. Whereas in the 1970s very few universities possessed survey capabilities, today most universities either have a survey capability or easy access to nearby organizations that do. Developments in microcomputer technology have brought about easily maintained address files, word processing, desktop publishing, and data analysis capabilities, which were once associated only with main-frame computing. In sum, small survey organizations can now do what was hardly imagined in the 1970s—conduct policy relevant surveys targeted to geographic areas and groups normally ignored by federally sponsored surveys.

Making Federal Surveys Responsive to Change

The same advances in mail and telephone survey capabilities that have fostered the development of small survey organizations are also available to the federal government. The federal government could therefore expand its survey interests and capabilities to conduct more targeted and geographically specific surveys that are responsive to emerging issues (e.g., making nonagricultural data more relevant to meeting rural data needs).

The federal government has enormous survey capabilities. The Bureau of the Census, Bureau of Labor Statistics, National Center for Health Statistics, National Center for Educational Statistics, and National Agricultural Statistics Service are among the organizations devoted to collecting and analyzing data that are relevant to rural areas of the United States. These organizations, separately and often in collaboration, conduct enormous national surveys—the decennial census survey of more than 100,000,000 households, the quinquennial agricultural census of some 5,000,000 farmers, the Current Population Survey of 60,000 households per month, and so on. However, there are four main reasons why it is unlikely that these or other federal government-sponsored surveys will become more responsive to providing new kinds of information, particularly for targeted groups or regions, or to perform studies more quickly.

First, the central tendency of the federal agencies is to think and act nationally. Their major emphasis is to produce accurate national estimates, not accurate regional or local estimates. As the nation continues to shift toward urbanization, it seems unlikely that sufficient sample sizes from rural areas and groups will be an important consideration in developing national data sets, particularly in a way that allows the incredible regional heterogeneity of rural areas to be revealed. This tendency was illustrated during debates on whether adjusted census counts should be used for the nation's population counts, and later the intercensal year estimates. Use of the estimates for these purposes, which ultimately was rejected, would undoubtedly have improved the accuracy for states and certain large cities, but would have done so only on average for rural and other small geographic areas. The expanded capability of other organizations to produce local data may, in fact, lead to less federal concern over being responsible for producing such information. Also, improved survey capabilities at state and local levels might lead the national government to deliberately avoid taking on such responsibilities and even divest those which it already has.

Second, it is extremely difficult to change federal surveys. Nearly every survey question has a legion of supporters ready to protest its removal from national data collection or, frequently, even the slightest changes in the wording of questions. Answers to individual questions are used by multiple users for widely disparate purposes, and even the slightest changes in wording may be actively resisted because of the impacts on longitudinal comparisons. For example, the 1990 census maintained use of the racial category "Black or Negro" despite the undesirable connotation of the latter term to many people. Also, individuals were asked to indicate whether their home was on "10 acres or more," even though most people today do not know how large an acre is. Another difficulty of national surveys is that questions have to be written for the widest possible audience of respondents as well as consumers, so that wordings of questions are often compromises among very disparate interests.

A third barrier to change in federal surveys is organizational momentum. Once a survey is conducted in a certain way, a proposal to change modes (e.g., from face-to-face to telephone), content, or specific procedures may mean massive reorganization for how that survey is conducted and, therefore, resistance. For example, changing a regularly conducted survey from face-to-face to telephone may mean putting regional interviewing offices out of business and creating a telephone-interviewing facility in one region of the country. These changes cannot be made without agency, employee, and congressional reactions. Interest groups also want a say in what is asked in surveys and how the surveys are conducted.

Fourth, even minor changes may have enormous cost implications. Adding a few questions to a mail survey of a million households could add another page of paper, increase postage, and complicate processing arrangements. Adding one minute of questions to a telephone survey of 60,000 households also has substantial cost implications. Planning for significant changes may take several years to coordinate efforts.

In sum, it seems unlikely that the federal government can or is likely to attempt to fill the need that exists for targeted, rapidly needed, small geographical area or group surveys that are important to meeting rural data needs. Further, any rapid change from rural agencies emphasizing agricultural or other kinds of statistics needed for rural development seems unlikely to occur. Adding new questions usually means removing old ones.

A Disquieting Look Toward the Future

It would seem, on the surface, that the federal agencies continuing to do what they do well, and new survey organizations using new methods to do what federal statistical agencies find difficult to do, would bode well for the future. A natural complementarity could develop between the regular federal provision of national data sets on enduring concerns and the quick provision by other organizations of regional and local data on emerging issues. Together, they could provide guidance for new and carefully targeted rural development policies. However, development of such complementarity of function will not be easy.

Survey procedures and methods, which in the 1970s and 1980s were on a trajectory of becoming easier to do, are now on a path of becoming more difficult to perform. Telephone interviewing, once viewed as the heir apparent to face-to-face interviews, is experiencing increased error concerns. Culturally, the telephone has changed from being an extension of personal interaction, which many people viewed as obligatory, to being a device under their control. Therefore, people increasingly consider it acceptable to hang up on unwanted calls. In addition, more and more household members are using answering machines while they are away from home and to screen calls when they are at home. These factors increase nonresponse rates and make them more difficult to determine accurately. Thus, response rates for telephone surveys are increasingly likely to be lower than are those for mail surveys. Further, telephones, which were once connected to individuals, are increasingly connected to households, where they are used for purposes other than voice communication (e.g., facsimile transmission and computerized data transfer). Because telephones can be quickly installed and removed, random digit surveys are likely to contact ever-increasing proportions of telephone numbers of unknown status.

One solution to these problems is to conduct mixed-mode surveys, whereby mail, telephone, and/or face-to-face methods are used in conjunction with one another to locate and survey respondents (Dillman and Tarnai, 1988). This trend has raised a new set of yet-to-be resolved questions about survey error and how to deal with it.

Four major sources of error threaten the accuracy of data obtained in surveys (Groves, 1989). The first and most common source of error, *sampling error*, is due to chance considerations involved in drawing samples. The second source is *noncoverage error*, which stems from all members of a population not having a known nonzero chance of being included in a sample (e.g., being excluded from the sample list). The third source, *nonresponse error*, results from those people who do not respond to the survey and from the fact that they are different from those who do respond. Response rate serves as the usual indicator of nonresponse error, although it is by no means a direct measure of it. The fourth source of error is *measurement error*, which results from respondents who give inaccurate answers, for whatever reasons, ranging from poorly worded questions to poor interviewing techniques.

A perfect survey could be described as one in which every person in the population of interest is included in the list from which the sampling frame is drawn and has an equal (or for some designs, a known nonzero) chance of being included in the sample to be surveyed, the selected sample is large enough to make estimates of desired accuracy, everyone in the sample responds to the request to be surveyed, and people understand exactly what is wanted by the questions and provide honest answers. It's against this standard that the importance of the trend toward replacing single-mode with mixed-mode surveys can best be understood.

Increasingly, no single survey mode by itself is likely to obtain a high enough response rate from many populations to alleviate concerns about nonresponse error. Some people who are unwilling to be surveyed by one mode are often willing to be surveyed by another mode. In addition, people who cannot be located by one mode (e.g., having an unpublished telephone number) can often be located by another. Therefore, by beginning with one mode and switching to another, both coverage and response rates can often be improved.

For example, in the 1990 decennial census, less expensive mail procedures were used to obtain responses from 65 percent of the households and, then, personal enumerators surveyed the nonrespondents, thereby greatly reducing costs. Also, the Census Bureau recently conducted a national test survey of college graduates by using the 1990 census records to illustrate the procedure of combining all three survey modes. A total of 54 percent responded to mail survey contacts (which included a prenotice, reminder, replacement questionnaire mailing, plus a financial incentive with the first questionnaire mailing); a telephone follow-up to nonrespondents improved the response rate to 66 percent; and personal interviews further improved the response rate to 86 percent (Mooney, Giesbrecht, and Shettle, 1993). Several factors were responsible for increasing the response rate: surveyors located people who could not be reached by earlier methods, convinced people who would not respond to earlier methods to answer the questionnaire, and determined the ineligibility of some individuals.

The tendency to use mixed-mode surveys to cut costs, improve coverage, and raise response rates raises the critical question of measurement error and, in particular, the possibility that different survey modes encourage respondents to answer questions in different ways. During the 1980s, it became abundantly clear that question order, choices of answer categories, order of answer categories, and other question attributes could dramatically influence respondents' answers (e.g., Schuman and Presser,

1981). More important, it became evident that the mode of presenting questions and answer choices had a direct effect on how people answered some questions. For example, mail survey respondents were found to more likely choose from among early categories (*primacy effect*) while telephone respondents were more likely to choose from among the last categories mentioned (*recency effect*) (Krosnick and Alwin, 1987). It also appears that different effects may interact. In a study of the number of hours per day that students study, the estimates of the percentage of those studying more than two and a half hours per day varied from 23 to 70 percent, depending on the survey mode and the range of response categories provided (Dillman, Sangster, and Rockwood, 1992). Use of one set of categories resulted in reports of 23 percent by mail and 43 percent by telephone. Our understanding of the causes of mode differences is as yet in its infancy; however, it is sufficiently advanced to clearly state they must be taken into account.

The increased importance of mixed-mode surveys as a means of reducing error raises some important concerns about who conducts surveys and how they get done. For many years, statisticians have conducted the majority of surveys. Their skills for sample design and analysis were crucial for conducting high-quality surveys, particularly when multistage, clustered samples were so critical for lowering the cost of face-to-face interviewing. Indeed, as presented in the media, statements about sample size (e.g., samples of this size are accurate within plus or minus "x" percent), have often been taken as synonymous with survey data quality.

Statisticians are generally not trained to deal with the problems of improving response rates and controlling measurement error. These problems are usually attended to by academicians in other disciplines such as cognitive psychology, social-psychology, and sociology. To conduct accurate surveys, it is increasingly important for people trained in different disciplines to work together and to influence one another in the survey design process.

Small survey organizations are generally not large enough to involve people from multiple disciplines with the needed diverse survey skills on their staffs; thus it's not surprising that concern with one source of error sometimes dominates the others. An informal look at survey results produced by small organizations across the nation suggests that some organizations are greatly concerned about response rates but are willing to mostly ignore sample coverage issues; some are fixated on sample size and tend to ignore response rates; still others emphasize response rates above all other concerns.

On the surface, it would seem that the chance that multiple facets of error are taken into account is better in the large national survey organizations. That may or may not be the case. Some agencies are dominated by statistics, the traditional professional occupation associated with surveying, and perspectives on the other sources of error are being introduced slowly. A tendency to deal with sampling error and coverage as the critical issues, leaving the others to a residual category of "nonsampling" error, may exist.

Partnerships for the Future

The emerging data needs of rural America are quite different than those which the nation's federal data system is capable of providing. That system, designed for an earlier, simpler time, and held in place by an assortment of strong interests, cannot easily be changed. In particular, it will be exceedingly difficult to change it in the direction of responding to the necessity of asking new kinds of questions, on new issues, that are responsive to the problems and possibilities for rural development.

Simultaneously, the emergence of new survey technologies makes it possible for quality surveys to be conducted by local and regional university-based survey organizations as well as by others. Further, development of this capability is critical for meeting the data needs of rural America.

A division of labor is needed. The emerging data needs of rural America are too important to leave solely to the federal government. They are also too important to leave solely to universities and locally oriented survey organizations. That which can be done federally often cannot be done locally, and vice versa. Each has an important role in building a responsive data system to meet rural needs. It's also important to recognize that this is a time of dramatic change for how surveys are conducted. The emerging trend is toward surveys of greater, rather than less, complexity. Above all, it is necessary to recognize that individual disciplines (e.g., statistics, sociology, cognitive psychology, and economics) are, by themselves, inadequate for influencing how surveys are conducted. Without consideration being simultaneously given to multiple sources of error, we run the risk of poor and inaccurate data being used to influence policy issues. This situation in some cases may be worse than the previous lack of data.

Federal agencies are sufficiently large for all the relevant specialties to be gathered under one roof. Yet, the traditional dominance of statistics, and the reluctance to change, may mean that measurement and nonresponse error become downplayed or ignored. State agencies and university survey research centers typically do not have enough professionals in the disciplines needed to assure quality data collection and to control for multiple sources of error.

Federal agencies have considerable inertia, well protected by interest groups, that may prevent discontinuing the collection of data on some topics so that the resources can be devoted to other topics. State and local survey organizations, on the other hand, may be tempted to run from hot topic to hot topic, so that longitudinal data sets never accumulate to tell us where we have come from and where we seem to be going.

Universities should take the lead in recognizing that surveys are subject to multiple sources of error and build the interdisciplinary bridges that will lead to the training of survey methodologists who understand and appreciate the various threats to collecting quality data. The survey research laboratories now emerging nationwide in universities provide a mechanism for accomplishing that, but they must be accompanied by joint efforts in graduate training, which does not seem to be developing.

Finally, universities, state governments, and the federal government should join hands to encourage development at all levels of improved survey methods. Only a partnership offers promise that the emerging rural data needs of our country are likely to be met.

Notes

Work on this paper was supported under Western Region Project W-183, Rural and Agricultural Sample Survey Methodology, of the Washington Agricultural Research Center. This paper was partly written while serving a two-year assignment as the senior survey methodologist at the Office of the Director, Bureau of the Census, U.S. Department of Commerce. The opinions expressed in this paper are those of the author and should not be attributed to Washington State University or the U.S. Bureau of the Census.

1. Agricultural statistics, although very important to collect and analyze as industry or economic sector statistics, are no longer justified as critical to understanding the causes and consequences of rural development in most rural areas of the United States.

References

Blankenship, Albert B. 1977. *Professional Telephone Surveys*. New York: McGraw-Hill.

Dillman, Don A. 1978. *Mail and Telephone Surveys: The Total Design Method*. New York: John Wiley and Sons.

______. 1990. Information technology in agriculture: The United States experience. In M. Harkin, ed., *Information Technology in Agriculture Food and Rural Development*. Luxembourg: Commission of the European Communities.

______. 1991. The design and administration of mail surveys. *Annual Review of Sociology* 17:225–249.

______. 1992. Recent advances in survey data collection methods and their implications for meeting rural data needs. Pp. 52–71 in Reuben Buse and James Driscoll, eds., *New Directions in Data and Information Systems*. Ames: Iowa State University Press.

Dillman, Don A., and Donald M. Beck. 1988. Information technologies and rural development in the 1990s. *Journal of State Governments* 61(1):29–38.

Dillman, Don A., and John Tarnai. 1988. Administrative issues in mixed-mode surveys. Pp. 509–528 in *Telephone Survey Methodology*. New York: John Wiley.

Dillman, Don A., Jon Clark, and Michael Sinclair. Forthcoming. Effects of questionnaire length, respondent-friendly design, and a difficult question on response rates for occupant-addressed mail surveys. *Public Opinion Quarterly*

Dillman, Don A., Roberta Sangster, and Todd Rockwood. 1992. Overview of results from 14 experiments on question form and survey mode effects. Paper presented at the annual meeting of the American Association of Public Opinion Research. St. Petersburg, Florida.

Fox, R. J., M. R. Crask, and J. Kim. 1988. Mail survey response rate: A meta-analysis of selected techniques for inducing response. *Public Opinion Quarterly* 52(4):467–491.

Goyder, John. 1985. Face-to-face interviews and mail questionnaires: The net difference in response rate. *Public Opinion Quarterly* 49:234–252.

Groves, Robert M. 1989. Research on survey data quality. *Public Opinion Quarterly* 51:S156–172.

Groves, R. M., and Kahn, R. L. 1979. *Surveys by Telephone: A National Comparison with Personal Interviews*. New York: Academic Press.

Groves, Robert M., Paul B. Biemer, Lars E. Lyberg, James T. Massey, William L. Nicholls II, and Joseph Waksberg. 1989. *Telephone Survey Methodology*. New York: John Wiley and Sons.

Heberlein, Thomas A., and Robert Baumgartner. 1978. Factors affecting response rates to mailed questionnaires: A quantitative analysis of the published literature. *American Sociological Review* 43:447–462.

Krosnick, John A., and Duane F. Alwin. 1987. An evaluation of a cognitive theory of response order effects in survey measurement. *Public Opinion Quarterly* 51:201–219.

Mooney, Geraldine, Lee Geisbrecht, and Carolyn Shettle. 1993. Influence of questionnaire length and financial incentives on response rates and quality for a government-sponsored survey of scientists and engineers. Paper presented at the 1993 annual meeting of the American Association for Public Opinion Research. St. Charles, Illinois.

Schuman, H., and Presser, S. 1981. *Questions and Answers in Attitude Surveys: Experiments on Question Form, Wording, and Context*. New York: Academic Press.

U.S. Office of Management and Budget. 1984. The role of telephone data collection in federal statistics. Statistical Policy Working Paper No. 1. U.S. Government Printing Office.

10

New Social Science Research Technologies

Edwin H. Carpenter

Changing research technologies allow university researchers and local, state, and federal officials to significantly impact how data can be gathered, stored, accessed, analyzed, and presented in order to better inform rural policy. This chapter examines some of these changing technologies. For example, prior to the conference that gave rise to this book, a questionnaire was sent to all conference participants. During a conference session, the results were tabulated and graphically presented. This quick turnaround time may not seem out of the ordinary until it is known that the questionnaire was sent to conference registrants on microcomputer floppy disks. In other words, the traditionally labor intensive and lengthy task of collecting, managing, and analyzing data, and presenting the findings graphically was accomplished with a fraction of the effort and time that was required only a few short years ago.

How Changing Research Methods Can Inform Rural Policy

The basic parts of the research process (as discussed below) have not changed appreciably; rather, it is how the process is conducted that has changed.[1] Figure 10–1 depicts the increase in the parts of the research process that are now computerized as well as the amount of time it takes to accomplish the research endeavor. Since about 1980, changes in the research process have been dramatic and the outlook for the future suggests that change will continue to accelerate.

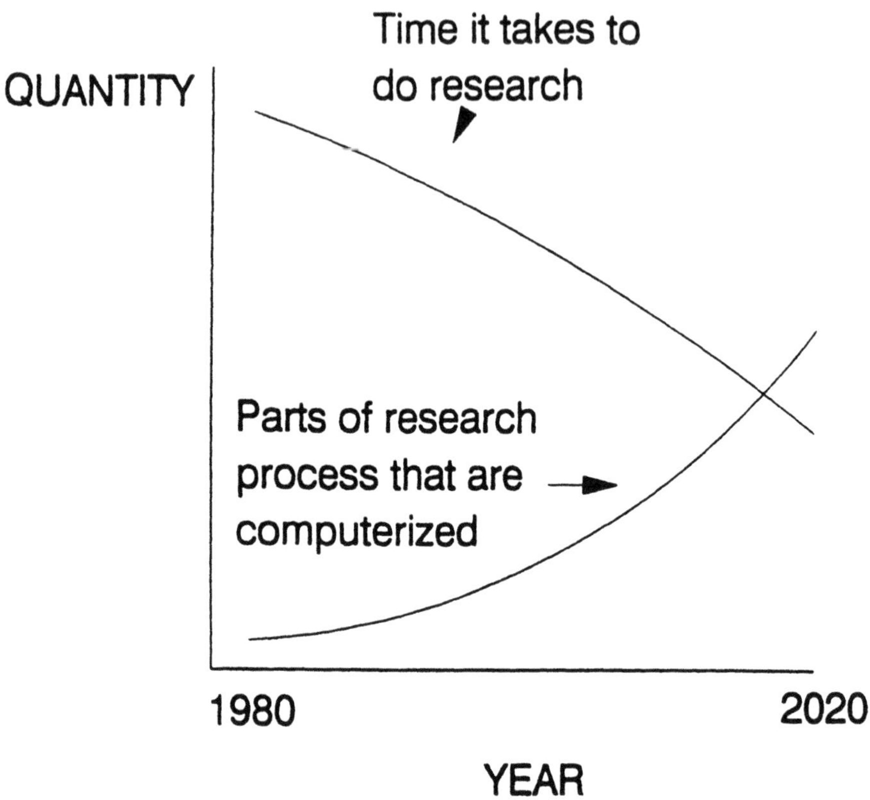

Figure 10–1. The computerization of social science research methods.

In this chapter, the entire research process is discussed in the context of how it can be aided and advised by software that runs on microcomputers. The chapter provides an overall picture of the process and, thus, should allow readers the opportunity to see how they fit into the process and, in turn, impact the process that informs rural policy. Although each stage of the research process is discussed, emphasis is given to two of the stages that have the greatest potential impact on rural policy formulation: data collection and the visual presentation of findings. Three closely allied areas are also discussed: (1) linkages among software packages that aid the stages of the research process, (2) the recently available programming software (called authoring software) that allows nonprogrammers to write software, and (3) some of the advances in hardware and software that will facilitate the storage and retrieval of vast quantities of data and information. As a point of departure, a brief explanation of the importance of each of these topics is presented.

Data Collection

Three somewhat different aspects of computer-assisted data collection are important for the changing impact that social science research can have on informing rural policy. First is the ability to conduct data collection quickly, accurately, and relatively inexpensively. As Dillman points out in Chapter 9, we live in the information age where the half-life of data is sometimes as short as a few minutes. This short period for which data or information are of use makes it imperative to collect, process, analyze, and present information quickly—tasks that can now be performed with the appropriate microcomputer hardware and software.

The right to privacy that must be given to respondents of data collection efforts is a second reason why computer-assisted data collection should be aided by the new technologies. The problem arises when national samples of rural households are taken. The samples are often designed to allow generalization of results to the nation, a region, or a state. This means that the number of cases from any particular small rural area, such as a county, are quite small and any summary statistics could reveal important, and perhaps sensitive, information about respondents. As a result, data for small geographic areas are either not released or they are aggregated with other small areas so that the respondent's identity is not revealed. Even if the data were not aggregated, the small number of respondents in a national survey that would be selected randomly from a given area would not adequately represent the area. Both of these considerations suggest that additional surveys in these small rural areas is a good alternative, especially because technological advances have made undertaking such surveys much more feasible and affordable.

A third important aspect of computer-assisted data collection is the ability to coordinate question asking to provide the same data across several different studies or across time for the same sample. Several smaller studies can include a similar set of questions so the resulting answers can be aggregated to represent a larger population. For example, a study conducted to represent each county of a state could be aggregated to represent the entire state for those questions that were used in common. The use of a similar set of questions across time can provide data that are useful for establishing trends as well as monitoring change. The major focus of the studies need not be the same at each time period, but the questions that are included to monitor some specific change or trend need to be the same. Both of these capabilities are more easily achieved with the computerization of the questions which allows for their easy placement in different study questionnaires.

Linking Stages of the Research Process

Linkages among different software packages that are used for different parts of the research task are fast becoming important capabilities in the microcomputerization of the social science research process. Such linkages are important for informing rural policy in two distinct ways. On the one hand, the linkages allow quick movement through the research process while reducing errors. This means that the time from conceptualization of a project to graphical presentation of findings may be as short as a few days. The other important role of linkages is the ability to connect data sets that were collected using different software systems, to analyze a data set collected by someone else (who was using a different system), and to analyze a data set using different statistical software.

Visual Presentation of Findings

Chambers et al. (1983) are probably correct in asserting that there is no single statistical tool that is as powerful as a well-chosen graph. It is far easier to understand a well-done graphic than to understand a table of numbers or percentages. That graphics can help inform rural policy seems to be a given. Presenting research findings graphically to an audience of policymakers is more effective than presenting the same findings in tables or text. Graphics have been used for many years to convey information, but only recently have they become widely available to the researcher in an easy-to-use form.

Experts and Authoring Software

Experts in a field write books and articles on topics of their expertise. This seems reasonable and apparent. What if an expert were to decide to communicate something in a software program, such as an easy way to interpret and understand demographic data or trends that will affect a rural area or community? The difficulty of programming the software would likely delay such an effort. Not only would this person have to be an expert in a particular topic of a substantive field, like demography, he or she would also have to be a master of a programming language, or hire a programmer.

Storing and Accessing Data and Information Resources

Sometimes good ideas do not catch on until a technological mechanism is developed that can provide an easy-to-use, inexpensive, and effective means of moving forward with the idea. One such example might be the development of the birth control pill. Zero population growth was a good idea for the planet, but little was accomplished toward that end until an easy-to-use and inexpensive means was found to carry the idea into practice. The same can be said about creating a database of information that is inexpensive and can be easily updated and accessed. Today, inexpensive microcomputer hardware and software can create data and information bases that can be updated and accessed and that provide storage in the multiple gigabyte capacities.

The Research Process

The research process can be divided into seven distinct stages—conceptualization; analysis selection, sample, or experimental design; data collection; data entry, cleanup, or transfer; data transformation and management; data analysis; and result presentation. Two of these stages are especially applicable to informing rural policy—data collection and visual presentation of results—along with the relatively new capabilities, linking (automating) the various parts of the research process, the ability for nonprogramming experts to program or author software, and the arrival of technology to make data and information bases a reality.

The seven stages of the research process cover a lot of research methods. Because of the extensive amount of information and knowledge required to be highly proficient at each stage of the research process, an individual rarely is an expert in all stages. As a consequence, the researcher must either obtain help from a knowledgeable colleague, a hired consultant, or a textbook, or simply make an educated guess at the solution. While the latter is less than optimal, it is often the course that is taken, leading to incorrect or inappropriate research process specification and conduct.

Fortunately, researchers no longer have to make such guesses during the research process. Microcomputer software is now available that can advise or help the researcher at every stage, providing as little or as much help as necessary. Equally important is that the ability to receive help from microcomputer software is changing rapidly. The pace of trying to provide helpful software is quickening as the competition for market share drives providers to implement increasingly capable software. This goes hand in hand with the increasingly powerful hardware that continues to be developed.

Problem Selection and Conceptualization

This stage of the research process is probably the most difficult. It requires an understanding of the phenomenon to be studied, familiarity with results of prior research, and likely some personal reason as to why the phenomenon is chosen as a topic of interest. Human thought skills are essential and microcomputer software is underdeveloped in this stage.

Analysis, Sample, or Experimental Design Selection

Most of us were taught in a research methods class that after conceptualizing the research problem, plans for analyzing the research project needed to be developed. Presumably, so the lecture went, if you lay out your analysis plans in advance, then you are less likely to forget to include a question that provides a measure for a particular variable. Also, you will have some notion of the type of measurement needed on that variable—such as ordinal instead of categorical. To help determine the type of analysis that is appropriate for the planned research, an expert system software package—Statistical Navigator—is available that can help with the selection of the appropriate statistics. Once the statistical analysis is selected, a next step may be to assure that the sample size or experimental groups are correct. This can be accomplished with Power Analysis and Sample Size, or an expert system sampling package (e.g., ExSample) is also available. The expert system package EXPERtIMENTAL Design helps select the appropriate experimental design system. Other software packages that can help with analysis selection and sample or experimental design are listed in the note 2.

The software can serve as a substitute for an expert and at the same time provide an interface that nonexperts can understand and use to their advantage. In all three of the above expert-system software packages, the user can get terms defined or can find out why a question was asked. The user can even tell the program the level of certainty of a response using the certainty scale that appears at the bottom of the screen. Depending on the answers, either singly or in combination with the certainty score, the software decides the next appropriate question. The process goes on and the answer is given regarding which experimental design is appropriate given the needs of the research project.

One of the most appealing features of these packages is to be able to clarify words or questions by pressing appropriate keys. This makes interaction with the software easier because explanations are provided only when requested; the software thus becomes an important pedagogical tool.

Data Collection

There is no substitute for accurate, appropriate, and timely data. Microcomputerization of data collection has helped in all three of these areas and has provided the additional benefits of lower costs and ease of use. As a point of departure, the types of data collection that are well suited to being assisted by microcomputer and why will be discussed. Probably the best use of computer-assisted interviewing (CAI) is when the telephone is used to collect data. In this mode of collection, the computer's capabilities can be maximized by keeping records of what transpires when a number is called and must be called again, implementing branching instructions so that a respondent is not asked an inappropriate question, and building the database so analysis can commence as soon as the final interview is completed.

In-person interviews can also be conducted with the help of a computer. Major advantages of this method are the ease of tailoring the questions asked of the respondent (using branching instructions) so that respondent burden is kept to a minimum and the automatic formation of a database as interviews are completed. Notebook-size microcomputers are sufficiently portable and powerful to allow the use of highly complex and detailed in-person interviews.

A variation on the above modes of data collection is the use of diskettes by mail. For this mode, the questionnaire is placed on a microcomputer diskette and mailed to the respondent in the same way that a mail questionnaire would be sent. The respondent then places the diskette in a microcomputer, instructs it to begin, answers the questions, and mails the diskette back to the researcher. The researcher then takes the diskette and copies the answers to a database. This data-collection mode reduces respondent burden through the use of branching questions and allows the respondent to choose a convenient time to answer the questions. A disadvantage is that respondents will not always have access to a microcomputer.

Advantages of Computer-Aided Interviewing. Some of the advantages of using the microcomputer for data collection were mentioned above, but a more detailed assessment is warranted. To make data timely, it is essential that the time it takes to collect and process data be shortened. This process can be accomplished by using computer-aided interviewing software that automatically writes the responses to questions to a database and, thereby, eliminates the data-entry step that is required when paper and pencil questionnaires are used. Automation of this step also helps eliminate errors caused from the transcription of data from paper forms to computer. Additional errors can be eliminated by making the CAI software to accept only answers that fall within a preset range or that meet other logic criteria that are programmed into the data-collection instrument. For example, a respondent would not be allowed to answer a question with a response other than "yes," "no," or "don't know," if those are the only appropriate responses. Also, the software can be programmed to balk at a response of "pregnant" if the respondent has indicated in a earlier question that he is a male.

Another benefit that has resulted from the use of microcomputers is the ability to reduce interviewer and respondent burden. This can happen when the CAI software is programmed to branch or use skip patterns when a question that is not appropriate for a respondent is encountered. For example, if a respondent is male, then there is no need to ask if he is pregnant. There are numerous times when skipping or branching can, if designed skillfully by the researcher, cause a respondent to feel that the questionnaire was tailored just for him or her. This makes the respondent feel more cooperative because questions that make no sense are eliminated, leaving only those questions about which the respondent may feel knowledgeable or have an opinion. Also, the reduction in inappropriate questions reduces the interviewer's effort.

Disadvantages of CAI. There are also disadvantages to using CAI, but they seem to be of increasingly less concern as computers and CAI software become easier to use and hardware prices continue to decline. One of the first concerns is the technical skills needed to operate microcomputers and, similarly, to program the CAI software. Depending on the particular CAI software, the skill and time necessary to prepare a questionnaire can be great (but it should be noted that the computerized preparation of a questionnaire, along with branching instructions, causes the researcher to give careful consideration to the content and usefulness of the questions that are included). However, to maintain a competitive market position, the CAI software vendors are continually improving their softwares' capabilities and ease of use. Likewise, the user interface on microcomputers has become significantly easier to use.

Hardware costs and maintenance are declining. However, as CAI software becomes increasingly capable and easier to use, it also demands more capable hardware. This newer and more capable hardware also costs more.

Searching for the Correct CAI Software. Locating the best CAI software for the needs at hand can be a trying exercise. A good place to start is to read articles like the one by Carpenter (1988) and those cited by

Carpenter. If telephone interviews are the goal, then books like the ones by Babbie (1989), Frey (1989), and Lake (1987) are good sources for some of the things that need to be considered. For surveys to be conducted by mail, the book by Dillman (1978) is a good reference. Once a list of possible software packages is obtained, the vendors can be called to request literature, a demo disk, or an evaluation copy. In this way, the most current information about the software will be in hand for consideration.

Questions to ask yourself and the vendor include the following:

- What initial training and skill levels are required to use the software effectively?
- What is the cost of retraining the personnel if the initial software purchased cannot accomplish the job?
- What is the cost of reconducting a study if the software fails or easily allows incorrect usage and thereby causes the collected data to be erroneous?
- What is the cost of spending endless hours trying to make software work when good user support should be a phone call away?
- What is the cost of having needed features go unused because the manual is poorly organized or incomplete?
- What is the cost of abandoning a package once it is in use for one with more advanced survey capabilities?

Naturally, there are other questions regarding specific capabilities desired for the specific objectives of the data collection enterprise, and these questions are probably best answered through the use of some or all of the resources mentioned above. (Software packages for computer-assisted interviewing and data entry are listed in note 3.)

One package, QPL, is worth pointing out. It costs $150, is quite capable in terms of desired attributes, and is exceptionally easy to use. The questionnaire is created using any word processor or text editor that saves the file in ASCII or text mode. After the questionnaire is drafted, QPL converts the questionnaire file that was created in the word processor into a file that uses the QPL format. If there are errors in the file, QPL will stop the process and produce a file that explains what is incorrect. This error checking will continue until the questionnaire is correct. The resulting file drives the computer that is used for the telephone interviews. The questionnaire can also be printed, in a preformatted style that includes skip patterns, so that it can be used in a mail or in-person interview.

While preparing the questionnaire, it is a good practice to make sure that branching instructions branch to the correct question. This can be accomplished by telling QPL to cross reference the questions. This cross-reference capability augments the check system that operates when the questionnaire is compiled in the first step above. If, during the compilation, a skip instruction is found for which there is no target question, an error message is produced and an error file is written to the disk so that the preparer can easily see what changes need to be made.

The QPL produced database is a standard ASCII file. As an interview progresses, QPL writes the responses to the database that it automatically creates. Returned paper copies of the questionnaire (if a paper questionnaire is used) can have the answers entered into the database using the QPL data entry system. The entry system has the ability to check for data entry errors, such as out of range responses, and inappropriate logic, such as a response of "pregnant" when the sex of the respondent is recorded as "male."

Once the database is created, the next step is to make preparations for analysis. It is at this point that QPL really excels. In order to prepare the data for analysis in SPSS/PC+, SAS, or some other statistical package, the user makes the appropriate selection from a pull-down menu. This simple command causes QPL to write the input file for either SPSS or SAS in the correct form with the correct variable format, variable names, value labels, missing data information, and name and location of the database. All that remains is to conduct analysis. In addition, QPL will output data and open-ended question responses in a form that can be used by askSam, a software package that can analyze the content of text based information sets. QPL really excels at this point by linking the data-collection step and the analysis step. This linkage is accomplishing a task that is quite tedious and error prone for a person to do. These are the kinds of tasks that are best left to a computer.

To summarize the data-collection section, a few final considerations are worth mentioning. Data-collection capabilities can be improved by taking advantage of the contingent questioning and the other capabilities that are available in most CAI software. Consider doing mixed-mode surveys (perhaps a mixture of telephone and mail data-collection modes) to obtain acceptable response rates. Also, think about the linkages between the CAI software and the analysis software which can be used to analyze results of the survey. A linking capability that prepares the input file (which instructs the statistical package regarding data format, variable names, and value labels) can save a lot of time and decrease the likelihood of errors. One additional capability that is available with some CAI software, and is a welcome addition, is a procedure for sampling telephone numbers that are randomly generated.

Data Entry, Cleanup, and Transfer

Data from mail surveys; from phone links from other computers; and from CD-ROMs, floppy disks, or tape reels may need to be entered, cleaned-up, and transfered before they can be analyzed. Note 3 lists software packages that may be useful. Two of the most capable packages for entry and/or cleanup are QPL and SPSS/PC+ Data Entry II. The key feature is the ability to apply simple tests to verify values and to apply complex cleaning rules to relationships among variables. For example, a check can be made for sex, pregnancy status, and age that raises a flag when certain conditions are met, like pregnancy at age 82 or male pregnancy. The rules can be applied in an interactive session, or a report can be generated so that flagged records can be identified and handled appropriately.

Most statistical packages can transfer data and variable names to a Lotus 1-2-3 or a dBase format and also import those formats. If data format, variable names, and value labels need to be transferred, consider Stat/Transfer or DBMS/Copy Plus, software packages that specialize in transfer. At present, DBMS/Copy Plus can transfer data, variable names, and value labels among 60 different statistics, econometrics, spreadsheet, and database packages, which makes it the more capable than Stat/Transfer.

Data Transformation and Management

One of the most tedious jobs in social science research is data transformation and management. Most statistical software packages have routine capabilities available. However, if you need data aggregation or similar advanced capabilities, then one of the advanced packages listed in note 4 will help. These packages have data transformation and management capabilities to accomplish the task set forth in the following example. Three years of data on more or less the same 1,400 clients are available in four data files: two files for the first year (when people signed up for the program at two different research installations); one for the first follow-up year; and one for the third year (when there was a possibility that some clients had been seen up to 40 times with a separate record for each visit). Fortunately, each client has a unique identification number;

unfortunately, each client also has somewhere between 1 and 43 records full of information. The data need to be in one file for analysis to proceed. To accomplish the task, case-sorting, file appending, nonparallel file-merging, record-aggregation, and record-mapping capabilities are required. The two data files from the first year are joined into one file, which becomes the base data file for the 1,400 cases. The second-year file, with 1,340 cases, is merged into the base file, and missing data codes are given to variables for the 60 cases that do not exist in the second-year file. Data from the third year is subjected to the aggregate procedure, which produces one record containing summary data for each of the variables collected in the third year for each client. A mapping of each record is produced so that all the actions above can be checked. With capable data transformation and management software in hand, what could have been a frustrating task becomes a tractable one. While most statistical packages have routine data transformation and management capabilities, the packages listed in note 4 have advanced capabilities like aggregate.

Data Analysis

Data analysis is where the action is. It is the stage in the research process that is often foremost in researchers' minds. While the actual data analysis may occupy only a small portion of the total time it takes to accomplish research, it is the key step to making the data meaningful. The ability to analyze data easily has increased dramatically in the past few years (analysis software is listed in note 5).

Let's imagine we are analyzing the data file that was created by aggregating the results of the survey that was sent to conference participants on floppy disk using the QPL. Let's assume we have already run the QPL software command that creates the file that contains the job control information that tells the data analysis package, SPSS/PC+, the variable format, names, and value labels for the data in the database. I will use the menu mode in SPSS, which is one of the three modes available, to provide the commands necessary to run the software. The other two modes are batch and interactive. One of the hallmarks of a user-friendly software package is the ability to choose how you would like to interact with the package. For example, if you use the software package on a regular basis then batch or interactive modes are probably the best because you will be likely to remember the commands. If you use the package infrequently and do not remember all the commands, then menu mode is quite handy. However, to be forced to use a menu each time you use the package is quite tedious, so it is important to be able to change modes easily.

The beauty of this type of interface is that the user is prompted with only one set of commands and the information about those commands necessary to accomplish a given objective. Using the manual will most likely become a thing of the past, except for examples of how to interpret findings from specific analysis procedures. One other point—if you ask for help, the help you receive will be keyed to the place in the command list that you asked for help, known as "context-sensitive help."

Knowledge Seeker is a software package that provides a usable user interface that automates the analysis of data often used by social scientists. The software uses the classification and decision tree approach to analysis. The user prepares a data set with QPL, SPSS/PC+, or some other package that can export the data set in a Lotus 1-2-3, dBase, or ASCII format. This data set is imported by Knowledge Seeker at which point the user specifies the dependent variable. The user has the option to run the analysis in fully automatic mode or to exercise precise control. Some would argue the procedures are better than multiple linear regression, and most would agree the output is easy to interpret and therefore advances understanding.

Visual Presentation of Findings

The research is not complete until the results are shared with others. There is no reason to expect anything less than high-quality text and graphical presentation to suffice for findings so diligently sought. While microcomputer software is changing the way research is conducted at every stage of the research process, there are some stages where a virtual revolution is underway. That happens to be the case for statistics and graphics, as will be discussed below.

Two developments are allowing this rapid change in statistics and graphics to occur. On the one hand is the phenomenal growth that has recently taken place in the graphics software industry. While statistics and graphics are important for academic researchers, that market is minuscule when compared to the business user market demand for graphics. The business market seems to have taken off with the recent mass adoption of Microsoft Windows, a user interface that provides IBM and compatible microcomputers with a graphical mouse-oriented approach to computing. This graphical approach, which was until recently the exclusive domain of the Apple Macintosh, is now available to DOS users who have Windows version 3.0 or higher. The new graphics capabilities, along with the statistical capabilities of DOS software, provide a set of capabilities that meet or exceed those available on the Macintosh. This means that researchers can now use the graphics to communicate their own research findings instead of turning the graphic idea and data over to a graphic artist.

The other development that is helping to propel the computing world into graphics is the capability of moving among software packages, both statistical and graphical, with both data and graphics. If a graphic cannot be accomplished fully in one package, then either the data or the graphic can be moved to another where annotations and embellishments can be added.

The principal types of graphics are analytical, charting, drawing, and animation—each of which can play an important role in aiding the understanding of research results as they potentially impact rural policy formation.

Charting Graphics. This type of graphic is probably the most common and is often found in newspapers, news magazines, on television news, and in reports to our bosses and colleagues. Data are presented in a format that typically punctuates what the data represent by including in the graphic a picture of what the data are about. For example, the number of hospital beds per 1,000 population in various rural counties might be depicted by stacking pictures of hospital beds to make a bar chart where each bar represents a separate county. The addition of visual images to a data chart helps the user remember what information is being conveyed. Software packages that provide charting graphics are found in note 6.

Analytical Graphics. Charting graphics are designed primarily for lay audiences, while analytical graphics are for the analyst or researcher and technical audiences. Graphics that accompany statistical software are often analytical and are designed to help the analyst understand the structure or meaning of the data. While analytical graphics can be rather austere, it is suspected that with the proper annotation or embellishment that can be added in a drawing software package, analytical graphics could be presented to lay audiences as well. The following analytical graphics packages are designed primarily for physical science and engineering applications but do contain powerful features that will benefit social science research: Surfer, Grapher, Sigma Plot, Graftool, and Stanford Graphics.

Drawing Graphics. Drawing software packages will play an increasingly larger role in the graphical presentation of data. With their rather phenomenal ability to create or manipulate artwork that accompanies the software, they become powerful allies to telling a story with data and graphics. A graphic that is created in a statistical package can be embellished or annotated much like a graphic that is drawn on a blackboard. Arrows or extra comments that make the graphic easier to understand can be added with relative ease. A list of drawing packages is found in note 7.

Animation. If a still graphic can take the place of words, then an animated graphic can take the place of words and several still graphics. Animated graphics are of particular value when the presentation is being made with a computer and a projection system that displays what is on the computer screen. The advantage of animation is that a complicated process can be depicted and a lengthy story shortened to a few moments. In addition to animation capabilities, most animation software packages also have the ability to do screen captures, create graphical and textual visuals, as well as present slide shows. This means that text, graphics, and animation can be interspersed to create a professional presentation. Animation software includes StoryBoard Plus, Show Partner F/X, Grasp, and Animator.

Linking Statistical and Graphical Software

There are two ways that statistical findings can be linked to other software to provide the final output. One is to move data from one statistical software package to another. This type of transfer would likely occur because the original statistical package, while providing good data handling or analytical capabilities, did not provide the types of graphical capabilities desired.

Another type of transfer is from statistical software to charting, drawing, analytical, or animation software packages. In this situation, data and/or graphics images can be transferred. Between the statistical package and the analytical software a data transfer is appropriate. A data or graphics image transfer is appropriate for the link between statistics and charting software, while the link must be graphical between statistics and drawing and animation software. See note 3 for software that is available for transfer of data and note 8 for graphics transfer and screen capture software.

Experts and Authoring Software

Although hiring a programmer for a specific research project is not a bad idea, many of us will not do so. Barriers that keep us from hiring a programmer include financial resources, difficulty in communicating ideas to the programmer (it might be faster to do it yourself if the software were sufficiently easy to use), unavailability of good programmers, and unavailability of programmers with enough expertise in the substantive area so communicating ideas would not become intractable. The same barriers seem to exist when it comes to writing a book about research, which is why experts in research do not hire someone to write their research books.

In the final analysis, the expert needs to be the director of what is communicated. Books or software about research contain ideas, facts, and procedures that are difficult to understand and therefore express in a way that others can grasp. By the time this information is communicated to a "ghost" writer or programmer, the researcher could have written it. There are, of course, those fortunate individuals who have disciplinary knowledge as well as programming expertise, and they are in the enviable position of being able to move forward and put in software from their ideas, thoughts, and solutions.

For the rest of us, another option is at hand: programming languages that are easy to use and still powerful enough to allow us to accomplish a difficult task. As this form of programming software, which we term "authoring software," becomes increasingly easy to use, doing it yourself will be an alternative to the researcher who is an expert in a field other than computer programming. Just as these researchers are in demand to communicate on paper what they know about their part of the research world to colleagues, technicians, and students, they will have available a medium that moves beyond just paper. This new communication medium has the added dimensions of interactivity with the user, animation, real time video, and sound. Additionally, several authoring packages include expert system capability, which gives experts a way to incorporate into software their knowledge in the form of decision rules. This expert ability, coupled with a good user interface, provides the necessary ingredients for a software package that the user is more likely to accept in place of a live expert. Not only can the researcher talk about the research, it can be shown in action. This will make learning and doing research easier.

There is no readily discernible point at which programming becomes authoring. It is a matter of degree and can best be described as a continuum with the left end of the horizontal line representing low-level programming languages and the right end representing ultra-high-level programming (or authoring) languages. At the low-level end of the continuum, there is machine language which is the "native" language of computers. It is flexible and powerful but difficult to examine, understand, and use. Next on the continuum is assembly language, easier to examine and understand, but still rather difficult to use. The middle ground on the continuum is occupied by high-level languages such as Basic, Pascal, Cobol, Fortran, C, Lisp, Prolog, all of which were designed to allow software with different purposes to be created more easily. At the extreme right end are very-high-level languages such as Lotus 1-2-3, and dBase, as well as the ultra-high-level authoring languages.

Authoring software, then, is software that can be used by a programming novice in a reasonable period of time—they will spend more time creating the end product than in learning how to create the product. By this definition, there are many people who are experts in their areas and should now be able to create a product that better enables the research process to be accomplished through computerization (see note 9). Paul Allen (1990:1), president of Asymetrix Corporation, the company that produced Toolbook, summarized the notion of authoring software when he stated, "We want to enable mainstream PC users to create their own software solutions, to focus on what they want to do rather than on how to get there."

Storing and Accessing Data and Information Resources

For a fraction of what it would have cost ten years ago to store and access large quantities of data and information, today's microcomputer user can implement a system that can store virtually unlimited amounts of data and information that can be searched and retrieved almost instantaneously. At present, there are several approaches to implementing such systems. The core ingredient is the microcomputer. It could be a desktop or tower unit with several empty card slots and drive bays, or it could be a six-pound notebook computer with an external expansion capability. What turns the microcomputer into a data and information system are the mass storage devices that can be connected to store the large quantities of data and information and the software that allows the user to easily update and retrieve the data and information.

There are several issues to be concerned with when considering mass data and information storage and retrieval. Large amounts of storage space, probably in the thousands of megabytes or multiple gigabytes (one thousand million is a gigabyte, or one billion) are needed. The data will be stored for long periods, so the media they are stored on will have to have a long shelf life. Fast search and retrieval will mean the access time for the storage device should be quick. The storage devices should have multiple disk capacity to reduce labor requirements. For security, removable media may be required.

Magnetic media storage devices are in widespread use today. Floppy disks, hard drives, tape cartridges, and removable large capacity floppy cartridges (Bernoulli and Syquest) are typical magnetic media storage devices. This form of media is typically thought to have a relatively short shelf life and is easily destroyed by magnetic fields or when disks touch the device read head on the surface of the media (head crashes). Large amounts of information (several gigabytes) can be stored on hard drives and tape drives. Retrieval times are very slow on tape, whereas hard drives provide the fastest retrieval speeds. Cost per unit stored is moderately low for tape.

Other options are optical disks that are read by a laser beam, eliminating the problem of head crashes. The read/write optical disk probably has the greatest potential for data storage and retrieval. The disks have a life expectancy of 15 to 25 years, the access speed is almost as fast as a hard disk, and they have a capacity of 128 megabytes (3.5-inch size), 600 megabytes, and 1.2 gigabytes (5.25-inch size). The multiple disk versions can access 120 gigabytes of data and information. The writes-once read-many-times (WORM) disks are similar to the read/write optical except they can only be written to one time and then they can be used to retrieve data. Their advantage is the security that comes with being unable to alter the information once it is written. The CD-ROM is a 600-megabyte, 5.25-inch disk that is read only (like the CDs that music is recorded on). The big advantage is the low cost to make inexpensive copies of the master disk if distribution of data and information is desirable. The access time and longevity are similar to other optical media.

In addition to the computer and the storage devices, there needs to be a way to connect them together so they will operate. One of the popular options is the small-computer systems interface (SCSI). This hardware system allows the connection of up to seven devices to the parent microcomputer through a card that is placed inside the computer or through a parallel-to-SCSI adapter that plugs into the parallel port of the computer (this adapter is especially useful for portable computers). While other connection systems are available, the SCSI interface seems to be the more widespread.

With the hardware specified, the next and important step is to take advantage of software that can further the usefulness of the data and information system. One such package is Stacker, software that will double the capacity of a hard disk, or removable media like the read/write optical drives. This means that for about $100, a 1.2-gigabyte drive could be doubled to 2.4 gigabytes. This is far less costly than any existing alternative.

Another software package that is potentially useful is DBMS/Copy. It can transfer data, variable names, and value labels among 60 different software package formats. Briefly, this means that if a user were interested in analyzing data that were on the data system in a format that was different from the one that was needed, then there is a very good chance that DBMS/Copy would be capable of making the transfer to the format that is needed.

Perhaps the software that provides the most potential for data and information systems is software that catalogues and retrieves the data and information. It is easy to imagine that if hundreds of billions of numbers and letters are stored on mass media, the most important step after they are placed there is their retrieval in a systematic and timely fashion. Two products that accomplish this task are askSam and SmarText for Windows and both can manage data and information files in the multiple gigabyte-size range. As a first step, the software searches and catalogues the material in the files. This process, which takes a bit of time but is done only once, prepares the data and information for very rapid access by the users. A user might want to know something about waste management for rural areas, but is not concerned with nuclear waste. In this instance, the user would query the information system to locate the paragraphs that contain the words waste and rural, but not nuclear. The paragraphs where this combination was found would be noted and the user could then investigate each in a full text context.

With the currently available software and hardware, a data and information system that would focus on informing rural policy is easily within reach of university researchers as well as personnel working for a community. High powered mainframe computers and highly skilled programmers are no longer required to put a data and information system in place and keep it updated and easily accessible for the user.

Conclusion

To improve data we need (1) data that do not now exist, (2) longitudinal data and information, and (3) data that are more reliable and valid. In additional, data should represent the population under study, if that is the goal, and other nonsampling errors should be minimized. Another area of data improvement is in the linkages that can be made between the software packages that are used for data collection, data analysis, presentation of results, and data storage and retrieval.

These capabilities will help us reach our overall goal of providing data as a basis for informing rural policy decisions. To this end, it is hoped that this chapter, as it regards informing rural policy via primary data collection, linkages among stages of the research process, the graphical presentations of results, authoring experts' capabilities into software, and storing and accessing information, will provide assistance to university and community researchers. Numerous hurdles in achieving this goal remain. And just as the software and hardware help to eliminate the hurdles that loomed so large a few years ago, the future will bring more capable, less expensive, and easier-to-use systems.

Notes

1. For more detail about software available at each step of the research process see Carpenter, 1985a, 1985b, 1987, 1988, 1991; Carpenter and Axelson, 1989; and Dahlgran and Carpenter, 1988.

2. Analysis Selection: Statistical Navigator, Spring Stat; Sample Design: Ex-Sample, Number Cruncher, Statpac Gold, Systat Design, StatGraphics. Experimental Design: EXPERtIMENTAL Design, Number Cruncher, Stat-Graphics, Systat Design, CADE, JASS, Design-Ease, E-Chip.

3. Data Collection: ACS Query, Athena, CAPPA, CASES, CASS, Ci2, Ci2 CATI, ISSA, MaCATI, MATI, PCRS, PC Survent, Q-Fast, QPL, Quancept, Question Writer, Quiz Whiz, Reach. Data Entry: Costat, QPL, SPSS/PC+ Data Entry, MPA, Statpac Gold.

4. Data Transformation and Management: BMD/PC, Crunch, SAS, SPSS/PC+, Statpac Gold, Systat.

5. Data Analysis—IBM World (PC & MS DOS): Abstat, A-Cross, Analytica, BMD PC, BMDP Solo, Costat, Crunch, CSS, GB-Stat, Knowledge Seeker, Minitab, Mathematica, Number Cruncher, NWA Statpak, P-Stat, SAS, Sigstat, SPSS/PC+, Stata, Stat Chek, Stat80, StatGraphics, Statpac Gold, Systat, Turbo Springstat. Apple World (Macintosh): Systat, Statview 512+, Stat80, NWA Statpak.

6. Charting Graphics: Chart (Microsoft), Charting Gallery, Draw Applause, Excel, Fox Graph, Freelance Plus, Graph-in-the-Box, Graph Plus, Graph-Writer II, Harvard Graphics, Perspective Jr. and Option Pak, Pixie, Slide Write Plus, Stanford Graphics.

7. Drawing Graphics: Adobe Illustrator, Arts and Letters, Corel Draw!, Designer, Drawing Gallery, Draw Plus, Freelance Plus, Slide Write Plus.

8. Graphics Transfer: Hijaal, Metafile, TGL Plus. Screen Capture: Appart, Collage Plus, Hijaak, Pizazz Plus, Inset, TGL Plus.

9. Actor, Demo II, Hyperpad, Hyperwriter, Instant Replay Professional, Knowledge Pro DOS, Knowledge Pro Windows, Grasp, Guide, Object Vision, Quest, Spinnaker Plus, Toolbook, Visual Basic.

References

Allen, Paul. 1990. *Asymetrix Corporation: Redefining Software of the 1990s*. White Paper. Bellevue, Wash.: Asymetrix Corporation.

Babbie, Earl. 1989. *The Practice of Social Research*. Belmont, Calif.: Wadsworth.

Carpenter, Edwin H. 1985a. Statistical packages for microcomputers: New vistas for social science researchers in 1985. *Social Science Microcomputer Review* 3:183–204.

______. 1985b. The future for 'user friendly' microcomputer statistical software: SPSS/PC and SPSS/PC+ as examples. *Social Science Microcomputer Review* 3:352–361.

______. 1987. The evolving statistics and research process using microcomputer statistical software. *Social Science Microcomputer Review* 5:529–545.

______. 1988. Software tools for data collection: Microcomputer-assisted interviewing. *Social Science Computer Review* 6:353–368.

______. 1991. The research process: Additional automation via authoring software. *Social Science Computer Review* 9:624–654.

Carpenter, Edwin H., and Rick D. Axelson. 1989. Statistical and graphical research methods: State of the art. *Social Science Microcomputer Review* 7:503–534.

Chambers, J. M., W. S. Cleveland, B. Kliner, and P. A. Tukey. 1983. *Graphical Methods for Data Analysis*. Belmont, Calif.: Wadsworth.

Dahlgran, Roger A., and Edwin H. Carpenter. 1988. Econometric-forecasting microcomputer software: Capabilities, ease of use, and cost. *Social Science Microcomputer Review* 6:410–428.

Dillman, D. A. 1978. *Mail and Telephone Surveys: The Total Design Method*. New York: John Wiley & Sons.

Frey, J. H. 1989. *Survey Research by Telephone*. Newbury Park, Calif.: Sage.

Lake, C. C. 1987. *Public Opinion Polling*. Washington, D.C.: Island Press.

Software Cited

AbStat. Anderson Bell Corp., 11479 South Pine Drive, Suite 400-AR, Parker, CO 80134 (phone: 303-841-9755, ext. AR).

A-Cross. Strawberry Software Inc., 42 Pleasant St., Watertown, MA 02172 (phone: 617-923-8800).

ACS Query. Analytical Computer Software, Inc., 640 North LaSalle Drive, Chicago, IL 60610 (phone: 312-751-2915).

Actor. The Whitewater Group, 1800 Ridge Ave., Evanston, IL 60201-3621 (phone: 800-869-1144; Fax: 708-328-9386).

Adobe Illustrator. Adobe Systems, Inc., 1585 Charleston Rd., P.O. Box 7900, Mountain View, CA 94039-7900 (phone: 415-961-4400).

Analytica. New England Software, Inc., Greenwich Office Park #3, Greenwich, CT 06831 (phone: 800-633-2252, ext. 7008). *See also* GB-Stat, Graph-in-the-Box.

Animator. Autodesk, 2320 Marinship Way, Sausalito, CA 94965 (phone: 415-332-234).

Arts and Letters (Graphics Composer and Graphics Editor). Computer Support Corp., 15926 Midway Rd., Dallas, TX 75244 (phone: 214-661-8960).

Appart. Eric Juvet Software, 411 North 46th St., Seattle, WA 98103 (phone: 206-632-3522).

askSam. askSam Systems, 119 S. Washington, Perry, FL 32347-1428 (phone: 904-584-6590).

Athena. CRC Information Systems, Inc., 435 Hudson St., New York, NY 10014 (phone: 212-620-5678).

BMDP. BMDP Statistical Software, Inc., 1440 Sepulveda Blvd., Suite 316, Los Angeles, CA 90025 (phone: 213-479-7799). *See also* BMDP Solo.

BMDP Solo. BMDP Statistical Software, Inc., 1440 Sepulveda Blvd., Suite 316, Los Angeles, CA 90025 (phone: 213-479-7799). *See also* BMDP.

CADE. International Qua-Tech, 2820 Fountain Lane North, Plymouth, MN 55447 (phone: 612-887-0838).

CAPPA. The Scientific Press, 540 University Avenue, Palo Alto, CA 94301 (phone: 415-322-5221).

CASES. Computer Assisted Survey Methods Program, 2538 Channing Way, Berkeley, CA 94720 (phone: 514-642-6578).

CASS. Survey Research Center, University of Wisconsin, WI 53703 (phone: 608-262-3122).

Chart. MICROSOFT Corp., 16011 NE 36th Way, Box 97017, Redmond, WA 98073-9717 (pphone: 206-882-8089).

Charting Gallery. Hewlett-Packard Co., Inquiries, 19310 Pruneridge Ave., Cupertino, CA 95014 (phone: 800-752-0900). *See also* DRAWING GALLERY.

Ci2, Ci2 CATI. Sawtooth Software, Inc., 208 Spruce North, P.O. Box 3429, Ketchum, ID 83340 (phone: 208-726-7772).

Collage Plus. Inner Media, 60 Plain Rd., Hollis, NH 03049 (phone: 603-465-3216).

Corel Draw!. Corel Systems Corp., 1600 Carling Ave., Ottawa, Ontario K1Z8R7, Canada (phone: 613-728-8200).

Costat. CoHort Software, P.O. Box 1149, Berkeley, CA 94701 (phone: 415-843-9599).

Crunch. Crunch Software Corp., 5335 College Avenue, Suite 27, Oakland, CA 84618 (phone: 415-420-8660).

CSS. Stat-Soft, 2325 E. 13th St., Tulsa, OK (phone: 918-583-4149).

DBMS/Copy Plus. SPSS, Inc., 444 N. Michigan Ave., Chicago, IL 60611 (phone: 312-329-3300).

Demo II. Sage Software, Inc., 3200 Tower Oaks Blvd., Rockville, MD 20852 (phone: 800-547-4000).

Designer. Micrografx Inc., 1303 Arapaho, Richardson, TX 75081 (phone: 800-272-3729). *See also* Draw Plus, Graph Plus.

Design-Ease. Stat-Ease, Inc., 4108 Aldrich Ave. South, Minneapolis, MN 55409 (phone: 612-822-5574).

Drawing Gallery. Hewlett-Packard Co., Inquiries, 19310 Pruneridge Ave., Cupertino, CA 95014 (phone: 800-752-0900. *See also* Charting Gallery.

Draw Applause. Ashton-Tate, 20101 Hamilton Ave., Torrance, CA 90502-1319 (phone: 800-437-4329).

Draw Plus. Micrografx Inc., 130 Arapaho, Richardson, TX 75081 (phone: 800-272-3729). *See also* Designer, Graph Plus.

ECHIP. ECHIP, Inc., Hockessin Mill Plaza, Suite 6, 7460 Lancaster Pike, Hockessin, DE 19707 (phone: 302-239-5429).

Excel. Microsoft Corp., 16011 NE 36th Way, P.O. Box 97017, Redmond, WA 98073-9717 (phone: 800-227-4679). *See also* Word.

EXPERtIMENTAL Design. Statistical Programs, 9941 Rowlett, Suite 6, Houston, TX 77075 (phone: 713-947-1551).

ExSample. The Idea Works, Inc., 100 W. Briarwood, Columbia, MO 65023 (phone: 314-445-4554). *See also* Statistical Navigator.

Foxgraph. Fox Software, 118 W. South Boundary, Perrysburg, OH 43551 (phone: 419-874-0162).

Freelance Plus. Lotus Development Corp., 55 Cambridge Parkway, Cambridge, MA 02142 (phone: 617-577-8500). *See also* GraphWriter II and Lotus 1-2-3.

GB-Stat. New England Software, Inc., Greenwich Office Park #3, Greenwich, CT 06831 (phone: 800-633-2252). *See also* Analytica, Graph-in-the-Box.

GrafTool. 3-D Visions, Inc., 2780 Skypark Dr., Torrance, CA 90505 (phone: 213-325-1339).

Graph Plus. Micrografx Inc., 1303 Arapaho, Richardson, TX 75081 (phone: 800-272-3729. *See also* Designer, Draw Plus.

Graph-in-the-Box. New England Software, Inc., Greenwich Office Park #3, Greenwich, CT 06831 (phone: 800-633-2252). *See also* Analytica, GB-Stat.

Grapher. Golden Software, Inc., P.O. Box 281, Golden, CO 80402 (phone: 303-279-1021). *See also* Surfer.

GraphWriter II. Lotus Development Corp., 55 Cambridge Parkway, Cambridge, MA 02142 (phone: 617-577-8500). *See also* Freelance Plus, Lotus 1-2-3.

Grasp. Paul Mace Software, 400 Williamson Way, Ashland, OR 97520 (phone: 503-488-0224).

Guide. Owl International, 2800 156th Avenue S.E., Bellvue, WA 98007 (phone: 206-747-3203; Fax 206-641-9367).

Harvard Graphics. SPC Software Publishing Corp., 1901 Landings Dr., P.O. Box 7210, Mountain View, CA 94039-7210 (phone: 415-962-8910).

Hijaak. Inset Systems Inc., 71 Commerce Dr., Brookfield, CT (phone: 800-828-8088. *See also* Inset.

Hyperpad. Brightbill-Roberts & Company, Ltd., 120 E. Washington St., Suite 421, Syracuse, NY 13202 (phone: 315-474-3400).

Hyperwriter. Ntergaid, Inc., 2490 Black Rock Tpke., Suite 337, Fairfield, CT 06430 (phone: 203-368-0632; Fax 203-334-5658).

Inset. Inset Systems Inc., 71 Commerce Dr., Brookfield, CT (phone: 800-828-8088. *See also* Hijaak.

ISSA. Institute for Resource Development, Westinghouse, Demographic and Health Surveys Project, P.O. Box 866, Columbia, MD, 21044 (phone: 301-992-0066).

Instant Replay Professional. Nostradamus, Inc., P.O. Box 9252, Salt Lake City, UT 84109-0252 (phone: 800-388-8086).

JASS. Joiner Associates Inc., 3800 Regent Street, P.O. Box 5445, Madison, WI 53705-0445 (phone: 608-238-9106).

Knowledge Seeker. 1st Mark Technologies, Suite 608, 16 Concourse Gate, Ottawa, Ontario, K2E-7S8, Canada (phone: 613-723-8020; Fax: 613-723-8048).

Knowledge Pro DOS. Knowledge Garden Inc., 473A Malden Bridge Rd., Nassau, NY 12123 (phone: 518-766-3000; Fax: 518-766-3003).

Knowledge Pro Windows. Knowledge Garden Inc., 473A Malden Bridge Rd., Nassau, NY 12123 (phone: 518-766-3000; Fax: 518-766-3003).

MaCATI. PSRC Software, Bowling Green State University, Bowling Green, OH 43403 (phone: 419-372-2497).

Mathematica. Wolfram Research, Inc., P.O. Box 6059, Champaign, IL 61826-9905 (phone: 217-398-0700).

MATI. Social and Economic Sciences Research Center, Washington State University, Pullman, WA 99164-4014 (phone: 509-335-1511).

Metafile. Zenographics, 19752 MacArthur Blvd., Suite 250, Irvine, CA 92715-9976 (phone: 714-851-6352). *See also* PIXIE.

Minitab. Minitab, Inc., 3081 Enterprise Dr., State College, PA 16801 (phone: 814-238-3280).

MPA, Statchek, Data Utilities. Detail Technologies, Inc., Emmons Drive A-2, Princeton, NJ, 08540 (phone: 609-452-8228).

Number Cruncher. NCSS, 329 North 1000 East, Kaysville, UT 84037 (phone: 801-546-0445).

NWA Statpak. Northwest Analytical, Inc., 520 N.W. Davis, Portland, OR 97209 (phone: 503-224-7727).

ObjectVision. Borland, 1800 Green Hills Rd., Scotts Valley, CA 95067 (phone: 408-438-5300).

PCRS. M/A/R/C Inc., 7850 North Belt Line Road, Irving, TX 75063 (phone: 214-506-3400).

PC Survent. Computers for Marketing Corp., 547 Howard St., San Francisco, CA 94105 (phone: 415-777-0470).

Perspective Junior. Three-D Graphics, 860 Via de La Paz, Pacific Palisades, CA 90272 (phone: 213-459-8525).

Pixie. Zenographics, 19752 MacArthur Blvd., Suite 250, Irvine, CA 92715-9976 (phone: 714-851-6352). *See also* METAFILE.

Pizazz Plus. Application Techniques Inc., 10 Lomar Park Dr., Pepperell, MA 01463 (phone: 508-433-5201).

Power Analysis and Sample Size. NCSS, 329 North 1000 East, Kaysville, UT 84037 (phone: 801-546-0445).

P-Stat. P-Stat, Inc., 271 Wall St., P.O. Box AH, Princeton, NJ 08542 (phone: 609-924-9100).

Q-Fast. Statsoft, Inc., 2325 E. 13th St., Tulsa, OK 74104 (phone: 918-583-4149).

Quancept. Quantime, 4010 Executive Park Drive, Suite 226, Cincinnati, OH 45241 (phone: 513-563-8800).

Quest. Allen Communication, 5225 Wiley Post Way, Salt Lake City, UT 84116 (phone: 800-325-7850).

Question Writer. Concurrent Marketing System, Inc., 205 State Rd., Princeton, NJ 08540 (phone: 609-683-7702).

Quiz Whiz. Quiz Whiz Enterprises Inc., 790 Timberline Drive, Akron, OH 44313 (phone: 216-922-1825).

QPL. Questionnaire Programming Language. Available through (NTIS) National Technical Information System, U.S. Department of Commerce (phone:702-487-4650). Produced by Kevin Dooley, Human Resources Division, U.S. General Accounting Office, Washington, D.C. 20548 (phone: 202-275-5848).

Reach. World Research Systems, P.O. Box 1009, Palatine, IL 60078 (phone: 312-991-1122).

Realizer. Within Technologies, Laurel Corporate Center, Suite 201 South, 8000 Midatlantic Dr., Mount Laurel, NJ 08054-5080 (phone: 609-273-8881).

SAS. SAS Institute, Inc., SAS Circle, P.O. Box 8000, Cary, NC 27512-8000 (phone: 919-4367-8000).

ShowPartner F/X. Brightbill-Roberts and Co. Ltd., 120 Washington St., Suite 421, Syracuse, NY 13202 (phone: 315-474-3400).

SigmaPlot Graphics Software. Jandel Scientific, 2656 Bridgeway, Sausaleto, CA 94965 (phone: 415-331-3022).

Sigstat. Significant Statistics, 3336 North Canyon Road, Provo, UT 84604 (phone: 801-377-4860).

SlideWrite Plus. Advanced Graphics Software Inc., 333 E. Maude Ave., #105, Sunnyvale, CA 94086 (phone: 408-749-8620).

SmallTalk/V for Windows. Digitalk, 9841 Airport Blvd., Los Angeles, CA 90045 (phone: 213-645-1082).

SmarText. Lotus Development Corp., 55 Cambridge Parkway, Cambridge, MA 02142 (phone: 617-577-8500).

Spinnaker Plus (Windows and Macintosh). Spinnaker Software, 201 Broadway, Cambridge, MA 02139-1901 (phone: 617-494-1200).

SPSS/PC+. SPSS, Inc., 444 N. Michigan Ave., Chicago, IL 60611 (phone: 312-329-3300).

SPSS/PC+, Data Entry II. SPSS Inc., 444 N. Michigan Ave., Chicago, IL 60611 (phone: 312-329-2400).

Stanford Graphics. 3-D Visions, Inc., 2780 Skypark Dr., Torrance, CA 90505, (phone: 213-325-1339).

Stata. Computing Resource Center, 10801 National Blvd., Los Angeles, CA 90064 (phone: 800-782-8272 in CA, AK, and HI; all others 213-470-4341).

Stat80. Logiciel/Eustat, Inc., 306 Douglas Street, P.O. Box 520283, Salt Lake City, UT 84152-0283 (phone: 800-STAT-80-S or 801-521-9309).

StatGraphics. STSC, Inc., 2115 E. Jefferson St., Rockville, MD 20852 (phone: 301-984-5123).

Statistical Navigator. The Idea Works, Inc., 100 W. Briarwood, Columbia, MO 65203 (phone: 314-445-4554). *See also* Ex-Sample.

Statpack Gold. Walonick Associates, 6500 Nicollet Ave. So., Minneapolis, MN 55423 (phone: 612-866-9022 or 800-328-4907).

Stat Transfer. Circle Consulting, 10 Arnold Circle, Cambridge, MA 02139 (phone: 617-491-4511 or 617-864-9233).

Statview 512+. BrainPower, Inc., 24009 Ventura Blvd., Suite 250, Calabasas, CA 91302 (phone: 818-884-9233).

Storyboard Plus. International Business Machines Corp., P.O. Box 28331, Atlanta, GA 30358-0331 (phone: 800-IBM-2266). *See also* Presentation Manager.

Surfer. Golden Software, Inc., P.O. Box 281, Golden, CO 80402 (phone: 303-279-1021). *See also* Grapher.

Systat/Sygraph. Systat, Inc., 1800 Sherman Ave., Evanston, IL 60201 (phone: 312-864-5670).

Systat, Logit, Probit, Design. Systat, Inc., 1800 Sherman Ave., Evanston, IL 60201 (phone: 312-864-5670).

Turbo Springstat. Spring Systems, P.O. Box 10073, Chicago, IL 60610 (phone: 312-275-5273).

TGLPlus. Harvard Systems Corp., 1661 Lincoln Blvd., Suite 101, Santa Monica, CA 90404 (phone: 213-392-8441).

ToolBook. Asymetrix Corp., 110-110th Ave. N.E., Suite 717, Bellvue, WA 98004 (phone: 206-637-1500).

Visual Basic. Microsoft Corp., One Microsoft Way, Bellvue, WA 98052 (phone: 206-882-8080; Fax: 206-883-8101).

Windows (ver. 3.0). Microsoft Corp., 16011 N.E. 36th Way, P.O. Box 97017, Redmond, WA 98073-9717 (phone: 800-227-2679). *See also* Excel and Word.

11

Geographic Information Systems and Rural Data

Steven D. Shultz and Robert MacArthur

A geographic information system (GIS) is a computer-based spatial database system that can capture, store, edit, manipulate, and display geographically referenced information. The use of GIS technology can greatly increase the quantity and quality of rural data by (1) making a wide variety of natural and physical resource data readily available in compact form; (2) permitting rural policymakers and other users of rural data to integrate such data with sociodemographic information; and (3) enabling these users to access census data at a level of geographic specificity and to integrate this data with the other forms of data mentioned above.

GIS Technology and Rural Data

California Congressman George Brown (1991:69), who is chairman of the House Science, Space, and Technology Committee, recently noted that "the majority of issues on today's political agenda are subject to analysis and study with the aid of GIS technology." In fact, almost all the rural data issues identified in *Rural Policies for the 1990s* (Flora and Christenson, 1991) have a "spatial component" and, therefore, the potential for more comprehensive analysis with the help of GIS technology. Five of the most specific and pressing issues are as follows:

1. Local governments are being flooded with data from new sources, much of it generated by the 1990 census, without a good way of integrating it. Fortunately, much of this new data is "spatially

referenced" (i.e., tied to a coordinate system). These files are called the *TIGER* files. A geographic base provides a foundation for integrating all data, including data from a variety of other sources, and for doing comprehensive, multivariate analysis.

2. Local governments can use GIS technology to improve the accuracy and level of meaning of their census data and, thus, to capitalize on the political and financial benefits (such as political redistricting and reapportionment) that are directly tied to having accurate census data.
3. Survey data dealing with rural issues are often startlingly more revealing when analyzed in a spatial context.
4. GIS technology is adept at detecting and improving infrastructure services, which in many rural areas are falling into disrepair.
5. Finally, GIS technology is well suited for inventorying and modeling many of the natural resources. Caretaking for these resources is becoming an increasingly prominent rural issue. Traditionally, rural communities have been regarded as the stewards of the nation's natural resources, but they are receiving more and more advice from their urban neighbors, advice which does not always take into account the complexities of balancing ecological protection with the commercial use of rural natural resources. A GIS can provide the rural policymaker with a powerful and convincing tool in these dialogues.

An Overview of GIS Technology

A GIS is often mistakenly thought of as a tool for creating and displaying appealing and colorful maps. In fact, it is the analytical capabilities rather than the cartographic output of a GIS that make it such a unique and valuable technology. More specifically, the use of GIS enables users to interactively model many quantitative and qualitative features of the physical and sociodemographic world.

GIS technology has historically been divided into vector and raster systems. A *vector GIS* regards an area and the objects contained within it as points, lines, and polygons. Hence, it is a sort of object-oriented approach to spatial representation. *Raster GIS* uses a grid or cell matrix to describe an area. Here each object is a collection of these cells, similar to the way that a computer's screen represents objects as collections of pixels or picture elements. Although most GIS software packages are predominantly one or the other, they have the means to transfer data between the two systems. Generally, vector GIS programs are better suited to planning and raster GIS programs are better for modeling and research. Hence, vector GIS programs are favored by city planners, land managers, and the like, whereas raster GIS programs are favored by academicians and researchers.

Spatial Data

Both types of GIS systems require data, which come from various sources including satellite and aerial photos and tabular records. Sometimes data are already collected into a GIS format, as with the TIGER files from the 1990 census or the DIME files from the 1980 census. Data are often brought in from paper maps by digitizing them, an arduous and expensive process. More than two-thirds of the cost of a GIS project can result from digitizing data. Sometimes maps can be scanned, but this procedure often requires extensive editing. Fortunately, data-capture tasks are getting easier as better digitizers and scanners evolve at lower cost and as agencies and other GIS users begin to share data with each other.

All data need to be given a spatial reference by tying them to some real world or artificial location via a coordinate system (e.g., longitude-latitude, Universal Transverse Mercator, or some system you design). This computerized coordinate system defines an area of study and is called the *base map*. Because all other data are tied to it, it is important to build a base map that reflects the scale and accuracy required by a specific study. The data that are tied to this base map make up the *GIS database*. This database is actually many tables or "layers," each one representing some theme or attribute which is of interest, such as soil type, roads, or vegetation.

Also, because the data are tied to the base map, they are topologically related, or given "geographic intelligence," so that each object or attribute knows where everything else is. This is another way of distinguishing GIS technology from simple cartography; that is, all data in a GIS database are related so that the user can perform analyses rather than just make maps. Hence, a GIS database can, for example, not only tell how many houses, inhabitants, and miles of road exist in a given area, but what route is fastest to a given location in the area, what parcels are zoned for a certain type of housing and are within a certain distance of a school and a major highway, what types of soil vegetation exist in an area, and where the hydrology is and how it might be affected by a housing project. This interrelatedness of things in a GIS database is what gives it analytical strength.

GIS then, is a tool for creating and using a spatial database. In this database are various tables, each representing a theme such as vegetation, soil type, population, income, age, and so on. These themes are also referred to as *data overlays or layers*. With a GIS, these layers can be manipulated with various computer operations (e.g., search and sort; logical Boolean functions; mathematical, geometric, and network analyses; and a variety of other spatial and temporal modeling procedures). Together, these are the analytical dimensions of a GIS. In a planning situation, GIS database layers might include streets, lots, zoning areas, soil types, hydrology, water supplies, school districts, and census regions. Community planners attempting to locate ideal sites for new construction (such as industrial parks, schools, airports, and hazardous waste dumps) can then overlay and analyze these layers. In academic research, a more sophisticated application might be to develop a model of a complex ecological process such as water-runoff and soil-erosion patterns for a given area.

Another basic function of a GIS is to display data for a report or tabular format or, more properly, for a GIS map. GIS can produce high-quality color maps that can be viewed on a computer monitor or transferred to paper with a plotter. The appeal of such illustrative and colorful maps is their suitability as study tools and informative public-relation mediums which may easily be changed to present alternative interpretations of the data. This flexibility in displaying alternative interpretations of spatially related data (e.g., many views of an area and its surroundings that has been proposed as a landfill) may potentially help resolve many complex natural resource/human conflicts facing rural America in the 1990s.

Trends in GIS Software and Hardware

By 1992, the GIS software and hardware industry will have revenues of approximately $3.5 billion and an expected total eight-year growth rate of almost $100 billion (*The Economist*, 1992). GIS software is now available for use on personal computers, work stations, minicomputers, and mainframe computers, and is advertised and reviewed frequently in journals such as *GIS World* and *Geo Info Systems*. The types of GIS software that are presently available can be divided into three basic categories: sophisticated and expensive products, public domain software, and desktop mapping packages.

Advanced GIS software such as ARC/INFO, Intergraph, and GeoVision usually costs several thousand dollars. These state-of-the-art packages utilize a variety of data types (including raster and vector GIS formats); conduct a wide range of GIS manipulation and analytical functions; and produce high-quality, detailed colored maps. However, besides their costly price tags, these programs are usually difficult to learn and often require expensive training sessions.

The two most prominent examples of public domain GIS software are GRASS and MOSS. MOSS was developed by the U.S. Forest Service, the Bureau of Land Management, and other federal government agencies. GRASS was developed by the Army Corps of Engineers and the Soil Conservation Service. These software packages are powerful and, perhaps most importantly, are free (users are required to pay only distribution costs). Source code is also available for those interested in writing custom GIS applications. Public domain GIS software has become the vehicle for many GIS modeling-applications. Unfortunately, for the average rural user, these programs are often written for relatively expensive work stations running the arcane UNIX operating system. Further, because these are "home-brew" software, technical support may be hard to find, and they are not always wholly compatible with other GIS formats. The academic researcher can possibly afford to work around these limitations, but the local planner cannot.

The third category of GIS software, often referred to as *desktop mapping* packages, is relatively inexpensive (usually less than $3,000) and quite easy to learn. Some of the more commonly known packages of this type include MapInfo, Atlas GIS, MapMaker, and GeoSpreadsheet. These packages run on personal computers and can usually import a variety of GIS data types. The main limitations of these packages are that they often lack advanced GIS analytical functions and they cannot handle very large data sets. These packages are better suited to persons and institutions who do not have an interest in creating complex GIS data sources by themselves but, rather, want to perform relatively simple analyses of already existing spatial data sources. The rural planner finds these packages especially appealing because of their affordability and relatively short-learning curve.

Until recently, hardware requirements for a GIS have been prohibitively expensive to most rural users. But it is now possible to get up and running with a microcomputer that costs less than $2,000, a digitizer between $1,000 and $2,000, and a plotter or laser printer between $1,000 and $1,500, for a total cost of between $4,000 and $5,500. However, some additional expenses are likely to occur. For example, fine-quality maps may need to be produced by outside professionals. Also, as GIS users become more adept with the technology, they will likely experience a growing need for bigger, better, and more costly equipment.

Once software and hardware are acquired, the next step is to look at what types of data are available and where they can be found.

Types of Rural-Specific GIS Data

Regardless of the specific software that is used, many different sources of rural data may be captured by a GIS, including natural-resource, socio-demographic, and cadastral-based data.

Natural Resource Data. The difficult and expensive task of inventorying natural resources has been a major driving force behind the adoption of GIS technology. Many federal, state, and local agencies responsible for land-use management have used a GIS for years because it improves the efficiency of storing, retrieving, and updating natural resource data. These agencies also help construct the models they need to manage their resources. Data available from these agencies include tables or "layers" of geological features, soils, vegetative covers, water sources, and wildlife populations for all public lands as well as many other areas.

Some states have made GIS management of natural resources a part of their mission. In several states (including Minnesota, Vermont, and Wisconsin), the adoption of natural-resource-based GIS data by state agencies has been mandated by law (Stutheit, 1990). In others, state agencies have been encouraged to voluntarily adopt GIS technology, which has resulted in collaborative efforts between many federal and state agencies. For example, the South Carolina Water Resources Commission has built a natural resource GIS database that policymakers use as a decision support system for environmental policies. This five-year project is being aided financially and technically by National Oceanic and Atmospheric Administration (NOAA), U.S. Geological Survey (USGS), U.S. Fish and Wildlife Service (USFWS), Soil Conservation Service (SCS), and others (Hale and Anderson, 1990). In Arizona, a variety of agencies have formed the Arizona Geographic Information Council (AGIC) to coordinate GIS use among state agencies, federal agencies, county and local governments, and universities. This council provides a medium for sharing data overlays, proposing standards, and sharing resources such as a high-quality electrostatic plotter (Shultz, 1990).

Sociodemographic and TIGER Data. A considerable amount of rural-based sociodemographic data are collected from the decennial census, which itself has been greatly improved with the use of GIS. In fact, the U.S. Census Bureau has created its own GIS database named TIGER (topologically integrated geographic encoding and referencing system) built from the 1990 census data.

TIGER is an extensive, national digital map database that contains important features such as roads, railroads, rivers, address ranges and zip codes, census statistical areas, and political and administrative boundaries, including 6.9 million census blocks. Not only did TIGER improve the efficiency and accuracy of the Census Bureau's 1990 enumeration procedures, but it has increased geographical specificity and permitted the analysis of census data in considerably greater detail than ever before (LaMacchia and Tomasi, 1990).

What this means is that persons using a GIS to manipulate 1990 census data can now easily relate these data to other types of data (such as natural resource data—soils, hydrology, vegetation, wildlife, etc.), using spatial reference as a base. Most of the GIS software discussed earlier will accommodate TIGER files, although in some cases additional data translation software may be necessary.

Cadastral Data. Ownership and taxation data are termed *cadastral data* in GIS parlance. GIS can be used to streamline much of the local government tasks associated with this type of data, such as administering taxes and settling boundary and ownership disputes. Federal agencies make extensive use of these data in granting leases and dealing with private leases of public lands. Public utility companies also use this type of information to settle right-of-way disputes and to work out rental agreements resulting from shared property (such as utility poles).

Examples of GIS Applications in Rural Areas

While the conceptual advantages of using a GIS to improve rural data and rural development applications have been documented (Reinsel, 1989; Wright, Harris, and Davis, 1989), specific GIS applications that integrate and utilize different types of rural data have not been widely reported. Primarily, this is because such GIS applications have, for the most part, been conducted by local governments and planners who generally do not write journal articles or participate in other traditional information exchange mediums. Presented below are some brief summaries of several GIS applications with relevance to rural areas. They are classed into three broad areas: inventorying and protecting natural resources, agricultural applications, and economic development and planning activities. Although these areas are likely to overlap substantially, a key feature of GIS technology is the ability to handle this complex integration.

Inventorying and Protecting Natural Resources

Environmental Risk Assessment. EPA researchers used GIS technology to integrate natural resource and sociodemographic data to determine efficient and accurate methodologies for protecting local human populations from various environmental risks (Mynar and Hewitt, 1989). A similar GIS application by an EPA contractor in a mining area near Butte, Montana, involved merging population estimates with GIS-based land-use and soil data to identify residential areas with the greatest need for soil decontamination (Daumiller, 1990). Finally, a GIS has been used at the county level to determine alternative routes for the transportation of hazardous wastes (Padgett, 1992).

Land-Use Change Dynamics. Three studies focus of the use of GIS and land-use changes. In the first study, a GIS was used to assess the impact of new town development on the environment of the New Territories of Hong Kong with regard to erosion and surface hydrology and to the settlement patterns of local populations. This historical study integrated aerial photographs of the town's development over several years into a GIS so that the dynamics of demographic growth on erosion could be revealed (Lo and Shipmann, 1990).

In another study, researchers at the University of New Hampshire used a GIS to integrate aerial photo and census data to quantify and analyze spatial land-use changes in two rapidly growing rural counties (Luloff and Befort, 1989).

In the third study, changing land-use patterns for nine rural counties in Georgia were examined with a GIS to build a historical database for policymakers and researchers. The purpose was to study the ecological effects on land that shifted from agricultural use to forest and back again. As part of this research, a broad-scale view of the regional rural landscape was built (Turner, 1990).

Agricultural Applications

Compliance with Agricultural-based Legislation. To meet California agricultural compliance laws, a GIS was used to examine the spatial relationships between various layers of agricultural and land-use data (Crichton, 1990). GIS technologies have also been used to help rural counties promote low-input sustainable agriculture and to cope with administrative law, specifically the 1985 Food Security Act (Bishop, Hines, and Mechelke, 1989).

Implementing Land Evaluation and Site Assessment (LESA) on a GIS. The LESA model was developed by the Soil Conservation Service to aid local planners in protecting important agricultural lands. It was designed for site-specific evaluations of the economic viability of farmlands. At the University of Kansas, such a GIS was used to conduct a county-wide evaluation of proposed zoning changes (Williams, 1985). This is one of several studies that points out how the impact of GIS on policy-making grows as the scale of implementation rises. Once LESA could be used for the whole of Douglas County, Kansas, it became a focus of rural policy, whereas at the farm level, it was implemented manually (without a GIS) with little attention to policy. At the regional, state, or national level the relationships between GIS analysis and resulting policy decision-making have literally unlimited potential.

Farm Planning Internationally. In Australia, a GIS was used for farm planning by "applying GIS as an interfacing mechanism between physical data, economic data, and personal data to facilitate better farm management decisions" (*GIS World*, 1990:17). A GIS was also used with remote-sensing techniques to improve regional rice production in Thailand (Karnchanasutham and Wongwantanee, 1991) and to improve the efficiency of planning activities among private and cooperative farmers in the Nicaraguan watershed (Shultz and Rosales, 1992).

Economic Development and Planning Activities

Census Studies. The Anchorage Economic Development and Planning Department used a cadastral GIS system containing property, tax, household, and other sociodemographic data to improve their community-wide database and provide more detailed information for small areas not adequately reported by decennial census efforts (Breedlove, 1990).

Planners in Guilford, Connecticut, have combined census data with their own survey data in a GIS framework to model the spatial differences in residents' attitudes and opinions toward various local policy issues (Berry et al., 1981).

Finally, in Tucson, Arizona, city planners have undertaken a comprehensive land-use study based on aerial photographs and a GIS to verify and improve 1990 census data.

Integrated GIS for Comprehensive Economic Planning. Planners in Sutton, Massachusetts, developed an integrated GIS database consisting of soils, farmlands, watersheds, infrastructure, and land-use data to assist their comprehensive planning efforts. Researchers at the University of South Carolina, along with state planners, developed a statewide GIS database containing some 17 different layers of information. The purpose of this GIS was to assist in site suitability modeling, infrastructure improvements, and economic development (Shirley, 1990).

Obstacles to Improving Rural Data with a GIS

The above examples show how GIS technology can improve the quality and quantity of rural data by increasing geographical specificity and integrating a wide variety of natural resource information with socio-demographic and cadastral data. However, several obstacles are delaying the widespread adoption of GIS technology for use with rural data.

The most significant constraints delaying the adoption and use of GIS technology for rural data applications are the high start-up costs and the technical complexities of the technology, which are simply examples of the "rural-urban continuum." While GIS technology has been adopted in most urban areas, rural areas have been slow to follow suit because they cannot as readily absorb the high start-up costs. Ironically, such investments in GIS technology in the urban areas have been returned many fold.

In addition, GIS technology can be very labor intensive; that is, substantial investments in training and human capital may be required. Further, once personnel become trained in the technology, they are likely to become a target for employment by urban or other GIS centers. These financial and technical constraints associated with GIS technology in rural areas are very similar to the problems that have been associated with the adoption of telecommunications and other "information age" technology in rural areas (Dillman and Beck, 1988). Fortunately, GIS software is becoming easier to use as vendors develop more user-friendly interfaces to the software.

One final obstacle facing the adoption of GIS technology to improve rural data is that different public agencies often resist the idea of sharing data with their fellow agencies and users. This is especially true of social and economic data. Data sharing is required to help ensure data format compatibility and to provide repositories where data from many sources can be accessed for integrated policy-making. The real payoff of GIS lies in its ability to integrate data from many sources and to offer holistic policy-making opportunities.

These are formidable obstacles to GIS adoption, but rural development practitioners and policymakers have the potential to address them if they employ the same determination they exhibited when dealing with similar rural issues in the past, such as rural electrification. However, before this is likely to occur, it will be necessary for the benefits of using GIS technology to be more fully understood, for more cooperation to exist between various agencies using GIS technology, and for direct financial or technical GIS support to be made available to local rural communities. Who can provide this support? The next section will explore some options.

Institutional Roles in Rural GIS Development

With the spread of GIS use among different government agencies has come the discerned need to share data and other resources. Recognition of this need has led to some cooperative agreements and arrangements that have helped to create several rural-based GIS databases. There has also been some recognition by various agencies and educational institutions that they must give others help in spreading GIS technology. These collaborations and programs are listed below.

Federal

Some federal agencies such as the Bureau of Land Management and the Forest Service have worked collaboratively to define their GIS needs, and they have drafted a joint procurement for hardware and GIS software. The procurement process for this huge multimillion dollar outlay has come under the scrutiny of federal procurement officers in the Government Service Administration, but the process has helped set some standards for the hardware and software. These standards should provide guidelines for those setting up a GIS system. For example, these requirements specify that the GIS runs in a distributed data-processing environment (i.e., it is able to assimilate data from many sources and over networks) and that the text data are based on Structure Query Language (SQL, an IBM mainframe environment). Users who adhere to these standards can be assured of access to the tremendous amounts of GIS data generated by these two agencies. This is especially important to users of rural data in the West, where these agencies have most of their holdings.

Other federal agencies such as the Bureau of Reclamation are also prolific users of GIS data, although the Bureau's data, used in the construction of dams and the like, are often of a much finer scale than is necessary for most applications. USDA, through the American Farmland Trust, has spawned the National Center for Resource Innovation (NCRI), whose purpose is to establish regional GIS centers. The mission of these centers is to inventory all retired farmlands and wetlands, as well as to build models for managing them. The five centers to date are Washington, Chesapeake Bay, Georgia, Arkansas, and North Dakota, and there are plans for at least two more. Potentially, these centers can be a tremendous aid to rural users who are involved with the management of retired farmlands or lands earmarked for retirement under the Conservation Reserve Program. Over the next few years, models for looking at these lands at different levels of ecological sensitivity in different regions of the country will hopefully evolve from this program. NCRI models will also enable rural resource managers to deal with some complex ecological processes such as erosion over large areas.

State

Many states have already adopted leadership roles by embarking on organized programs to coordinate and enhance GIS use in their own environments (Warnecke, 1991). Good examples of these programs exist in Massachusetts and Arizona. In Massachusetts, the METLAND Project, which ran from 1985 to 1987, researched the feasibility of a workstation-based GIS that various public land-use planners could affordably install and use to manage the resources in their domain. METLAND was model-driven; rather than focus on coordinating GIS use in the state, it attempted to provide a paradigm for the state's budding GIS users. METLAND defined desirable features of GIS software and hardware and suggested approaches to land-use planning with GIS.

Arizona's Land Resource Information System (ALRIS) is a more formal attempt to coordinate GIS activities among state agencies. Under ALRIS, the State Lands Department, designated as a lead GIS agency, provides training, support, and some hardware and data exchange facilities. It also organizes regular meetings of local, state, and federal agencies to share overlays and information (Shultz, 1990).

Sometimes one environmental issue can bring together a multiagency approach to GIS. In Kansas, a GIS initiative involving 14 agencies and three University of Kansas departments originally focused on water issues, but ended with the legislature's endorsement of a statewide GIS program.

Local Groups and Educational Institutions

On the local level, groups of communities sometimes join together to form associations. These associations are often eager to sponsor rural GIS projects, sometimes with seed money. Often seed money is also available from private funding sources (such as the Pew Charitable Trust Fund, the Kellogg Foundation, Successful Communities, the Ford Foundation, and the Rockefeller Foundation) for environmental or natural-resource management applications. Cooperative agreements with community colleges can also be useful vehicles for developing technology.

At the university level, many past efforts have applied GIS to local development and resource planning, but they have mostly been directed overseas. One example, Comprehensive Resource Inventory and Evaluation System (CRIES), developed at Michigan State University, intended to make technology like remote sensing and GIS available to communities in underdeveloped countries through a university.

This idea is currently being tried in the United States by encouraging rural Americans to use GIS via the university system. The Cooperative Extension Service (CES), which is associated with state universities, is often the vehicle for this transmission. CES is well-suited to this task because it already has a network of specialists in place in local communities. Also, selling GIS is largely an educational function, which is the mission of CES.

Such GIS education and assistance has already been undertaken by at least two state CES organizations. The Wisconsin CES launched a program called LOCALIS, which is specifically directed at gearing up local governments with GIS. Aided by a $2 million equipment and software grant from IBM, ESRI, and ERDAS, Wisconsin boosted its Land Information and Computer Graphics Facility into a local government support group. They have already created a model land base for the town of Westport in Dane County. The model includes layers in soils, wetlands, floodplains, zoning, parcel ownership, and land cover. Dane County has been targeted for development of Conservation of Natural Resources through Sharing of Information Layers (CONSOIL), a GIS prototype to integrated resource management at the local level.

LOCALIS will undoubtedly experiment with ARCVIEW from ESRI, a future product of GIS. ARCVIEW is an affordable read-only GIS interface that is networked to a spatial database somewhere else. Its purpose is to allow the novice user, like the local government in Dane County, to access the much more sophisticated host software on the university campus, to make queries, and so on; it is the university's job to create and update the database.

Elsewhere, the Rhode Island CES has started a program to provide town officials with educational programs and technical guidance and support for GIS adoption and use (McCann and Husband, 1990). Similar programs are under way in other states, all pointing toward a larger role in rural GIS development for CES and the universities.

Conclusion

This chapter has described the potential advantages and related policy implications associated with using GIS technology to improve the quantity and quality of many types of rural data. Several of the most serious obstacles delaying the successful adoption of GIS technology in rural areas were also discussed. Finally, various institutional roles and strategies that would help to overcome such obstacles were presented.

The authors hope that as the ability for GIS to improve rural data and analysis becomes more apparent, and as the cost of this technology continues to decrease, such obstacles will be removed. At some point, it will probably become a way of doing business for every agency and planner to have their data spatially referenced within a GIS. One can also expect to see a continuation of the trend whereby the adoption of GIS technology for planning activities is implicitly or explicitly legislated by state governments. All of this makes GIS an important issue for persons with a continued interest in using rural data.

Rural data users need a tool that will permit them to make complex policy and planning decisions involving may interrelated variables. GIS can do this. The hitherto prohibitive cost of using GIS is rapidly disappearing. At the same time, GIS data sources, such as TIGER, are growing. All of this bodes well for the continued improvement of rural data with GIS technology.

Note

Parts of this chapter are modified from Shultz and Regan (1991).

References

Berry, J. K., J. K. Sailor, C. E. Youell, and J. G. Warren. 1981. Analysis of the spatial ramifications of the comprehensive land use plan of a small town. *American Congress on Surveying and Mapping 41st Symposium Proceedings*. Reprint.

Bishop, M., M. Hines, and R. Mechelke. 1989. Using PC ARC/INFO to develop an automated system to meet the conservation provisions of the 1985 Farm Bill. Pp. 561–568 in *GIS/LIS 1989 Conference Proceedings*. Vol. 2. Bethesda, Md.: American Society for Photogrammetry and Remote Sensing.

Breedlove, M. J. 1990. Utilization of a parcel-based geographic information system for small area estimates. *1990 ESRI Conference Proceedings.* Redlands, Calif.: Environmental Sciences Research Institute (ERSI).

Brown, G. E. 1991. California congressman has GIS vision. *GIS World* 4(6):68–69.

Crichton, W. 1990. PC-based GIS approach for performing agricultural land assessment. Pp. 18–24 in *1990 URISA Conference Proceedings.* Vol. 1. Edmonton, Alberta: Urban and Regional Information System Association.

Daumiller, G. 1990. Land use allocation model for estimating study area populations". *1990 ESRI Conference Proceedings.* Redlands, Calif.: ESRI.

Dillman, D. A., and D. M. Beck. 1988. Information technologies and rural development in the 1990's. *The Journal of State Government* 6(1):29–38.

The Economist. 1992. The delight of digital maps. *The Economist* (March 21–27):69–70.

Flora, C. B., and J. A. Christenson, eds. 1991. *Rural Policies for the 1990s.* Boulder, Colo.: Westview Press.

GIS World. 1990. GIS investigated for farm planning. *GIS World* 3(2):17.

Hale, A. M., and E. Anderson. 1990. A cooperative approach to natural resource planning and building a geographic information system database. In *GIS/LIS 1990 Conference Proceedings.* Anaheim, Calif.: GIS/LIS.

Karnchanasutham, S., and S. Wongwantanee. 1991. Provincial agricultural planning in Thailand. *GIS World* 4(3):98–100.

LaMacchia, R. A., and S. G. Tomasi. 1990. Planned TIGER system products. Paper presented at the 1990 annual spring conference of The Government Publications Librarians of New England. Amherst, Mass., March.

Lo, C. P., and R. L. Shipmann. 1990. A GIS approach to land-use change dynamics detection. *Photogrammetric Engineering and Remote Sensing* 56(11):1483–1491.

Luloff, A. E., and W. A. Befort. 1989. Land use change and aerial photography: Lessons for applied sociology. *Rural Sociology* 54(1):92–105.

McCann, A., and T. P. Husband. 1990. The role of GIS in Rhode Island Cooperative Extension programs. *1990 ESRI Conference Proceedings.* Redlands, Calif.: ESRI.

Mynar, F., and M. J. Hewitt. 1989. Population estimation for risk assessment: A comparison of methods. *1989 ESRI Conference Proceedings.* Redlands, Calif.: ESRI.

Padgett, D. 1992. Assessing the safety of transportation routes for hazardous materials. *Geo Info Systems* 2(2):48–48.

Reinsel, E. I. 1989. The potential for geographic information systems in agricultural economics. *American Agricultural Economics Association Conference Proceedings.*

Shirley, W. L. 1990. An economically focussed statewide GIS database design using DLG and TIGER. *1990 ESRI Conference Proceedings*. Redlands, Calif.: ESRI.

Shultz, S. D. 1990. The creation of a Cooperative Extension information system that is compatible with GIS technology. Report prepared for the University of Arizona Cooperative Extension Service, Tucson, Ariz., June.

Shultz S. D., and J. Regan. 1991. "The 1990 census, GIS technology, and rural data needs." *TRS* 2(1):23–29.

Shultz, S. D., and J. Rosales. 1992. Using a desktop GIS for agricultural planning: A case study of the Lake Managua Watershed in Nicaragua. Unpublished report, Advanced Technology Program, University of Arizona, Tucson, Ariz.

Stutheit, J. 1990. Wisconsin legislates innovative new LIS program. *GIS WORLD* (October):90–91.

Turner, M. G. 1990. Landscape changes in nine rural counties in Georgia. *Photogrammetric Engineering and Remote Sensing* 56(3):379–386.

Warnecke, L. 1991. State leadership increasing in GIS circles. *GIS World* 4(5):62–63.

Wright, J., T. Harris, and L. Davis. 1989. Exploring the feasibility and utility of geographic information system technology for rural development applications. Project Report of the Western Rural Development Center, Corvallis, Ore., October.

Williams, T. H. L. 1985. Implementing LESA on a geographic information system. *Photogrammetric Engineering and Remote Sensing* 51(12):1923–1932. Reprinted in William J. Ripple, ed., 1987, *GIS For Resource Management: A Compendium*. Falls Church, Va.: American Society for Photogrammetry and Remote Sensing and American Congress on Surveying and Mapping.

Epilogue

This book illustrates how important it is for researchers to gather information about people in rural areas to help policymakers formulate informed decisions at the national, state, and local levels. Although data sets are available and much independent research is conducted, a great deal of information about rural people and communities remains unavailable, uncollected, or incomparable. With today's technology, researchers have many more opportunities to collect data to benefit rural Americans. An underlying assumption of this book is that universities and university researchers must play a key role in gathering, processing, and cataloging appropriate data on rural populations to facilitate better informed political decisions.

The three themes described in Chapter 1—complementarity, cooperation, and responsiveness—are exemplified in the subsequent chapters. Complementarity is perhaps the most difficult goal to achieve. The nationally collected secondary data sets provide the only comparable data on a state-to-state basis. However, "rural" is a problematic category, as the authors have pointed out numerous times. State governments collect large amounts of secondary data, but the collection, storage, and use of these data are not consistent among states. But complementarity is certainly much more than comparability. Public universities must continue to demonstrate both the ability and the willingness to extend and restructure the information systems that are important for a national rural policy.

This book also discusses the importance of cooperation among disciplines, universities, and agencies in building a comprehensive rural information system. While cooperation is certainly not impossible to obtain, specific efforts will be required. It is very common for researchers and agency personnel to use data from other sources, but this is a long way from cooperating in defining, formulating, and collecting data. Indeed, it is generally the goal of universities, agencies, individual disciplines, and individual researchers to develop independent data and results. It will take major shifts in the way our universities and agencies are organized, along with how individuals within these organizations are recognized and rewarded, for this cooperation to be truly integrated as a normal means of operation in our data efforts.

Responsiveness to rural populations and policy decisions related to such areas should be the driving force behind researchers' efforts to collect, analyze, and utilize data. Public universities and public agencies are formed with the ultimate goal of serving citizens. Unfortunately, public organizations are becoming increasingly criticized because they do not serve the public. Public universities cannot ignore this charge. Land-grant universities especially have the mission to serve the citizens of their respective states. Part of this mission includes the attention historically given to rural people and communities. The needs for rural data expressed throughout this book provide a tremendous opportunity for universities to demonstrate the capability to respond to public citizen needs. The very individuality present in university faculty research which has made complementarity and cooperation a problem provides the flexibility needed to make necessary changes relatively quickly. Universities must seize this opportunity to respond.

Part One of this book explains how rural areas are extremely diverse and can no longer be considered as a catch-all category for data that must meaningfully describe the various rural conditions. The "politics" of data must also be overcome to maintain our focus on rural areas. A decreasing proportion of our population lives in rural America. University researchers have been instrumental in calling attention to the deficiencies and needs for specific rural data, including diverse situations. Now university researchers can expand this role into the rural data systems that will fill in the current gaps.

Part Two includes several examples of existing data sets and data-collection methods that address the rural data needs expressed in this book. These examples are encouraging because they reveal the depth of information that research can provide about rural people. The remaining challenge is for university researchers, working with the relevant public agencies, to develop the rural data systems that can complete the pictures of rural areas at national, state, and even local levels. The coordination needed to integrate existing and future databases will be large, but the benefits of informed rural policy development will be equally large.

Part Three gives us a glimpse of how we can combine rural data into a comprehensive system. As survey methods continue to evolve, the complementary roles among universities and government agencies will become more and more apparent. A national survey approach developed with rural areas in mind will prove invaluable for rural data needs. In addition, the technological advances in computer systems have expanded the capabilities of all types of research and data management and analysis at an unbelievable rate, and will continue to do so. The chapters that discuss computer technology show some of the most exciting possibilities that exist for both research at the universities and the coordination of data among universities and agencies. Although there is much work to be done, these directions offer us a chance to truly move toward a comprehensive rural information system.

Let us revisit the proposals offered in Chapter 1 in light of the discussions presented in subsequent chapters. Proposal 1 suggests allocating a one cent per dollar of federally funded research for archiving data and making research data available to the public. While university researchers often feel that there are already enough restrictions attached to the public funds they receive, the authors here argue that research results must be made widely available to be used in data systems. As with any changes that must occur in the research system, some financial incentives must be offered. One cent of every dollar is only a small portion, but it represents a positive approach to making data available across all the geographic levels and interested groups. This small but significant positive approach is certainly preferable to additional requirements that could force standardized formats or federally centralized collection points.

Proposal 2 recommends enhancing the position of university libraries to systematize research findings into rural data systems. Many such efforts are already in progress, such as the recent programs of the National Agricultural Library. Computer and communications technology has radically changed the way libraries operate and thus this trend will continue into the future. For example, public universities are linked with both individual and document communications systems. University libraries are natural locations for data retrieval and access systems because they already exist at the same institutions. Designated funding sources, such as the one-cent allocation, would provide the recurring dollars necessary to ensure a commitment to such a system.

Proposal 3 calls for mandating land-grant universities to develop and make available information systems relevant to rural populations and rural issues in their respective states. In fact, land-grant universities already have such a mandate. The aim of this proposal is to return the land-grant universities to this mandate by the specific contribution of rural data systems. Once again, the authors show that university researchers recognize this need and are committed to developing useable research results, consistent with the information needs of rural policy at the national, state, and local levels.

In summary, this book shows that universities, especially public universities, and most especially land-grant universities, have the unique expertise and positioning to be the predominant developers of a rural information systems so desperately needed to adequately analyze our rural areas. This role represents both a major challenge and a major opportunity for universities. Meeting the challenge will restore university research to its place of relevance and prestige among the citizens for whom universities were founded to serve. It is hoped that the examples included here will allow the discussions to continue and the directions to emerge to guide our rural information system into the twenty-first century.

James A. Christenson
Richard C. Maurer
Nancy L. Strang

About the Editors and Contributors

Janet L. Bokemeier is associate chair and professor of sociology at Michigan State University. Her research and teaching focus on farm family operations, gender differences in work experiences, children in rural poverty, urban encroachment on dairy families, and urban-rural differences in women's health. She is on special appointment with the MSU Outreach as faculty coordinator for State Issue Responses in the areas of children, youth and family, the environment, and economic development.

James T. Bonnen is professor of agricultural economics at Michigan State University. His research and teaching focus on public policy, primarily for agriculture. His research interests also include information systems theory, the design and management of statistically based policy decision systems, and agricultural research policy. He has served as chairman of the National Academy of Sciences' Panel on Statistics for Rural Development Policy, director of the President's Federal Statistical System Reorganization Project, and senior staff economist with the President's Council of Economic Advisors. He has served as president of the American Agricultural Economics Association (AAEA) and was made a fellow of AAEA, the American Statistical Association, and the American Association of the Advancement of Science. He also received the Julius Shiskin Award for Outstanding Achievement in Economic Statistics from the American Statistical Association's Washington Statistical Society.

Edwin H. Carpenter is professor and research methodologist of agricultural and resource economics at the University of Arizona in Tucson. His research interests include improving survey research and bringing automation, via computers and software, to the social science research process. He is associate editor of statistics and research methods for the *Social Science Computer Review*, is a past president of the Social Science Computing Association, has served on the National Review Panel to judge EDUCOM higher education software award competition, and has won the Masters of Innovation national software competition. Recently he became director of the Computer Multimedia Lab for the Office of Academic Programs in the College of Agriculture, where faculty are trained and assisted in the use of computing technology for instructional research.

James A. Christenson is director of Cooperative Extension and associate dean of the College of Agriculture at the University of Arizona. He is former chair of sociology at the University of Kentucky. He has served as editor of *Rural Sociology* and president of the Rural Sociological Society. He has co-authored or edited five books, including *Rural Policies for the 1990s, Community Development in Perspective,* and *The Cooperative Extension Service.*

Rand D. Conger is director of the Center for Family Research in Rural Mental Health, director of the Social and Behavioral Research Center for Rural Health, and a professor of rural sociology at Iowa State University. He conducts research in family research methods, family stress and individual well-being, the social context of family relations, childhood and adolescent development, and families and health.

Don A. Dillman is professor of sociology and rural sociology and director of the Social and Economic Sciences Research Center at Washington State University, Pullman. He is also serving as senior methodologist in the office of the director at the Census Bureau under an Intergovernmental Personnel Act (IPA) appointment. He is past president of the Rural Sociological Society. He has authored more than 100 articles and books on survey methods, information technology, and rural development issues, including *Mail and Telephone Surveys: The Total Design Method.*

Melissa Latimer is a doctoral student in the Work, Gender, and Inequality program of sociology at the University of Kentucky. Her dissertation integrates both spacial and feminist analysis of inequality to examine how local and regional opportunity structures intersect with gender, race, and ethnicity to influence an individual's position within the occupational structure and the welfare system. The data she uses for this research come from the National Longitudinal Survey Youth Cohort.

Frederick O. Lorenz is associate professor of sociology and statistics at Iowa State University. He is also director of the Statistics and Measurement Lab in the Center for Family Research in Rural Mental Health. His research includes methodological issues in modeling family data and rural family resilience to stress.

Robert MacArthur is director of the Computer Applications Group in the College of Agriculture at the University of Arizona. He helped found the Advanced Research Technology program of which he is now director. He has written articles and conducted studies using GIS, AM/FM, and spacial data modeling. He is a member of the Arizona Geographic Information Council's Technology Subcommittee and assisted in drafting the Arizona Geographic Information Systems Strategic Plan.

Richard C. Maurer is assistant director of the Cooperative Extension Service for Rural and Economic Development Programs and professor and associate chair of sociology at the University of Kentucky. He administers extension and research programs in the general area of social and economic education for development. He has written numerous publications and conducted educational programs in the areas of community needs assessment, leadership development, and local strategic planning.

Glenn L. Nelson is research coordinator of the Rural Policy Research Institute—Coordinating Center at the University of Missouri, Columbia. His research concentrates on policy analyses relevant to policymakers and includes models of rural economies and studies of specific policy initiatives. He is directly involved in government policy-making as well as in academic research and teaching. He was the state economist of Minnesota, senior staff economist with the President's Council of Economic Advisors, and economist with the Office of Economic Opportunity and the Cost of Living Council. He is editor of a recent book on the foundations of rural development and of a major study of rural data needs published by the National Academy of Sciences.

Steven D. Shultz is a resource economist at the Tropical Agriculture Research and Teaching Facility in Costa Rica. He received his doctorate from the University of Arizona in 1992. His dissertation concerned the development of hedonic land-use models based on GIS. He has also written articles describing government uses for GIS and using TIGER census tract data in resource management projects. He presented a paper entitled "The 1990 Census, GIS Technology, and Rural Data Needs" at the Rural Sociological Society annual meeting in 1990.

Jerry R. Skees is professor of agricultural economics at the University of Kentucky. His research and teaching programs focus on agricultural policy. He has served on congressional staffs and as the research director for the Congressional Commission on Crop Insurance, as a visiting scholar for USDA's Economic Research Service, and on Secretary Yuetter's task force on Disaster Assistance Policy Options for the 1990 Farm Bill. Skees advises a number of agencies in USDA, OMB, and the Senate and House Agriculture Committees, as well as farm leaders in Kentucky and the nation. He is co-author of *Sacred Cows and Hot Potatoes: An Inquiry into Agrarian Myths and Agricultural Policy*.

Nancy L. Strang is a research specialist in sociology in the College of Agriculture at the University of Kentucky. Her interests include rural sociology, community development, environmental sociology, and food safety. She is a member of the Cooperative Extension Service's Food Safety and Quality Task Force at the University of Kentucky. She has copy-edited eight books on rural sociology and community development and three medical technology textbooks.

Louis E. Swanson is professor of sociology in the College of Agriculture at the University of Kentucky. He has written or edited several books in the area of agriculture and rural development policy: *Agriculture and Community Change in the U.S.: Congressional Research Reports*, *American Rural Communities*, *Rural Communities: Legacy and Change*, and *Sacred Cows and Hot Potatoes: Agrarian Myths in Agricultural Policy*. He was also a resident scholar at the National Center for Food and Agricultural Policy at Resources for the Future.

Ann R. Tickamyer is professor of sociology at the University of Kentucky. She has published extensively in the areas of rural poverty, gender, work, and labor markets. Recently, she served as chair of the Working Group on Women and Persistent Rural Poverty of the Rural Sociological Society Task Force on Persistent Rural Poverty.

Robert D. Tortora is associate director for Statistical Design, Methodology, and Standards at the Census Bureau. His is responsible for statistical and survey methods including the design of the 2000 Census of

Population and Housing. He came to the Census Bureau as chief of the Statistical Research Division. Prior to that he worked at the National Agricultural Statistics Service in a variety of technical and management positions, including director of the Research and Applications Division.

Kristen R. Yount is assistant professor of sociology at Northern Kentucky University. She has conducted both ethnographic and survey research on social relationships in rural boom towns and gender relations among workers in traditionally male blue-collar occupations. Her professional interests focus on environmental sociology. She is currently conducting research on social processes determining risk perceptions and investment decisions among potential developers of contaminated inner-city properties.

Name Index

Subject Index

For Product Safety Concerns and Information please contact our EU representative GPSR@taylorandfrancis.com
Taylor & Francis Verlag GmbH, Kaufingerstraße 24, 80331 München, Germany

www.ingramcontent.com/pod-product-compliance
Ingram Content Group UK Ltd.
Pitfield, Milton Keynes, MK11 3LW, UK
UKHW022000180926
475701UK00003B/124
9780367301729